PARKSTONE

BY

DAVID DAVIES

FOREWORD
JEREMY WATERS

Published by David Davies in 2021

British Library Cataloguing-in-Publication Data
A catalogue record for this book is available from the British Library.
ISBN 978-1-8-0068-160-6

Available from good bookshops and from the Author on danecourtworld@aol.com
All trade enquiries should be addressed to the Author

Production by Graphic Editions Ltd, Poole. Printed by Ashley Press, Poole, Dorset

Foreword

Today the original Parkstone Village, clustered around St Peter's Church at Ashley Cross, is so densely built up that there is no space for further development. It is therefore hard to imagine that, only a stone's throw from the church, once stood a substantial mansion with three acres of garden, a private chapel, lodge, gardener's cottage and stabling. What eventually came to be named *Dane Court* was built in 1862; it bankrupted its original developer and throughout its chequered existence was variously a grand private house, a convalescent home and, for 35 years, a boy's preparatory school, before being demolished for redevelopment in 1936.

The Author grew up in one of the thirty or more dwellings which were built on the site of *Dane Court.* When his family garden revealed relics of the previous occupation, his childhood imagination was fired by thoughts of what might have been there in the past. This extremely detailed record, extending to more than 200 pages and 170 illustrations, is the result of seventeen years of meticulous research to unearth the history of the house itself, and of virtually everyone who was ever associated with it. The principal occupiers are not only covered in considerable depth, from their origins to any subsequent history, but also every individual, regardless of status, and especially the many boys who attended as pupils, has been researched, and recorded. Many of the names will be familiar to people in Poole, such as Pike, Aldridge, Curtis, Sturdy, Scutt and Yeatman and even include the children of the Painter, Augustus John.

The text is enhanced by a wonderful collection of period photographs. Many of these are, unusually for the time, informal snapshots rather than formal portraits, and give a fascinating glimpse into everyday life in Edwardian Parkstone. The school archives have also brought to light many individual portraits of the pupils, as well as the traditional group photos of staff and boys. However, it is the amateur snaps of sports days, staff and pupils, school plays and picnics on Sandbanks that, in my experience, are so unusual and evocative of the time.

I believe this book will be of interest to local historians, to those interested in the social history of the period, and particularly to those whose family history can be traced to the many pupils and staff who passed through the doors of *Dane Court.* David Davies has published a most interesting addition to the existing body of research on the history and growth of Parkstone, and especially of Ashley Cross.

Jeremy Waters

June 2021

Preface

From the bedroom window of my childhood home in Chapel Road, Parkstone, Poole, Dorset I could see a giant fir tree, the last relic of *Dane Court*. The house and grounds occupied most of the three-acre site bounded by Danecourt Road, St Peter's Road, Church Road and Chapel Road. Demolished in the 1930s, it was replaced by the thirty or so properties we see today. As a boy, I wondered where *Dane Court* was, who lived there and what happened in the house and grounds: the joys and sorrows the fir tree saw. Then one sad day in 1965 when I was 10 the tree was felled, my last witness lost.

I imagined the house was in the middle of the site. Digging over the garden in the 1960s with my father, we would come across broken clay smoking pipes, rusty stirrups and fragments of pottery, but no house. Then forty years later my father suddenly hit brickwork while removing a small tree near the top fence. His neighbour over the fence in Danecourt Road said she always seemed to hit concrete when digging. Little did she know *Dane Court* lay beneath.

Seventeen years ago, I began my search for the lost world of *Dane Court*. I examined my father's property deeds which showed some names from the Victorian and Edwardian eras but robbed of significance. After many years research, I can now tell the extraordinary story of *Dane Court*: from its construction in 1862 as *Brontë House*, its calamitous early years, the addition of a mysterious private chapel in the early 1870s, the establishment of the first convalescent home in the country for children with tuberculosis of the hip, the residents who featured in Victorian novels and the affluent merchant who eventually called it *Dane Court* then its later years when as a boys' preparatory school many notable people passed through its portals and spent their formative years there. Over 300 people lived or spent significant time at *Dane Court*. This is their remarkable story.

At the book's core is a wonderful collection of photographs depicting life at the house and local excursions over 100 years ago. While some are a little grainy, this is compensated by their spontaneity and social interest. Many are rare of their type, even rarer as a collection with the names of the people and dates known. There are numerous enchanting reminiscences from those who were there. I trace the residents' journeys to the house, whether as owners, tenants, children, servants, tutors or pupils, and find out what became of them in later years. Further information on the boys known to have lived at and/or attended *Dane Court* are set out in the Supplement.

The history of Parkstone has been covered in several other books as listed in the Bibliography. I do not recover that ground. The space is needed for the story of *Dane Court*. Parkstone's history, wider social history aspects and events such as the First World War are referred to where relevant to the story of the house. I use the form *Dane Court* as this is how it was shown on contemporary Ordnance Maps, postcards and the deeds though it was sometimes referred to as *Danecourt*, as in the road name. I use the name 'Parkstone' throughout, unless the context requires otherwise, even though in earlier centuries it was known as 'Parkston'.

I am most grateful to Robin Pooley and Robin Phipps who have given generously of their time and allowed me to make use of their photographs, drawings, documents and publications. I thank the proprietors of the *Glynhir Mansion* in Llandybie, Alan Sim, a Research Volunteer at The Gordon Highlanders Museum in Aberdeen, Maureen Cummings at Saltash Heritage, Phaedra Casey at Brunel University London Archives, Janice Parker and Karen Bourrier at the University of Calgary, Kate Jarman at Barts Archives, Bev Davidge, Curator and Archivist at the Hilton College Museum in Natal and the many helpful staff at Bournemouth Local Studies, Poole Local Studies, the Dorset History Centre, Lambeth Palace Library, The British Library and The Lyon Office in Edinburgh.

The following pictures have been provided by Robin Pooley: 7, 8, 10 to 12, 20, 21, 36 to 42, 49, 55 to 60, 62, 63 to 68, 70 to 93, 95 to 97, 99 to 140, 156, 157, 162, 165, 166 and 170. The photographs and drawings numbered 141, 143 to 151, 153 and 169 were provided by Robin Phipps.

Picture 1 is reproduced with the permission of Agnew's. Map 3 is reproduced with the permission of the Dorset History Centre. Maps 4, 6 and 18 are reproduced courtesy of the Ordnance Survey. Map 5 has been reproduced courtesy of Poole Borough Council, adapted to show the approximate positions of the previous dwellings.

Picture 15 had been provided by the proprietors of *The Glynhir Mansion*. Illustration 16 has been reproduced courtesy of Bournemouth Library. Illustration 19 is reproduced with the permission of the Dorset History Centre. Pictures 22 and 158 to 161 and 163 are reproduced under license from the National Portrait Gallery. Picture 23 is reproduced courtesy of Wareham Museum. Picture 24 is reproduced courtesy of the late R W Kinder's Estate. Pictures 28 to 32 are reproduced with the kind permission of the Library of Birmingham (references MS 978/6/77 and MS 978/4/3/3/2) and the Trustees of the Sir Barry Jackson Trust. Picture 42 is reproduced by the kind permission of the Oxford History Centre. Picture 43 is reproduced courtesy of Dr Brian Cox. Picture 44 is reproduced courtesy of The Lyon Office in Edinburgh. Picture 48 is reproduced with the kind permission of the Surrey History Centre. Picture 69 is reproduced courtesy of the Finnish National Gallery. Pictures 94 and 98 are reproduced under license from the Tate Gallery, the former picture being copyright of the Estate of Augustus John / Bridgeman Images. Pictures 142, 152 and 168 are reproduced from various editions of *Paton's List of School and Tutors*. Picture 167 was provided by Peter Levey..

The following map and pictures come from the Author's collection, or the copyright holder is not known: 2, 9, 13, 14, 17, 25 to 27, 33 to 35, 45 to 47, 50 to 54, 61, 154, 155 and 164. Other sources are referred to in the Notes at the end of the book. A Bibliography and Index are also provided at the end of the book.

I thank Jeremy Waters, Author of *Parkstone-on-Sea: Salterns, Sandbanks and Sea Planes*, for reviewing and commenting on drafts of the book and for writing the Foreword. I also thank Philip Davies, Ruth Bebb and Ivan Seery for reviewing drafts and making helpful comments. If there are any mistakes of fact, they are mine alone and if any reader can offer any corrections, suggestions or comments, I would welcome hearing from them on danecourtworld@aol.com.

This book celebrates the lives of all those who lived or spent time at *Dane Court* and as such is dedicated to their memory.

David Davies

June 2021

Contents

Prologue

When Turner sat down with his sketch book in 1811 on Constitutional Hill overlooking Poole Harbour, Parkstone was sparsely populated. His watercolour completed the following year is consistent with the Ordnance Survey Map of 1811. The dwellings in the foreground are probably brick makers' cottages close to a known brick field, later a sports field where schoolboys happily played. Little did Turner know that his exquisite gem, measuring just 5½ by 8½ inches, would encapsulate some of the key places in our story: Poole, Wareham, the Purbecks and Parkstone.

1. J M W Turner's watercolour Poole, Dorset with Corfe Castle in the Distance c1812

For those not familiar with the area, the Ordnance Survey Map of 1811 shows how Parkstone and the site where *Dane Court* was later built fits into the wider landscape. The neighbourhood immediately to the right of the words 'Parkson Green' is the spot where just over 20 years later the first St Peter's Church and St Peter's School would be built in 1833. These formed the nucleus of the village that grew up, known as Parkstone Village and later Ashley Cross. The road running from west to east beneath the words 'Parkston Green' is what is now known as Commercial Road. The site on which *Dane Court* was built 50 years or so after the 1811 map was just under the letters 'on' of 'Parkston Green', though the site was not defined at that time.

2. Extract from the Ordnance Survey Map of 1811 showing Poole and Parkton Green

A slightly later Canford Manor estate map, reproduced as illustration 3, shows the site of *Dane Court* much more clearly. It is the blank rectangular site above the letters 'TON' in the name 'PARKSTONE'. Again, the road running under that name is what is now known as Commercial Road. The site is believed to have been an uncultivated heath field. The green fields were arable land.

3. Extract from an early 19th Century Canford Manor Estate map

Before delving into more detail, it is important to say a few words about the house names and how and when they changed. *Dane Court* was originally called *Brontë House* from 1862 when it was built until January 1875. It was then called *Leymore* until June 1891. Thereafter the house was known as *Dane Court* until it was demolished in 1936.

On the same site were two cottages close to the house. One was called *Brunswick Cottage* from 1862 until August 1872. It was then purchased along with *Brontë House* and became known as *Brontë Cottage*. From January 1875 until June 1891, it was usually known as *Leymore Cottage*, although occasionally the original name of *Brunswick Cottage* was used, for example in the 1881 Census. After June 1891, it was usually known as *The Cottage*. The other cottage on the site was always used by the Coachman or Gardener employed at the main house. It was originally known as *Brontë Lodge* until January 1875, then as *Leymore Lodge* until June 1891 and finally as *Dane Court Lodge*. The property still exists in a modernised form.

There was also another house on the site, built by the same person at about the same time, called *Carlton Villa*. This property was owned separately to the main house and the above-mentioned cottages after 1872.

All these properties are shown on the first large-scale Ordnance Survey map of 1890 in illustration 4.

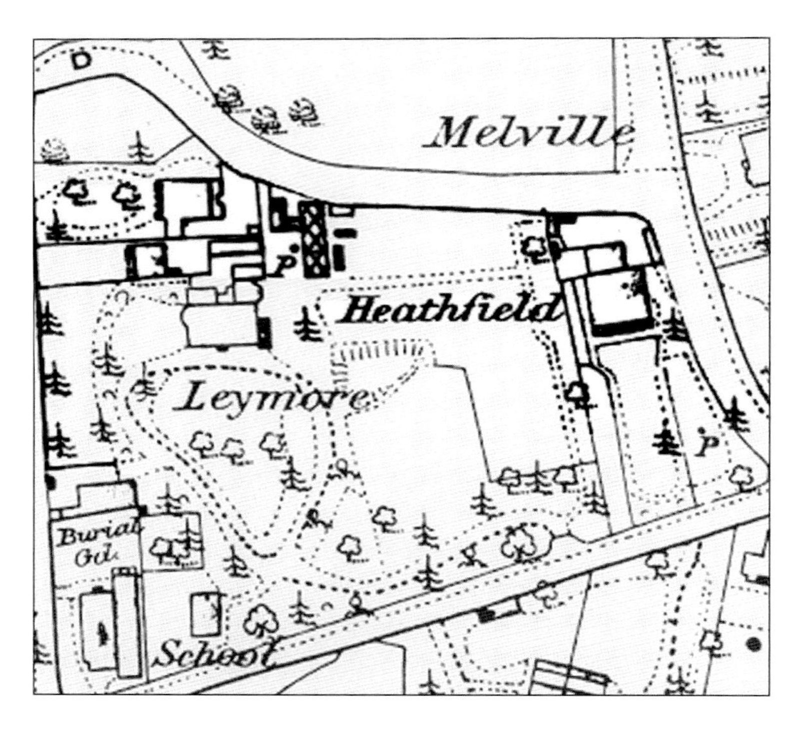

4. A section of the 1890 Ordnance Survey Map showing Leymore

As noted above, by 1890 the main house was called *Leymore*. The front gate of the house was in Back Lane (now Church Road) running along the bottom of the map. There was an impressive circular carriage drive leading to the front of the house. It faced south and had distant views of

Poole Harbour. By 1890, a glass Porch over the front door and a Conservatory on the south-east corner had been added. A large Greenhouse is shown to the north-east of the house.

The first building to be constructed on the site was the congregational Buckland Chapel on the south-west corner, the left part of the building beneath the words 'Burial Gd' on the map. This opened on 6 March 1839. The school room attached to its east side, used by the British School, was added around 1879. These buildings, much loved by roosting pigeons when the Author was a boy, survived until the 1960s after which the St Peter's Centre was built on the site. The building to the east of the chapel and school room, above the word 'School', was *Leymore Lodge*.

Heathfield on the north-east corner of the site was built as a private house around 1840. In 1855, an advert regarding its future as a school appeared, as included in the Notes. So began *Heathfield's* 70-year life as a school. It was later used as the Liberal Club then as some auction rooms before being tastefully converted into four flats in recent times.

Of the remaining buildings, *Leymore Cottage* (not named on the map but located to the north-west of *Leymore*) is believed to have been built around the same time as *Brontë House*. As noted, it was originally called *Brunswick Cottage*. *Carlton Villa* (also not named on the map) was situated to the north of *Leymore Cottage*. It had a carriage driveway.

The following modern 1:2500 map shows the approximate positions of *Leymore*, *Leymore Cottage* and *Carlton Villa* in relation to the detached and semi-detached properties that were built in the late 1930s and which still exist. Relevant house numbers in Chapel Road and Danecourt Road have been added.

5. A modern map with the outlines of Leymore *and other buildings superimposed*

The main part of *Leymore* was situated on what is now part of the back garden of 72 Danecourt Road, with the west side underlying the top end of the back gardens of 22 and 24 Chapel Road. The stable block and yard, above the word 'Burial' on the 1890 map, were located where 12 and 14 Chapel Road are now situated.

The front part of *Carlton Villa* on the north-west of the site was situated where the back gardens of 26 and 28 Chapel Road are now, while the rear part of the house was where the front garden of 72 Danecourt Road is now located. *Leymore Cottage*, (originally known as *Brunswick Cottage*), was located where the back garden of 24 Chapel Road is now.

The locations of the properties in relation to Ashley Cross and the surrounding neighbourhood are shown below. At the time of this 1890 map, all the large Victorian villas on the east side of Constitutional Hill Road (now St Peter's Road and North Road), such as *Melville* and *Montagu*, had been built. To the north and west of *Leymore* it was still mainly open fields.

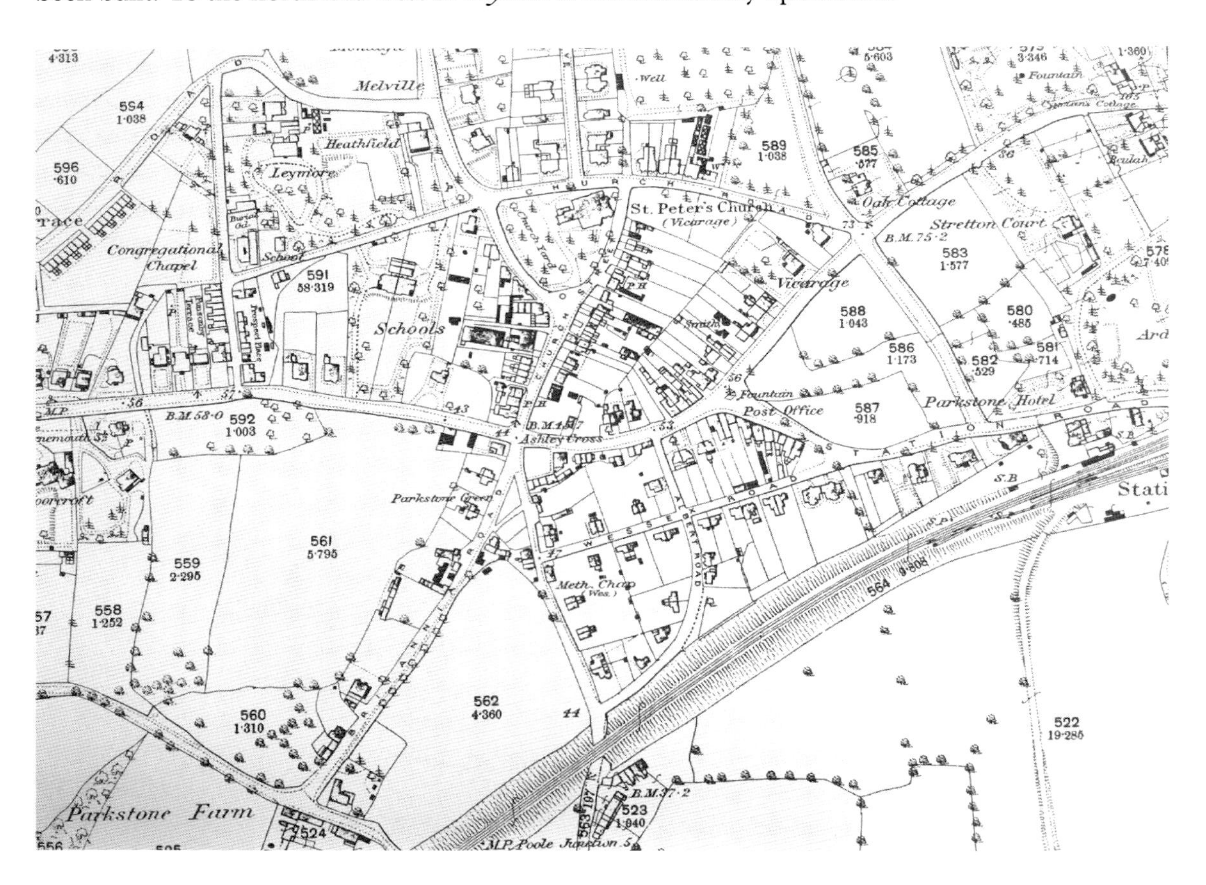

6. 1890 Ordnance Survey Map showing Leymore *and the village of Ashley Cross*

Chapter 1

CRABB'S FOLLY

On 6 October 1864, Alfred Crabb, an eminent Surgeon, left his home at *Pelham House* on Poole High Street to catch the train for London. The journey took nearly five hours along the winding route to Southampton known as Castleman's Corkscrew and then to the capital. Crabb spent his days examining others. On the morrow he would be the one to be examined.

As a Fellow of the Royal College of Surgeons, he had written learned papers on the diseases and brains of infants, diphtheria and, for wilder patients, the injurious effects of opium. He held several important public appointments: Surgeon to the Police, to the South-Western Railway Company, to the Admiralty, the Coastguard, the Naval Reserve and many others.

Aware of the fine residences built in Parkstone over recent years, he probably thought there was money to be made from property speculation. So, early in the 1860s when in his late 40s, he acquired several plots in Parkstone and Lytchett Minster and started to develop villas and cottages. On the *Brontë House* site, he clearly saw the potential for a truly grand residence that would later be described as follows:

'a well-built mansion nearly in the centre of Parkstone about three miles from the celebrated watering place of Bournemouth, truly delightful, facing south and commanding extensive coastal and inland views'.

The area north of what is now known as Ashley Cross was still largely undeveloped with agricultural small holdings occupying Constitutional Hill Road (now St Peter's Road) while the areas to the north and west of the proposed mansion were open fields or heathland.

So Crabb bought the site financed by a mortgage from The Blandford Building Society. By 1 January 1862, he had spent £700 on *Brontë House*. A further £1,472 was paid out during its construction with £977 still owing in mid-1864, totalling £3,149. There was only one snag: *Brontë House* was only worth £2,500 and had not sold. Many others had also financed Crabb, the great and the good of Poole, presumably believing that no-one could be more reliable than a Fellow of the Royal College of Surgeons.

The next day in London Crabb made his way to an imposing building in Basinghall Street. At the time it was described as *'a sort of purgatory through which a number of unfortunate victims of their own folly and extravagance have to be hoisted, shoved, squeezed, ground or propelled by some means or other in order that they may be liberated from the bondage of debt and left free to begin the world again'*. It was the London Court of Bankruptcy.

Crabb had filed his Petition for Bankruptcy a few months earlier on 18 May 1864. He attributed his predicament to a *'deficiency of funds by reason of losses arising from bad debts and unsuccessful building contracts'*. On 7 June 1864, the first sitting for the Proof of Debts and the Choice of Assignees had taken place, at which a long list of Secured and Unsecured Creditors was presented, the largest being The Blandford Building Society who were owed £3,842. The precise total of the Bankrupt's Creditors was not stated in the preliminary statement, but it was estimated to be in the region of £12,000 to £13,000 (or c£1½ million today). Creditors' Assignees (or representatives) were appointed, one being George Curtis of Poole, a Builder who was a Creditor and probably responsible for the construction of *Brontë House*.

7. The front of Brontë House *in a later photo when ivy-clad*

8. The front of Brunswick Cottage *with* Brontë House *in the background*

However, there was a glimmer of hope for Crabb. The Court reported: *'it is the intention of the Creditors to allow him to continue his practice for the benefit of the estate and remunerate him for his services'*. His formal Examination and Application for Discharge from Bankruptcy was arranged for 8 July 1864. In the meantime, he was granted *'enlarged protection from arrest'*.

Unfortunately, the Examination on 8 July 1864 did not go well. Counsel for the Creditors' Assignees considered his accounts to be unsatisfactory. He had committed the cardinal sin of not maintaining a cash book. Three months later the Final Statement of Accounts, presented on 7 October 1864, showed a deficiency of £3,624, when assets were compared to liabilities (or c£½ million today).

Nevertheless, the Court papers indicated that *'the Creditors think that Dr Crabb had reasonable grounds for believing that the building transactions into which he entered would realise the cost of the buildings'*. He therefore passed his Examination, was granted an immediate Order of Discharge and the proceedings were terminated. Crabb returned to Poole and for ever after stuck to what he knew.

Brontë House (including *Brontë Lodge*), and the other properties built by Crabb on the site, *Carlton Villa* and *Brunswick Cottage*, were at the time let to Richard Morgan Humfrey, Dr Richard Elgie and Mr De Charille, respectively. The properties were advertised for sale in the *Dorset County*

Chronicle on 4 August 1864: *'to be sold by auction by T M Park at the London Hotel, Poole on the 15th day of August 1864 at 3 o'clock in the afternoon'*. Presumably, all the properties had been repossessed by The Blandford Building Society who were no doubt keen to sell them on quickly at suitable prices.

Brontë House was described as *'a newly erected and well-built mansion'* as follows:

> *Brontë House* advert August 1864
>
> *Comprising entrance hall, drawing and dining rooms, 20' by 17', with noble marble chimney pieces, white and gold enriched ceilings and cornices, morning room with bay window, 19' by 15' 9", airy large-sized bedrooms, two dressing rooms, water closet, excellent light staircase with stained glass windows, good landings and passages, china pantry, larder, kitchen with pumps of spring and soft water, scullery and other necessary offices, large paved yard, 3-stalled stable, double saddle room, two productive gardens, lawn, double carriage drive, planted with choice evergreens. The mansion is fitted up with great taste and is in most excellent condition.*

As shown in the photograph, the house had three gables and curved Italianate-styled windows on the top floor characteristic of the period. The glass Porch and Conservatory shown in the photograph were added in the early 1870s.

Brunswick Cottage had a verandah on the front of the house. The grainy photograph shows its front elevation facing what was then Chapel Lane (now Chapel Road). The cottage was described as follows:

> *Brunswick Cottage* advert August 1864
>
> *All that brick and slate dwelling house called Brunswick Cottage now in the occupation of Mrs White and adjoining Lot 1 (Brontë House) comprising two parlours, four bedrooms, kitchen, scullery with pumps of spring and soft water, bricked wall in kitchen garden at the back of the house with lawn and flower garden at the front.*

Carlton Villa was described as follows:

> *Carlton Villa* advert August 1864
>
> *All that dwelling house with Portland cemented front called Carlton Villa, now in the occupation of Richard Elgie Esq., and adjoining Lot 2 (Brunswick Cottage), containing drawing room 19' by 16' with folding doors opening to the garden, dining-room, study, five good size bedrooms, dressing room, water-closet, kitchen, scullery, larder, pumps for spring and soft water, yard, large kitchen garden, well-stocked with fruit trees, enclosed with brick walls.*

No photographs of *Carlton Villa* are known to the Author. As regards the tenants, Dr Richard Elgie at *Carlton Villa* was a retired Surgeon who had previously practiced in Bournemouth. He lived there with his wife and daughters. Richard Morgan Humfrey at *Brontë House* was an ex-army invalid who had long been under the care of a Poole-based Surgeon, Howard Ellis. Maybe Crabb used his Surgeon contacts to find suitable tenants.

Brontë House almost certainly did not sell at the auction on 15 August 1864 as it was re-advertised two years later in the *Dorset County Chronicle and Somersetshire Gazette* on 7 June and 19 July 1866, for £2,500. The advert states 'erected four years' thereby confirming 1862 as the year of construction.

Brontë House advert 7 June and 19 July 1866

TO BE SOLD – A MODERN RESIDENCE, on three acres of land, contains eight bedrooms, two dressing rooms and a storeroom; drawing and dining rooms each 18' by 20'; breakfast ditto, two kitchens, three-stall stable, large coach house and loft, harness room and workshop, kitchen garden, lawn, shrubbery and paddocks; erected four years; fitted with every comfort; and fine sea views; near the church. Price £2,500.

Apply to R M Humfrey Esq., Brontë House, Parkstone, Poole.

Once again it may not have sold as the property was again put up for auction two years later, as follows:

Brontë House advert May 1868

A delightful FREEHOLD PROPERTY situated at the picturesque Hamlet of PARKSTONE within a short drive of the Fashionable Watering-place, BOURNEMOUTH, and near the Town and Port of POOLE. MESSRS ABBOTT & SON are favoured with instructions from the Proprietor to SELL by AUCTION at the BATH HOTEL, BOURNEMOUTH on Friday May the 29th 1868 at three o'clock, unless previously disposed of by Private Contract. A very desirable FREEHOLD PROPERTY consisting of a handsome newly and substantially erected residence distinguished as Brontë House seated on a gravel soil, approached from the road by a carriage drive, through prettily planted shrubberies and lawns and commanding diversified and beautiful views including the English Channel, Old Harry Point, the Purbeck Hills, the Poole Harbour and a variety of other interesting features.

The grounds are nicely disposed, studded with ornamental shrubs and a nice lawn, croquet ground, aviary, etc.

There are productive kitchen gardens, also a paddock together with excellent stabling, coach-house, saddle-room and a comfortable brick and slated cottage, the whole comprising about three acres.

The property did not sell and remained unsold until 1872.

Why a Fellow of the Royal College of Surgeons should have become involved in property development is not known. Clearly Crabb soon got out of his depth. He was lucky to be discharged. His Creditors probably thought it was better to have Crabb in Poole rather than in prison to cure their ailments.

As to why *Brontë House* did not sell, the size of the plot probably made it too expensive for the locality. Later villas nearby had half to one acre rather than three. Better use could have been made of the site. Architecturally, the house was not a masterpiece, largely based on a Builder's Pattern Book. It may have fared better if it had been built after the opening of Parkstone Station in 1874 when the area became attractive to a wider range of merchants who were then able to commute.

The photographer Frank Cathery who was later based in Ashley Cross once wrote that in the 1850s and 1860s large houses in Parkstone were often known as *'follies'*. In 1891, more than quarter of century after it was built, the property only fetched £2,925, still less than Crabb's costs. So maybe the locals were right when they nick-named it *Crabb's Folly*.

Chapter 2

A GAME OF BEZIQUE

One cold winter evening, on Thursday 5 January 1871, Richard Morgan Humfrey and his wife Elizabeth were in the Drawing Room at *Brontë House* enjoying a game of Bezique, a popular card game at the time. At half past eleven, Mrs Humfrey retired to bed. Her husband bid her good night and moved to the Breakfast Room to light his pipe. Fanny Legg, their Cook, acknowledged him as she went about her nightly duties. She had made up Mr Humfrey's bed and put his room in order.

Humfrey puffed away at his pipe for quarter of an hour before he too retired to his chamber, next to Mrs Humfrey's. They had not slept together since her illness five years earlier when doctors advised that she should not be disturbed.

Earlier that day Mrs Humfrey's Surgeon, Dr Ellis, had visited *Brontë House* to see how she was as recently she had not been in good health. He also spoke to Mr Humfrey who was under his care. He had suffered from paralysis for 22 years, since the age of 27, and frequently experienced excruciating neuralgia and the occasional epileptic fit. Recently though he had been enjoying better health.

9. Costume of the 67th Foot

Richard Morgan Humfrey was the son of an Army Surgeon, also called Richard Humfrey (1774-1843), who lived in Bristol. A commission for his son was purchased in 1839. He became an Ensign with the 67th Foot, or South Hampshire Regiment, in October 1839 when 17 years of age. On 10 March 1843, he was promoted to the rank of Lieutenant.

During the time he was in the 67th Foot he was in one of the depot companies based in Cork and remained with the 67th Foot until 1848 when he was invalided on half-pay. He had married his wife Elizabeth Hayes in Liverpool in 1846. They did not have children. From 1849, his paralysis got worse.

Richard and his wife had resided at *Brontë House* as tenants since at least 1864, maybe a little earlier. They had been in Parkstone since 1850 or 1851. Prior to *Brontë House* they lived at *Beulah Villa* in Parkstone (on the right edge of illustration 6 in Ardmore Road just off Castle Hill). Living with them at *Beulah Villa* at the time of the 1861 Census was a niece aged 13 called Lucy Robinson. They appear to have been very close to Lucy as later in the 1860s she adopted their name, becoming Lucy Robinson Humfrey. She was not however at *Brontë House* on the night of 5 January 1871.

10. The house as seen from Back Lane (now Church Road) in a later photo

11. The entrance drive of Brontë House *leading to the circular carriage driveway*

After Mrs Humfrey retired to bed, she heard a noise and thought that her husband may have fallen. He often fell and he had told her not to come to him at such times unless he called as it distressed her to see him and he said that he could get up again very well by means of a chair. Mrs Humfrey called Fanny Legg, saying, *"Did you hear anything fall down, Cook?"* The Cook replied that she had not. Mrs Humfrey said, *"Then, I suppose it is your Master"*, telling the Cook that he had gone to bed.

On Friday morning the Cook took hot water to the door of Mr Humfrey's chamber and knocked. There was silence. She alerted Mrs Humfrey who immediately sent for the Coachman, George Masterman, at *Brontë Lodge*. He had been in their service for six years. She asked him to open the door. He peered in. Humfrey was hanging on the wardrobe door.

Masterman ran for help to the Village Police Constable, Joseph Allen who lived in Back Lane nearby. Aged 28, he was a Boot and Shoemaker as well as part-time Police Constable and Rate Collector. He hastened to the house with assistant, George Rennison. a Shopkeeper. The cord was on the right side of Humfrey's neck, his face towards the wardrobe door. His bed had not been slept in. Allen and Rennison cut down Humfrey. Meanwhile Masterman sped to Poole on horseback to summon Dr Ellis.

A Coroner's Inquest was hastily arranged for the next morning, Saturday 7 January 1871, at The Sloop Inn. George Braxton Aldridge was the Coroner for the Borough, residing at *Bonavista* in Parkstone. A Jury was sworn in *'consisting almost entirely of gentlemen residents in the locality'*. The Foreman was John Sidney Hudson, Manager of the South-Western Pottery who lived at *Holly Lodge* in Parkstone Road (now Commercial Road).

The Coroner said that the circumstances of the case were extremely sad. He first asked the Jury, before proceeding to the house to view the body, to consider whether it was necessary to examine Mrs Humfrey as they would have the evidence of Fanny Legg, the Cook, who last saw the deceased alive on the Thursday evening, the Coachman, George Masterman, who discovered him dead the next morning and Dr Ellis, the Surgeon. The Jury decided that Mrs Humfrey would need to be examined and concluded that the Inquest should be conducted at *Brontë House*.

So the Coroner and the Jury set off in a solemn procession. Once in Back Lane, *Brontë House* was on their left. They opened the front gate, passed along the entrance drive and around the circular carriage driveway to the front door. They silently viewed the body. Then they examined the witnesses.

Fanny Legg the Cook was first. She confirmed that Mr and Mrs Humfrey had been very friendly with each other all day and had had no words. There was nothing to lead her to think they quarrelled. Mr Humfrey was very cheerful. She said that Mr Humfrey had latterly enjoyed better health and seemed as well as usual on the Thursday. She had not heard reports from other servants that were likely to affect the mind of the deceased.

The Coachman George Masterson also confirmed that Mr Humfrey seemed more cheerful on Thursday than at any time since he had been in his service. He added that Mr Humfrey was very weak and never walked without assistance. Mr Humfrey did not like anyone to notice how weak he was. Masterson also knew of nothing unfriendly that had taken place between the deceased and Mrs Humfrey.

The Police Constable, Joseph Allen, said that he saw the deceased hanging by the cord of his dressing gown on the wardrobe door. The right toe of the deceased was touching the floor, his left leg resting on a chair. He cut him down and with assistance laid him on the bed. His extremities were cold.

Dr Ellis said Mr Humfrey had suffered from a form of paralysis throughout the eight to ten years that he had known him. He said that Mr Humfrey was always very unsteady on his legs and liable to fall at any moment. He commented that when he had visited him on the previous Thursday he spoke cheerfully.

He said that *'the appearance of the body was natural, with the exception of a deep cut as from a cord on the right side of his neck'*. He had then been shown his dressing gown, with the cord attached, by which he was told that he had been found suspended. He had no doubt that the death was caused by strangulation. The body was cold: *'in the present weather a body would become cold in seven or eight hours'*.

Elizabeth Humfrey was then examined. The newspaper reported:

'it needs scarcely be said that the witness was suffering from the most acute anguish of mind. At times she was so overcome with grief as scarcely to be able to proceed with her evidence and it was distressing to all present that the necessity of the case should have rendered her attendance before the Jury indispensable'.

She said that:

'she last saw her husband about half-past eleven on Thursday night. They were rather late that night having played a game of Bezique. He appeared quite happy and when she retired, he said, "Good Night." Nothing had occurred during the last few days to cause the deceased any uneasiness of mind, except her illness. He was extremely pleased when she was better and able to come downstairs again'.

She then explained how she had heard a noise and thought her husband may have fallen but her husband had told her not to come to him at such times unless he called.

Having heard all the evidence, the Coroner left the Jury to decide what verdict they should return: they might either find that the deceased was found hanged, or that he hung himself whilst in a state of temporary insanity. The Jury returned a verdict to the effect that the deceased *'destroyed himself by hanging whilst temporarily insane'*. On the suggestion of the Foreman, John Hudson, the Jury agreed to give their fees to the Bournemouth Dispensary.

Mrs Humfrey remained at *Brontë House* for some months. Fortunately, her devoted niece Lucy Robinson Humfrey joined her later in January. In the 1871 Census the house was shown as uninhabited so maybe they had gone away for a break. They also appear to have been away from the house in June, returning by 1 July 1871. Mrs Humfrey and her niece remained at the house until late October 1871. Thereafter, the property was temporarily let to a Mr & Mrs Harvey and their family, about whom nothing is known, until the end of June 1872 after which the freehold of *Brontë House*, including *Brunswick Cottage* and *Brontë Lodge*, was purchased by the Reverend Richard and Mrs Caroline Ley.

THE ENIGMA

The Reverend Richard Ley and his wife Caroline Ley (née Du Buisson) purchased the freehold of *Brontë House*, including *Brontë Lodge* and *Brunswick Cottage*, in August 1872. They were first listed as residing at *Brontë House* in the *Bournemouth Visitors' Directory* dated 26 August 1872.

The Leys are an enigma. One might even conclude that they were estranged as they were not caught living together in any of the censuses during their 32-year marriage. Soon after moving to *Brontë House*, they mysteriously added a private Chapel to the back of the house. The apse may be glimpsed through the trees in the next photo. Such a Chapel in a domestic property was very unusual. The Author knows of only one other property with a large private Chapel in the Parkstone, Poole and Bournemouth areas: *Stewarton Lodge* in Bournemouth, the Leys' previous home.

12. The apse of the private Chapel added to the back of Brontë House *in 1872 or 1873*

Later in *Brontë Cottage*, formerly *Brunswick Cottage*, a children's convalescent home was suddenly set up in 1874, then a few months later discontinued. No photographs of the Leys have survived, even though there are photos of most other ancestors on the Du Buisson side. There is only one mention of them in the family history but that is incorrect. It states that they had a son called Augustin Ley. In fact, he was the son of one of Richard Ley's elder brothers, the Reverend William Henry Ley and his first wife Mary Pritchard. Richard and Caroline Ley did not have children. However, even that turns out to be not quite the case as we shall see in the final chapter. Some background on their journey to *Brontë House* may help to solve the enigma of the Leys.

Richard Ley (1821-1886), pronounced 'Lee', was born in Maker, Devon (now in Cornwall), the son of Thomas Hunt Ley. Richard's father was initially the curate of Maker Church, then Rector of Rame Church on the Rame Peninsula for 40 years. The Earl of Mount Edgcumbe, the Lord of the Manor, was his Patron. Thomas Ley was the family's private Chaplain at the *Mount Edgcumbe* mansion close by throughout the time that he was Rector of Rame.

13. Rame Church where Thomas Hunt Ley was Rector for 40 years

Richard Ley was devoted to his father. He commemorated him in 1872 shortly after moving to *Brontë House* by installing a large stained-glass east window in Rame Church.

Richard Ley had a typical start to his clerical career. He was educated at Brasenose College Oxford, obtaining a BA in 1844 and an MA in 1847. In the 1851 Census he was lodging in Oxford, the year he became a Deacon. He was ordained as a Priest in 1852. He was then appointed as Curate of Boarstall Church near Brill in Buckinghamshire where he also ran a small preparatory school.

In January 1854, he officiated at the wedding of his younger sister, Charlotte Anne Dunning Ley and Caroline Du Buisson's elder brother, Reverend Edmund Du Buisson, at Sellack church in Herefordshire where Edmund was then the Vicar. This may well have been the occasion on which he met his future wife, Caroline Du Buisson. He may have liked what he saw and decided that he wanted some of the same. The couple married in Caroline's home parish of Llandybie, Carmarthenshire later that year in July. Richard Ley then became the Curate at Cumnor Church near Abingdon. Richard and Caroline Ley remained in Cumnor for the next 8 years until 1862.

14. Cumnor Church then in Berkshire now in Oxfordshire

15. A 19th century photo of part of Glynhir Mansion

Richard did not hold a clerical appointment after 1862. This may have been due to ill health as he was later recorded as having had a diabetic condition. Nevertheless, he remained a Priest of the Church of England. The couple do not appear in the 1861 Census. Maybe they spent some time abroad. Some of Caroline's relatives had undertaken grand tours. Alternatively, given Richard Ley's health, he may have spent time convalescing with his wife in a warmer climate abroad.

Caroline Du Buisson (1826-1898), pronounced 'Doobison', was the only daughter of William Du Buisson (1781-1828) and Caroline Henckell (1788-1869). Her father died when she was two. She grew up on the historic Glynhir estate of over 1,100 acres in Carmarthenshire, which her grandfather Peter Du Buisson had purchased in the 1770s. She lived with her mother Caroline Du Buisson and brothers William and Edmund.

Caroline's widowed mother, Caroline Du Buisson had a strong personality according to the family history and played a significant role in the community, for example, by setting up a school for girls at Banc-y-felin near Glynhir. Unlike most schools of the time, the schooling was free. She was also instrumental in the renovation of Llandybie Parish Church, where her daughter Caroline later married Richard Ley in 1854. Caroline Ley's brother, William Henry Du Buissson and his wife Mary Lawford, were also dedicated to fostering the education of children.

It is not known for certain where Richard and Caroline Ley lived between Cumnor in 1862 and Bournemouth in 1866 although there is some evidence from 1865 that they were living in Gloucestershire. The diaries of their niece Edith Caroline Du Buisson for that year record that she went to see *'Aunty Carry and Uncle Dick in Gloucestershire'* where she *'was taken to see many churches'*.

To summarise, the Reverend Richard Ley's family had a long-standing link with the influential Earl of Mount Edgcumbe. The two families were close. Although no longer responsible for a parish, he was still a Priest of the Church of England. While certain members of the Du Buisson family were wealthy, Caroline is not known to have had significant capital herself, although she may have received income from a trust. Her family had a long history of doing good work in the community.

Ascertaining why the Leys moved to Bournemouth, where they lived and what they did there will help to explain their later activities once they got to *Brontë House*.

The couple bought *Stewarton Lodge*, a new house located in what was then part of Branksome Wood Road (now St Stephen's Road). The house was located immediately behind the National Sanatorium, shown in the top left corner of *Sydenham's 1874 Map of Bournemouth* reproduced below. *Stewarton Lodge* is the house above the letter *'W'* in the word *'Wood'*, with the entrance drive starting above the letter 'O'. It was directly opposite the Chapel of the National Sanatorium, shown with a holy cross in it, built soon after they moved into *Stewarton Lodge*.

The Earl of Mount Edgcumbe and his family had a house in Bournemouth just a few doors away. It was called *Walton House*, originally built for the well-known stationer W H Smith. It was located on the corner of Branksome Wood Road and Richmond Hill (the house still exists). The Earl was a Vice Patron of the National Sanatorium and heavily involved in fund raising activities when he was in Bournemouth. Given the close connection between the Earl's family and Richard Ley's (his father had been the family's Chaplain for 40 years), this may explain why the Leys moved to a house in Bournemouth only a few doors away from the Earl and directly opposite the National Sanatorium in which he was a leading figure.

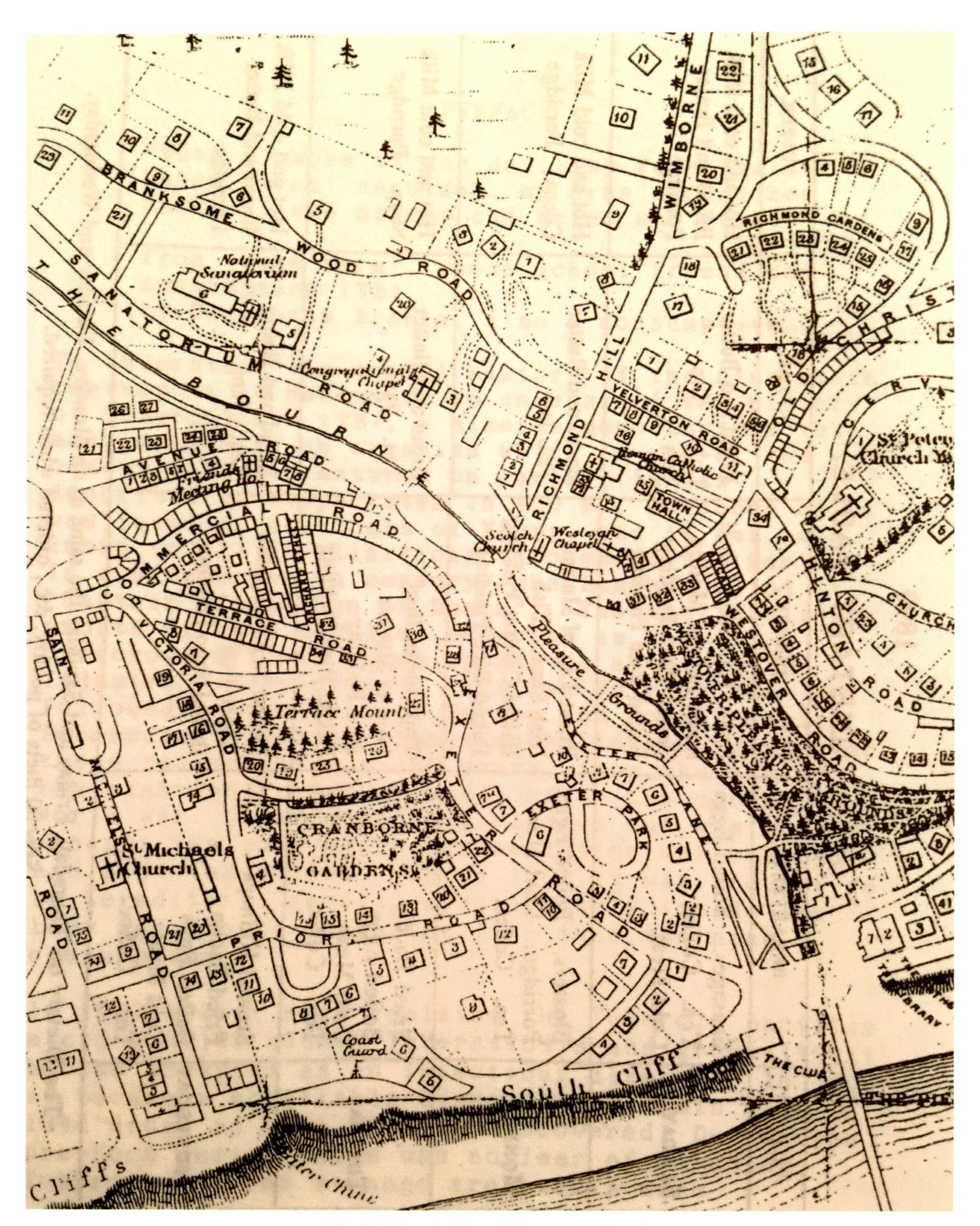

16. Sydenham's Map of Bournemouth 1874

Mary Graham has written the definitive history of the National Sanatorium. Briefly, in 1851 the Committee of the Brompton Hospital in London had recognised the need to offer convalescence to patients in the early stages of consumption who had some hope of recovery. The committee noted that the *'influence of climate in the restoration of health has clearly shown that in many cases the progress of consumptive disease can be arrested'*. Various places were considered, with Bournemouth being the one finally selected.

The National Sanatorium opened in 1855. It was the first institution of its kind to provide convalescing care for patients with tuberculosis. Mary Graham comments that *'locating the sanatorium in Bournemouth led to a great injection of national interest in the area'*. She adds that *'besides the medical interest many politicians and the gentry became aware of this little-known watering place through their attachment to Brompton Hospital. Hundreds of well-to-do people were governors of the Brompton Hospital'*. Numerous fund-raising events took place to fund the building and subsequent operation of the Sanatorium. It was entirely funded by private donations. She adds that the Matrons of the Sanatorium *'were from moneyed backgrounds, indicated by the fact they left generous donations to the institution on resigning and often left legacies in their wills'*.

17. The Royal National Sanatorium in Bournemouth

As regards the Chapel of the Sanatorium, it was built in 1866-1867 shortly after the Leys arrived, based on designs by the eminent Architect George Edmund Street (Architect of the Law

Courts on the Strand in London). It was heated and connected to the main building by a wide connecting corridor. Mary Graham makes the important point that *'religion was believed to go hand in hand with medicine in the curing of disease'*. The Sanatorium building (as later extended) and the Chapel still exist as retirement flats and a large residents' lounge, respectively.

Turning to the Leys, they may have helped with fund-raising activities, made donations, offered practical help to convalescing patients, or a combination of all three. There is no evidence that Caroline Ley was a Matron or Nurse or that Reverend Richard Ley was ever Chaplain of the Chapel at the Sanatorium.

The Chapel that the couple built at *Stewarton Lodge* had the same ground plan as the one at the National Sanatorium, although it was probably about two-thirds the size of the original. It was also heated and connected to the main house by a wide corridor.

The addition of the Chapel at *Stewarton Lodge* can be seen by comparing the original ground plan of the house, as shown in the first large scale Ordnance Survey Map of the area with a plan of the property attached to the Conveyance when they sold the property on 7 June 1873, shown below.

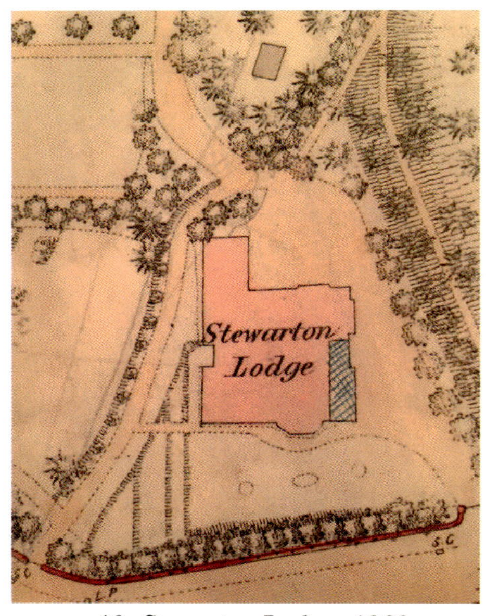

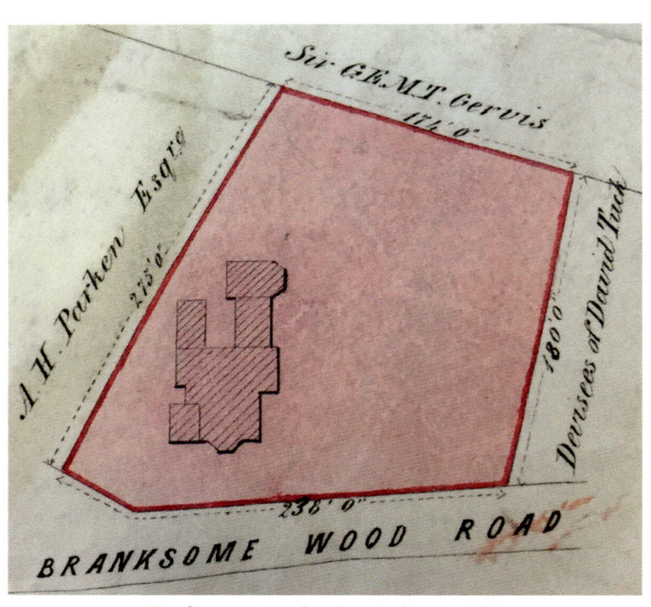

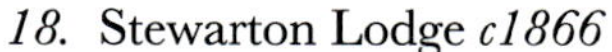
18. Stewarton Lodge *c1866*

19. Stewarton Lodge *in June 1873*

It is possible that the grounds or rooms of *Stewarton Lodge* were used on occasion by patients who were on the road to recovery, or when there was insufficient space in the main building. Mary Graham notes that *'the Chaplain at the Sanatorium led morning and evening prayers and services at regular intervals throughout the week. Attendance at these services was compulsory'*. While Reverend Richard Ley was not the Chaplain at the Sanatorium, he was still a Priest and may have led services in the private Chapel at *Stewarton Lodge*. Mrs Ley may have had a role in supervising the hosting of patients while they were at the house or in its grounds. Mary Graham notes that patients at the Sanatorium had to vacate their rooms by 10am each day, spending the day in the grounds or in the long, furnished corridors if the weather was inclement. The combination of fresh air and prayer was important.

In the 1871 Census, the Reverend Richard Ley is recorded as residing at *Stewarton Lodge*. However, Caroline was not there. It is not known where she was. As we turn to *Brontë Housë*, the themes of convalescing and prayer will continue.

While the Leys had moved into *Brontë House* by 26 August 1872, *Stewarton Lodge* remained on the market. It was put up for auction on 16 October 1872 but did not sell. A sale was only completed the following year on 6 June 1873.

Fairly soon after their arrival at *Brontë House* the Leys added the private Chapel already mentioned. During their stay they also added the Conservatory on the east side of the house. They are both mentioned for the first time in the advert when they sold it. They also probably added the matching Porch over the front door and the Greenhouse.

20. Brontë House *with the Conservatory and Porch added by the Leys*

While no photographs of the interior of *Brontë House* at this time have survived, we do know exactly how the main rooms were furnished as a house auction of all the contents was held when they left.

In the Drawing Room, there was a walnut couch covered in green rep, two easy chairs in walnut and papier-mâché, wicker seated, and other *'fancy chairs handsomely carved in walnut'*. There was a four-foot chiffonier with a marble top, plate glass back and three glass panels; two walnut whatnots, ottomans and a handsome oval-shaped walnut centre table, a walnut sofa and card, Sutherland and other fancy tables. There was also a four-tier bookcase and a handsome cable pattern plate pier glass 42" by 54" with a 44" gilt console table with marble top. On the floor was a Brussels carpet, hearth rug and on the chimney piece a japanned and gilt coal vase, a steel-mounted fender and on the windows rep curtains.

In the Dining Room there was a 10' by 4' ft 4" pitch pine dining table with 12 polished beech semi-circular chairs. There was a 10' 6" four-tier bookcase, a 6' Spanish mahogany pedestal sideboard, a plate glass mirror and *'a splendid marble mantle clock with bronze side-figures'*. There were striped rep curtains and ornamental items including a valuable collection of antique china.

The Boudoir had an oval-shaped walnut centre table, a 6' Spanish mahogany chiffonier-bookcase, walnut kidney-shaped writing table, walnut work-table and again a Brussels carpet, hearth rug, steel-mounted fender and set of fire irons, and about 220 volumes of books.

When the Leys moved in, the retired Surgeon Dr Elgie was still living at *Carlton Villa* next door with his two youngest daughters, his wife having died. *Brunswick Cottage* was let to a 39-year-old widow called Mrs Paul and her son, Alexander. They remained there until around 8 February 1873.

Then the next week's listing in the *Bournemouth Visitors' Directory* had the following surprising entry: *'Brontë Cottage – Sister Hilda'*. The 1 March 1873 edition threw more light on matters with the following advertisement (capitals as used in the original):

BRONTË COTTAGE, PARKSTONE

THE SISTERS will be glad to receive DAY PUPILS, or otherwise. LESSONS given in MUSIC and POINT-LACE; the latter worked to order. Illuminated texts, etc. may be procured.

The Sisters also have a HOME for GIRLS to be educated and trained for service. Terms, £12 a year after the age of 12; under 12, £10. Children in weak health for temporary care, 5s a week.

The Sisters remained at *Brontë Cottage* for about four months until the end of June 1873 when a Reverend E Norman Coles and family moved into *Brontë Cottage* for three months until mid-September 1873. Richard Elgie moved out of *Carlton Villa* around that time and in the *Bournemouth Visitors' Directory* of 5 July 1873, the entry for *Carlton Villa* becomes *'S. Katherine's Home – Sister Hilda'*. Presumably the Sisters' venture at *Brontë Cottage* moved to the larger house at *Carlton Villa* next door.

By 1 March 1874, the Sisters had moved again and *Carlton Villa* was vacant, listed under its original name. It remained vacant until 23 May 1874 when a Mr C E Pritchard and his family moved into the property. From at least that date the house appears to have been under separate ownership.

In the meantime, on 18 April 1874, an even more surprising entry appeared in the *Bournemouth Visitors' Directory: 'Brontë Cottage - Hip Hospital'*. A letter in the following week's newspaper provided the background:

HOME FOR SICK CHILDREN

I am anxious to engage the interest of the residents of Bournemouth in a small Convalescent Home for sick children recently established at Brontë Cottage, Parkstone, in the neighbourhood of your town. This house is a seaside branch of the hospital for hip disease in childhood, Queen Square, London. In that hospital sixty little children, boys and girls, all suffering from the painful complaint which gives its name to the hospital, are immured whilst they remain under medical treatment, and even under favourable circumstances their recovery is often a matter of some years. It will readily be imagined how beneficial to the health of those poor children is the change for a few weeks from the impure air of London to the health-giving sea breezes of Parkstone, and what immense delight they take in their little country home and fresh green landscape, and other country sights around them.

The cottage has, by the generosity of its owner been placed, rent free, entirely at the disposal of the hospital. But the committee, whilst gratefully accepting the offer for a time, have not considered themselves justified in taking advantage of it to its fullest extent, until it shall be seen whether sufficient funds will be forthcoming to meet the additional expenses entailed in such a home. The hospital is dependent solely upon voluntary contributions and the committee is not without hopes that the liberality of the residents at Bournemouth and the visitors of the town may provide them with funds sufficient to make the home a permanent institution.

The Lady Superintendent will have great pleasure in showing the home to visitors any afternoon between 2 and 6pm and will be very glad to receive the names of any ladies who will kindly volunteer to attend at the home on appointed days for the purpose of teaching and reading to the children. Gifts in kind, such as toys, old linen, etc. as well as donations in money will be very acceptable and may be forwarded to the Lady Superintendent at Parkstone. If you will kindly give this letter a place in your paper, you will be helping forward a good work. I remain, Sir, your obedient servant.

E. THURSTAN HOLLAND

Chairman of the Committee

According to Samantha Foot's study of the London hospital already referred to, The Alexandra Hospital for Children with Hip Disease, in the mid-nineteenth century tuberculosis was the largest single cause of death in England. It was the second highest killer, after diarrhoea, of children under five between 1861 and 1870. The most common form of non-pulmonary tuberculosis in children was tuberculosis of the bones and joints, including the hips. The House of Relief for Children with Chronic Disease of the Joints, later renamed the Alexandra Hospital for Children with Hip Disease, was founded in 1867 by two former nurses at the Hospital for Sick Children in London, Jane Perceval and Catherine Wood. Jane Perceval's family was prominent and wealthy. She bought 19 Queen Square, Bloomsbury as the hospital site. Like the National Sanatorium in Bournemouth, it was to be a voluntary hospital dependent entirely on public donations.

Foot comments that *'connections with the social elite enabled the hospital to attract noble and royal patronage, including Princess Alexandra, then Princess of Wales, to become its Patroness in 1870'*. Foot also refers to Frank Prochaska's study on philanthropy and the hospitals of London, noting that royal patronage was *'a virtual guarantee of prosperity'* for Victorian charities with subscribers and donors attracted either by a desire to follow royal example or because of the chance to become associated with the British aristocracy through common charitable interests. This provides a further clue as to why the

Leys may have been involved in the National Sanatorium and provided *Brontë Cottage* rent-free to The Alexandra Hospital as a convalescent home for children with hip disease.

The hospital's minutes first mention a lease on *Brontë Cottage* early in February 1874. Presumably, discussions had been taking place for some weeks prior to this. *Brontë Cottage* may seem a rather strange choice for a convalescent home for sick children, albeit it was in a part of the country famed for its health-giving properties. However, it was in the three-acre, secluded grounds of *Brontë House* and it had a homely character. Given the cottage only had a kitchen garden, the grounds of *Brontë House* would almost certainly have been used by the convalescing children when outdoors. The photograph shows a much later Lady Matron, Emily Bruun, in 1912 sitting under the verandah of the cottage with two healthy boys.

21. The verandah of Brontë Cottage with a later Lady Matron, Emily Bruun

The lease of *Brontë Cottage* dated 22 April 1874 between the Reverend Richard Ley and Howard Marsh, a Fellow of the Royal College of Surgeons, has survived. Marsh had married Jane Perceval in 1870 and provided his services as Surgeon to the hospital in London free of charge. *Brontë Cottage* was made available at a peppercorn rent. It was available during the lives of Richard and Caroline Ley and for a period of ten years thereafter, subject to three months' notice. If Richard Ley terminated the lease, he undertook to find similar premises. The lease was witnessed by a Dr Phillpotts of Parkstone, who was to be the local Surgeon who would look after the children, and the Ley's Gardener, John Coffen who was then living at *Brontë Lodge*.

A letter from the Director of the South-Western Railway Company was read out at the 10 February 1874 Committee Meeting *'granting the privilege of travelling 2nd class at 3rd class fares to the children and their attendants going from London to Parkstone'*. The station opened on 15 June 1874.

As regards the treatment of the sick children, it consisted of repositioning distorted joints, treating abscesses and nurturing patients' general health. The latter meant providing a good diet and fresh air where possible. Patients were expected to remain flat and in one position, sometimes for months, so as not to disturb a joint. Restless young patients were restrained in their cots by a chest band.

As with the National Sanatorium, it is not known what role Richard and Caroline Ley took in relation to the Hip Hospital at *Brontë Cottage*. Caroline Ley was certainly not the Lady Superintendent of the Hip Hospital. However, as the letter from Thurstan Holland states, there was a need for support from other ladies and she may have played a role in teaching and reading to the children. As regards the heated private Chapel added to the back of *Brontë House*, with an entrance from the house, its use may have been the same as the one at *Stewarton Lodge* as prayer was regarded as part of the treatment.

The use of *Brontë Cottage* was reviewed at meetings of the hospital's committee in London. At a meeting on 4 August 1874 its continued use was approved for a further three months with *'the question of permanent occupation to be referred to the next meeting'*. In the event, the meeting on 10 November 1874 agreed the occupation of *Brontë Cottage* for a further three months. However, unbeknown to the hospital, the 8 October 1874 issue of the *Poole & South-Western Herald* carried the following advert:

> *PARKSTONE*
>
> *FOR SALE a capital FREEHOLD RESIDENCE containing a large entrance hall, dining, drawing and breakfast-rooms, two private sitting-rooms, seven bedrooms and all the usual domestic offices; conservatory attached to the dining-room, flower and kitchen gardens and paddock; good stabling for three horses, coach-house, etc. An excellent entrance lodge. There is a private chapel, with entrance from the house.*
>
> *Full particulars to be obtained of Messrs Sharp and Co. Solicitors, Southampton.*

It is not known what triggered the Leys' move. On 8 December, a special meeting of the committee was held. The minutes stated:

> *MINUTES OF SPECIAL MEETING*
>
> *Agreed that the Committee accept Mr Ley's notice to terminate the lease of Brontë Cottage as from 17 December and his offer of £18 per annum in lieu of the condition that he should provide a new cottage. Resolved that as many of the children now at* Brontë Cottage, *Parkstone must be removed before the 17th instant in consequence of the cottage having been sold by the Reverend Richard Ley. This Committee approves of their being removed as soon as practicable to Bournemouth.*

Lady Eden agreed to provide £32 per annum to add to the £18 per annum given by the Reverend Richard Ley to make up a total of £50 to cover the rent, rates and expenses of the house proposed to be taken at Bournemouth. A lease was taken on a house in Lansdowne Road, Bournemouth.

On 8/9 December 1874, the entire contents of *Brontë House* were put up for auction in a house sale. Presumably, the Leys had already left otherwise they would have had no furniture to sit on.

A further twist in the story lies in the Indenture relating to the sale of the property dated 17 December 1874. This recorded that the sale of *Brontë House* (*Brontë Cottage* and *Brontë Lodge* were part of the property) was between Helen Emily Todd and Richard Ley on the one hand and William Joseph Pike (the purchaser) on the other. It is not known for certain who Helen Emily Todd was and why she was involved. The only candidate identified is a well-to-do spinster living near Southampton. It is not known whether she had provided a bridging loan to cover the period between the Leys buying *Brontë House* in August 1972 and the sale of *Stewarton Lodge* nearly a year later in June 1873. Maybe she had financed the difference in price between the two properties, as *Brontë House* was about £700 more expensive. Alternatively, she may have financed the building of the Chapel which would probably have cost around £700. The use of solicitors based in Southampton in the 8 October 1874 advert of the property suggests that this may have been the Helen Emily Todd concerned. The Reverend Walter Gill at *Heathfield* next door had obtained a 50 per cent mortgage on his property from a well-to-do widow in Oxfordshire in 1873, so maybe spinsters and widows with funds saw mortgages to Clergymen as a safe investment.

In both Bournemouth and Parkstone, the Leys were clearly committed to helping the sick to convalesce, prayer being a crucial part of the treatment hence the private Chapels. These themes will recur in the final chapter where the Leys will continue to surprise.

Meanwhile, the auctioneer cryptically remarked:

'the Reverend Ley is removing to a distance'.

Chapter 4

MARMADUKE

In 1877 the best-selling Victorian Novelist Dinah Mulock Craik visited the Pike family at *Leymore*. Twenty-five years earlier she had stayed at their former home at 16 North Street, Wareham while writing her early novel *Agatha's Husband*. She also wrote part of the novel which would make her rich and famous, *John Halifax, Gentleman*, while staying at the house. In 1877 she jotted in her diary: *'William and Anna Pike grown old. Children all men and women'*.

While no photographs of William and Anna Pike are known to have survived, we fortunately have Craik's affectionate portrait of William Pike in her character Marmaduke Dugdale, a Clay Merchant, in *Agatha's Husband*. Pike's obituary described the characterisation as a *'faithful and amusing picture of him... and while not sparing his peculiarities it has done full justice to his many noble qualities'*.

22. Dinah Craik aged 57 in 1883

At the time of Craik's visit in 1852, Pike was aged 43 and his wife, Anna 28, their children being Evelyn (6), William Lewison (4), Laurence Warburton (2), and Crystal Anna Pike (1). Craik first describes Marmaduke Dugdale as:

'a country-looking gentleman coming down the street in a mild, lazy, dreamy fashion, his hat pushed up at a considerable elevation from his forehead, leaving a mass of light hair straggling out at the back, his eyes bent thoughtfully on the pavement, and his hands crossed behind him'.

A little later she writes:

'Mr Dugdale walked in composedly through the sash window, beaming around him a sort of general smile. He never attempted any individual greeting, and Agatha offering her hand, was met by his surprised but benevolent 'Eh!' However, when required he gave a hearty grasp. After which, peering dreamily round the room, he pounced upon a queer-looking folio, and buried himself therein, making occasional remarks highly interesting of their kind, but slightly irrelevant to the conversation in general. Agatha amused herself with peeping at the title of the book – some abstruse work on mechanical science – and then watched the reader, thinking what great intellectual power there was in the head, and what acuteness of the eye. Also, he wore at times a wonderfully spiritual expression strangely contrasting with the materiality of his daily existence. No-one could see that look without feeling convinced that there were beautiful depths open only to Divinest vision, in the silent and abstracted nature of Marmaduke Dugdale. Nevertheless, he could be eminently practical now and then, especially in mechanics'.

23. 16 North Street Wareham is the large house with railings on the left-hand side of the road

Dugdale's wife, known as Harrie in the novel (Anna in real life), is described as:

'a merry-looking, pretty woman, of a style a little too pronounced perhaps, for her features were of a similar mould to Major Harper's. Still, there could be no doubt as to the prettiness, and the airy, youthful aspect, younger perhaps than her years. Agatha was perfectly astounded to find in this gay Harrie the wife of the grave and middle-aged Duke Dugdale!'

"How did Duke fall in love with me? Really, I can't tell. I was fifteen or so – a mere baby! He first gave me a doll, and then wanted to marry me! Somehow it all came quite naturally. We belonged to one another."

Craik was also close friends with William Joseph Pike's brother John William Pike and his wife Mary Pike (née Mayer). Mary was the daughter of Thomas Mayer of the Longhill Pottery and, like Craik, had spent her early years in Stoke-on-Trent and then Newcastle-under-Lyme, which is possibly where the friendship originated. Craik also had a close friendship with the couple's three daughters.

By the time of her visit to *Leymore* in 1877, Craik had completed 19 novels, numerous children's and travel books, short stories, poems and essays, including many on women's issues. *John Halifax, Gentleman* was an enormously successful book, published in 1856. With the proceeds over the ensuing years, she was able to commission the eminent architect Richard Norman Shaw in 1868/69 to design a large house in the Early English Style, the *Corner House* in Bromley. It still exists, sadly divided into seven flats around 1930.

Turning to William Pike and his business, he was just the sort of affluent merchant that Alfred Crabb probably hoped to attract in 1862 when *Brontë House* was built. Once Parkstone Station opened in June 1874, merchants like Pike, who had previously been based in Wareham close to his business, were able to commute from Parkstone.

In the 1871 Census, William Pike is described as a *'Merchant, Ship Owner and Worker for clay mines employing 220 men'*. He was then aged 61, residing at 16 North Street with his wife Anna, then 47. His sons William Lewison and Laurence Warburton Pike also still lived at the house, aged 23 and 21, respectively, both involved in the clay business. Also living there were Pike's youngest son Arnold (9) and his daughters Evelyn (25), Crystal Anna (20), Anna Lilian (16), Katherine Lewis (12) and Marion Lewis Pike (4). His son Wilfrid, born in 1856, had drowned in a tragic sailing accident in Studland Bay in 1863 while his daughter Edith, recorded as two months old in the 1851 Census, also appears to have died.

William Joseph Pike (1809-1884) and his brother John William Pike (1813-1869) were the third generation of Pikes to be involved in the Dorset ball clay business. Their grandfather, Joseph Pike had left the existing ball clay mining business in Chudleigh, south Devon in the 1750s to explore and then mine the deposits in Dorset. He established the ball clay business in Dorset around 1760. His son William Pike (1761-1833) continued the business on his father's death in 1807. When William died in 1833, his two sons William Joseph and John William Pike inherited the business, trading as *W & J Pike, Clay Merchants*. Their brother, Warburton Pike, became a barrister in London, and in his spare time was a noted translator of the Poet Dante.

The Ball Clay Heritage Society in their booklet *The Ball Clays of Devon and Dorset* note that *'unlike china clays – with which they are sometimes confused – ball clays are rather rare in the world. What are probably the world's most important deposits are found in Devon and Dorset. Ball clays from these deposits have been used by manufacturers of white-bodied pottery since the days of the famous 18th century potters such as Josiah Wedgwood, Asbury and Spode'*.

The booklet further explains that the term 'ball clay' *'derives from the former method of winning the clay by cutting it from the floor of an open pit in cubes. Due to the clay's high plasticity, the cubes held together but after being handled several times the corners became knocked in and the cubes were turned into balls – so to the potters, a plastic white-firing clay was a ball clay'*.

Joseph Pike originally took leases near East Creech in the Purbecks. In the 1790s, clay pits were dug at Furzebrook nearby. In 1791, Joseph Pike signed a contract with Josiah Wedgwood to supply ball clay for his pottery.

In 1840 a railway track was constructed to move the clay from Furzebrook to Ridge on the River Frome. The track had a gentle slope so that special braked wagons could gradually travel down the track to a wharf at Ridge on the River Frome, pulling a dandy wagon containing a horse which could then pull the empty clay wagons back to Furzebrook. Pike's obituary later commented: *'much of the machinery used in the works was designed by him and he was his own engineer in constructing the railway from the pits to the wharf; the barges were towed by tug to Wareham, then shipped to Poole where they were distributed to the potteries'.*

In 1866 the track was re-laid for a locomotive to pull the wagons up and down the line to Ridge. The first one was called *Primus*. It was followed in 1874 by a second locomotive, called *Secundus*. This is the only one of the seven locomotives purchased by the Pikes over the years to have survived.

Tragically, John William Pike died aged 57 in 1869, his wife Mary having died three years earlier at the age of 39. While their boys went to Rugby School and then to Oxford University, the girls were left in Wareham in the care of a guardian and a governess. The business was thereafter known as *W J Pike, Clay Merchant*. Chris Legg has written the definitive history of the mining operations and railways of the Pike brothers. His book and other relevant works are listed in the Bibliography.

24. Secundus *purchased by William Joseph Pike in 1874, shown here in 1938*

When William and Anna Pike arrived at *Brontë House* on or soon after 17 December 1874, aged 65 and 51, respectively, one of the first things they did was to change its name to *Leymore*. It was not unknown as a house name elsewhere, but it seems to be more than a coincidence that the previous owner was called Ley.

The Pikes' surviving children were still living at home: their sons William and Laurence Pike, aged 27 and 25, respectively, (known as 'Lew' and 'Larry' according to Chris Legg) together with their younger brother Arnold, aged 12, and their daughters Evelyn (29), Anna Lilian (19), Katherine Lewis (18) and Marion Lewis (17). Their daughter Crystal Pike had died earlier that year.

The Pikes had four servants at *Leymore*: Ellen Sherwood, a widow born in Poole, aged 35, as their Cook; Mary Dowland aged 28, from Swanage as a Parlour Maid; Annie Selby aged 23, born in Wareham, as House Maid; and Mary Jane Selby born in Church Knowle, aged 18, as Kitchen Maid. Various members of the Selby family had been servants with the Pike family since the 1850s.

William Pike brought his Coachman in Wareham with him to Parkstone, George Roe, who was then aged 56. Roe was a long-standing contact of William Pike, having previously worked for him as a Foreman. He and his wife Mary Ann, aged 34, their daughters Kate and Minnie and Mary's sister Elizabeth Hooper lived at *Leymore Lodge*. At *Leymore Cottage* (still called *Brunswick Cottage* in the 1881 Census), lived Pike's Gardener Thomas Best, aged 39, his wife Ethelred and three young children. Presumably with three-acres of grounds and a large Greenhouse, he had plenty to keep him occupied.

The area north of Ashley Cross had remained little changed since *Brontë House* was built in 1862. To the north and west of the house lay open fields. Constitutional Hill Road (now St Peter's Road) just had a few cottages and small holdings. The original St Peter's Church, built in 1833, was still standing along with the school of the same date, as shown in Paul Brannon's print of the 1850s. The Author began his schooling in this building over 100 years later in 1960.

25. St Peter's Church and School dating from 1833 in a print dating from the 1850s

However, as Canon H R Dugmore would later recall:

'in 1872 there were already signs that the population was likely to increase. The town of Bournemouth, within the memory of many people only a fishing village, was becoming an important health resort, while Poole, whose ancient trade with Newfoundland had almost ceased, was reviving by reason of the building enterprises at Bournemouth. There was no railway station nearer than Hamworthy on the one side, and what is now Bournemouth Central Station on the other; but a railway was in progress which should pass through Poole and join the main line to Weymouth at Broadstone and Parkstone was to have its own station'.

William Joseph Pike was probably only in semi-retirement as he is unlikely to have left the business, built up over three generations, in the hands of his two young sons, Lew and Larry, both still in their twenties. Parkstone Station enabled them all easily to commute to Wareham.

When walking to Parkstone Station a couple of years later in 1876, or travelling in his coach with George Roe, the Pikes would have seen the new St Peter's church beginning to take shape. It was recognised that the *'now inadequate and rapidly disintegrating old church'* would need to be replaced with a larger one. The foundation stone for the new church was laid on 1 August 1876.

In 1877, Pike's son Laurence and daughter Evelyn both got married. Laurence married Eleanor Sturdy from Trigon near Wareham on 30 April 1877. They moved into *Furzebrook House* close to the Furzebrook clay mines. Evelyn Pike married a merchant who is believed to have operated mainly in Chile, Walter Squire, on 26 July 1977 in Poole.

26. Parkstone Station in later photograph

It seems likely that Dinah Craik's visit to *Leymore* in 1877 coincided with one of these marriages, possibly the latter one. She would have remembered Evelyn and Laurence, as well as William Lewison, as small children when she stayed with the Pikes in 1852/3 while writing *Agatha's Husband* and parts of *John Halifax, Gentleman.*

On 19 June 1878, William Lewison Pike tied the knot with a local girl Jessie Aldridge Durrell, the ceremony being held at St Peter's Church, Parkstone. Given that parts of the new church had not been consecrated at that date, it is possible that the ceremony was held in what remained of the old church. The couple moved to *Mayfield*, an early nineteenth century house on Sloop Hill, on what is now called Commercial Road. When their daughter and son, Crystal and Joseph were born in 1879 and 1880, respectively, the family was still living at the house, William Lewison Pike being described as a *'clay merchant'*, as he would be in the 1881 Census when the family was still at the house.

In August 1879, the Parkstone British Mixed Infant School was opened in the Schoolroom belonging to the Congregational Buckland Chapel next door, rent-free. The Schoolroom had been added to the east side of the chapel shortly before. Although there is no specific evidence of William Pike funding the building of the Schoolroom, he is known to have had a deep interest in education, in particular the British School in Wareham, so he could well have done. His obituary noted: *'he took a deep interest in education. For many years he was treasurer of the British School. When this passed under a school board, he became chairman and filled this office to the last. He further gratuitously discharged the duties of clerk'*.

The first report of the Parkstone school, dated September 1880, indicates that the school opened with 13 children. By September 1880, 70 children were on the books with an average attendance of approximately 53. The report also shows that during its first year it received approximately £56 in donations and £26 in *'school pence'*, the one penny charges levied on pupils where their parents were able to pay. It records that the school mistress was a Miss Peckett. This was Margaret Peckett from Sydenham, then aged 21, who was boarding at 2 Fern Cottages in Church Street. She was paid £50 per annum. Desks, cupboards, paper, books and school materials accounted for nearly £30. The Committee was made up of local gentry and clergy interested in education including the lawyer Martin Kemp-Welch and the Reverend Walter Gill and Mrs Gill of Heathfield School on the opposite corner of the site.

27. Open fields still lay to the north and west of Leymore *in the 1870s*

After the death of John William and Mary Pike, Craik became closer to their daughters, Mary Constance, Isobel and Ada Violet Pike (known to Craik as *'Connie, Bel and Ada'*). Craik may have sympathised with the girls' predicament as on the death of her mother in 1845, Craik was abandoned by her errant non-conformist preacher father. A note in her diary dated 26 January 1880 records the Pike girls joining her in an ice-skating trip in Bromley. By 1881, Ada was at a private girls' school run by a Mrs Williams at a house called *Fir Grove* on Castle Hill in Parkstone (another of the 'follies' built in the 1860s referred to by Frank Cathery). A few years later, the three girls would move to a house in Shortlands Grove, Bromley close to Craik's *Corner House.*

In August 1881, Dinah Craik visited the Pikes again. Anna Pike was suffering from cancer at the time. Craik noted in her diary: *'Anna Pike changed but bright. William Pike just the same. Remembered me and Polly as girls this month 40 years ago'.* On 23 June 1882, Anna Pike died at *Leymore*. The *Parkstone Reminder* of 1 July 1882 noted: *'we record with much regret the death of Mrs Pike of Leymore. Her health had for a long time been giving way, but the end came suddenly and somewhat unexpectedly on Friday evening last. The funeral was on Tuesday last at Knowle'.* As regards William Joseph Pike, the paper later noted that *'the death of his wife affected him very deeply'.* Presumably, he was at work in Wareham at the time as his son Willliam Lewison was the one in attendance at the time of her death. William Lewison was by then resident at a new house called *Windholm* in Mount Road near the top of North Road.

By the following year, William Joseph Pike seems to have recovered his spirits a little as in November 1883 he visited Craik, apparently at the *Corner House* in Bromley. Craik noted in her diary: *'William Pike to tea. 80 but his old self of 40 years ago'.* In fact, he was 74 at the time but may have looked 80.

Sometime in the early 1880s, William Lewison Pike must have agreed with his father that he would retire from the ball clay business. When William Joseph Pike signed his will on 29 April 1884, it stated that the clay business would be left to his sons Laurence and Arnold Pike, then being 35 and 22, respectively. William Lewison was amply provided for in the will but soon removed to the impressive *Richmond House* in Appledore, Devon, referred to as a *'Retired Clay Merchant'.*

On 25 August 1884, William Joseph Pike died at *Leymore*, aged 75. His son Arnold Pike, who was still resident at the house, was present at his death. William Joseph Pike left £156,877, or around £10 million in today's money. As noted, the business was left to Laurence and Arnold Pike, being renamed *Pike Brothers, Clay Merchants. Leymore* and its contents were left to his three spinster daughters, Anna, Katherine and Marion Pike as tenants in common. All of his children were well provided for. The three Misses Pike are recorded in the *Bournemouth Visitors' Directory* as living at *Leymore* until February 1885. Thereafter, the property appears to have been unoccupied for long periods until it was sold to its next owner, James Jackson, in June 1891.

William Joseph Pike was buried in the churchyard at Church Knowle, the village where he was born. Meanwhile, the *Wareham Advertiser* did not hold back in its obituary:

'his excellence as an employer is shown by the fact that so many have grown grey in his service: the eight bearers had been with him from 20 to 45 years. It has been again and again said: "a better master there could not be." A gentleman very closely connected with him in business for over half a century speaks in the highest terms of his justice and fairness: he would stick to a bargain, though it might be a bad one; and if his word had been given, it was as good as a bond; and he was ever ready to do an act of kindness. He probably had no fixed views on religion, certainly he cared not for its forms; it was his conviction that our chief concern should be to fulfil the manifest duties that lie before us, to be truthful, upright, unassuming, he was every inch a man. The loss of such in a country district is not soon repaired. All honour to his memory:

He was a man, take him for all in all,
I shall not look upon his like again'.

THE DANISH CONNECTION

James Jackson bought the freehold of *Leymore* for £2,925 in June 1891, including *Leymore Lodge* and *Leymore Cottage*. Soon after moving in, he changed the name of the main house to *Dane Court* with the lodge and the cottage usually being referred to as *Dane Court Lodge* and *The Cottage*, respectively. The Danish connection will be explained later. As with William Pike, Jackson was just the sort of affluent merchant that Alfred Crabb probably hoped to attract when he built the house. Given Jackson's business commitments its proximity to Parkstone Station would have been most convenient.

28. James and Ada Jackson are third and fourth from the right - Betws-y-Coed in 1906

The photograph above dates from 1906 and is the only known picture in which James and his wife Ada Jackson (née Bailes) are believed to be shown. Taken in Betws-y-Coed in North Wales,

James and Ada Jackson are third and fourth from the right. His brother and business partner, George Jackson, is seated in the back of his new Lanchester Landaulette. He was a widower and not at all well at the time. On the far left is George's youngest son Barry (later Sir Barry Jackson, the Founder of the Birmingham Rep and a Director of the Royal Shakespeare Theatre and the Royal Opera House Covent Garden). James Jackson's sons Vincent and Alfred Gillingham Jackson are believed to be in the centre under the arch of the porch, with George Jackson's chauffeur on the far right. James and Ada Jackson were then aged 64 and 52, respectively.

In the conveyance of June 1891 relating to the purchase of *Leymore*, James Jackson is referred to as a *'Provision Merchant'* of *Pen-Craigh*, Branksome Park, Bournemouth. In the 1891 Census he is recorded at that address as a *'Butter Merchant'*. In fact, he and his family had only lived at *Pen-Craigh* for three months while looking for a property in Parkstone close to the station. On 11 June 1891, *The Poole & Bournemouth Herald* reported: *'we understand that the favourite residential property of Leymore, Parkstone, has been purchased by Mr James Jackson of Bristol, who is immediately taking up residence'*.

James Jackson came from a family that was entrepreneurial and had to live by their wits. This would stand him and his brother George in good stead in their future business careers.

29. Joseph Jackson (1809-1871)

30. Ruth Jackson (née Hawker)

James was born on 7 February 1842 in Hurstpierpoint, Sussex. He was the third and youngest son of Joseph and Ruth Jackson (née Hawker). His father was described in the 1841 Census as a *'Superintendent - Rail Road'*, the local line there being constructed at the time. Joseph was later described as a *'Contracting Surveyor'* relating to the building of the railways and as a *'Civil Engineer'*. Due to his work, the family moved around a lot: between 1835 and 1848 they resided in Hammersmith, Deptford, Hurstpierpoint, Worcester and Cambridge. By 1851 there may have been a dip in his line of work as we find Joseph and his wife running *The Plough Tavern* in Shoreditch for a couple of years. Their eldest son Joseph appears to have died by that time. The children at the *Plough Tavern* were George (12) James (9) and daughters Sarah (16), Mary Ann (14), Emma (6), Ellen (5) and Catherine (3).

By 1861, Joseph and Ruth Jackson had moved to the High Street in Teddington. Joseph is shown again as a *'Surveyor'*. George and James Jackson had left home by this time to find their fortunes.

At some point in the 1860s Joseph and Ruth Jackson split. With considerable resourcefulness, in her mid-50s, Ruth started her own business as a Stationer and Haberdasher at 83 Westbourne Park Road in Bayswater. In the 1871 Census she is shown at the shop aged 58 with three of her daughters as assistants: Mary Ann (30), Kate (23) and Fanny (19). The photograph of Ruth is taken at around that time by a professional Photographer in Westbourne Park. Meanwhile, James's brother George Jackson had acquired a small business, called Medova Dairies in Birmingham. He gradually built the business up by importing high quality Danish butter directly from Danish farms without a middleman. He traded under his own name, keeping the Medova name as one of his brands. Many of the shops later traded under the Danish Dairy Company name, mainly located in the industrial towns with large working-class populations. He was based in Birmingham.

James Jackson's movements in the 1860s and early 1870s are a mystery. He disappears from UK records. It is possible that he worked in Denmark. Given the important role he would later take in his brother's business from the mid-1880s onwards, and the need to source top quality butter from Danish farms, it seems quite likely. It is improbable that George Jackson would have employed him in such a key role later if James had not known the business well. During his time away, James got married and was widowed.

31. George Jackson in the mid-1880s

James Jackson reappears living at 3 Richford Street in Hammersmith at the time of his second marriage on 7 September 1878, close to his mother at number 32. He married Ada Maria Bailes, the daughter of a cabinet maker, in the St Andrews Presbyterian Church in Goldhawk Road, Shepherd's Bush. Ada was living at 86 Westbourne Park Villas in Bayswater close to Mrs Jackson's haberdashery shop. This may be how she got to know James Jackson.

Over the next six years James Jackson and his young family moved around in West London a good deal: his daughter Ada Ruth Jackson and first son James Frederick Jackson were born at 2 Portobello Terrace, Notting Hill on 6 January 1879 and 2 March 1880, respectively; Vincent Jackson at 73 Shepherd's Bush Avenue, Shepherd's Bush on 12 March 1881 and Alfred Gillingham Jackson at 19 Addison Terrace on 15 May 1884. Throughout this time James Jackson worked in London in the wine trade, variously described as *'a Wine Merchant's Clerk'*, *'a Cellar Clerk'* and finally as *'Managing Clerk of a Wine Merchant'*.

By the mid-1880s his brother George Jackson had developed his butter business across the country with over 60 shops. James Jackson appears to have joined, or re-joined, his brother in the business around this time. By 1888 James Jackson was in Bristol, referred to as *'the District Manager'*, probably an Area Manager in today's parlance. He was responsible for identifying suitable premises and opening stores. An informative article appeared in the *Western Daily Press*:

THE DANISH DAIRY COMPANY – JAMES JACKSON

A practical proof of the substantial development of the operations of the Danish Dairy Company, the district manager of which is Mr James Jackson, is afforded by the fact that today a large branch business is to be opened at 18 Old Market Street for the convenience of residents in the thickly-populated districts in the eastern part of the city.

This company which first introduced the products of the Danish farms into this city (in High Street) about three months ago has about seventeen large businesses situated in fifteen of the principal towns of the United Kingdom, the object being to supply the butter to consumers without the intervention of middlemen. In Denmark, the company have agents who devote the whole of their time to the selection of the best butter from the principal farms. The butter, having been examined and passed by those experts, is then packed into small barrels and the name of the farmer having been inscribed inside the cover, it is then despatched to the nearest port and conveyed to the English branches of the company.

Consumers are thus enabled to obtain the best Danish butter in excellent condition within a few days after it is made. The accommodation at the premises in High Street, owing to the rapid increase of business, has been found to be inadequate, and this has led to the acquisition of the shop and warehouse in Old Market Street. In connection with the central shop, it may be mentioned there are large, cool cellars which are filled with casks of butter. These cellars are especially suitable for the purpose, the butter - which, however, does not for obvious reasons, remain longer than a few hours there – being kept in pristine condition.

At the present time about 10 tons of butter pass weekly through the establishment and, with the provision of additional facilities, it is expected that this quantity will be materially increased. In another part of the premises employees of the company are busily employed in weighing the butter and enclosing it in parchment wrappers. The new shop is conveniently arranged, is well-lit and admirably fitted, marble having been freely utilised on the counters and in the windows and everything is scrupulously neat and clean. The premises have a depth of about 120 feet, affording on a line with the shop extensive warehouse facilities. There are also rooms upstairs and the cellars are commodious and cool.

It is not known what prompted James Jackson to move to Parkstone. Perhaps he needed a central location in the south of England close to a train station from which he could commute in his role identifying sites for and opening new stores. In June 1891, he and his wife were aged 49 and 37, respectively with their family Ada (12), James (11), Vincent (10) and Alfred Jackson (7). It is not known who their servants were as the family moved to the house just after the 1891 Census and left before the next one. However, we do know that he travelled about locally in a landau with two bay horses, of which more later. One of his first actions was to change the house name to *Dane Court* given his involvement in the Danish Dairy Company.

It was a lucrative time for the business and numerous shops continued to be opened. By 1893 George Jackson was reputedly the largest retailer of butter in the world with 30,000 tons sold every year. James Jackson would have been a busy man and probably away on business a good deal. George Jackson's main competitor was the Maypole Diary which by 1895 was the largest retailer of margarine in Britain.

Alongside his business activities, James Jackson became a pillar of the community. He was Chairman of the Branksome Conservative Club for many years. He was also involved in fund raising for the new Congregational Church on Commercial Road in 1892. With the growth of

Parkstone, attendance at the Buckland Chapel had been increasing. Densham and Ogle in their 1899 book called *The Story of the Congregational Churches of Dorset* comment:

'the memorial stone was laid by T J Hankinson Esq of Bournemouth on 10 November 1892 and a large meeting was held in the evening, James Jackson of Dane Court in the Chair. Strenuous efforts were made by paster and people to raise the requisite funds'.

The Reverend Walter Gill and his wife of Heathfield School *'rendered valuable assistance to the Parkstone church and their sterling worth and kindly sympathies won for them many friends'.* Given Jackson's connections with the Congregational Church and the Gills, he may well have sent his three sons, James, Vincent and Alfred, to Heathfield School next door to *Dane Court*.

32. James and Ada Jackson in 1906

During the 1880s the area north of Ashley Cross changed a good deal. Several large villas had been built on the east side of Constitutional Hill Road (now St Peter's Road and the upper part of North Road). Also, during the 1890s similar but smaller villas were built on the north side of what is now the east end of Danecourt Road. The backs of these new villas can be seen on the upper right of the next photo. No houses had yet been built on the new section of North Road, between what is now Danecourt Road and St Peter's Road. The completed St Peter's Church may also be seen.

There had also been developments in Ashley Cross. New Dutch-style villas had been built on Commercial Road at the corner with Church Street (now Parr Street). There was a Bookseller and Newsagent, A & H Jarvis, where previously H C Palmer's grocery shop had stood. To the west of these were several terraced villas. The photo was taken a few years after 1900 just after Jacksons had left. A new parade of shops had been erected in the distance. Further shops were added to the fronts of the villas a few years later and the Central Hotel was built on the corner.

On 7 December 1894, the following appeared in the *Western Gazette*:

FIRST ELECTION OF GUARDIANS - TO THE ELECTORS OF PARKSTONE

LADIES AND GENTLEMEN – I rejoice to observe that the Legislature has provided the means whereby the wants of those amongst us who are poor and needy will have a more careful and attentive supervision than in the past. The election of a greater number of Guardians who are earnest and painstaking in their duties, will, I feel sure, have a most beneficial effect in the working of our Poor-law system, both as regards the poor themselves and the pockets of the ratepayers – a desideratum which it will be admitted is greatly needed. Feeling as I do the immense importance of this subject, I have, in response to a number of requests from my fellow ratepayers and neighbours, gladly allowed myself to be nominated as a Candidate for the office of a Guardian for Parkstone District, and I now appeal with confidence to the Electors for their interest and support in securing my return, assuring them that should I be elected my sole object will be to see that the work of the Union is well and efficiently carried out with economy and justice to all concerned.

I have the honour to remain, Ladies and Gentlemen,

Yours faithfully,

JAMES JACKSON

Danecourt, Parkstone 6 December 1894

According to historian Mark Blaug, the Poor Law system provided *'a welfare state in miniature, relieving the elderly, widows, children, the sick, the disabled, the unemployed and the underemployed'*. The functions of Poor Law Unions (or districts) were exercised by Boards of Guardians elected by ratepayers.

33. Villas on the east side of Constitutional Hill Road (now North Road) c1905

On 25 March 1896, James Jackson purchased *Heathfield* from Charles Ernest Gill of Heathfield School, his father Walter Gill having died. As noted in Chapter 3, there was a mortgage on the house of £800 with a widow in Oxford, Alice Lucy of *Thornleigh*, Woodstock Road, Oxford. She was repaid as part of the transaction. The purchase price for *Heathfield* was £1,600. Thereafter, Heathfield School leased the property from James Jackson.

James Jackson took the opportunity to use some of the front garden of *Heathfield* to adapt the driveway of *Dane Court* so that the front gates were on St Peter's Road rather than in Church Road although this may have been done in the early 1920s when trees on the east side of the site were cleared for a cricket pitch. The plan below was attached to the Abstract of Title in 1936, by which time *Heathfield* was being used as the Liberal Club.

34. Commercial Road looking westwards c1900

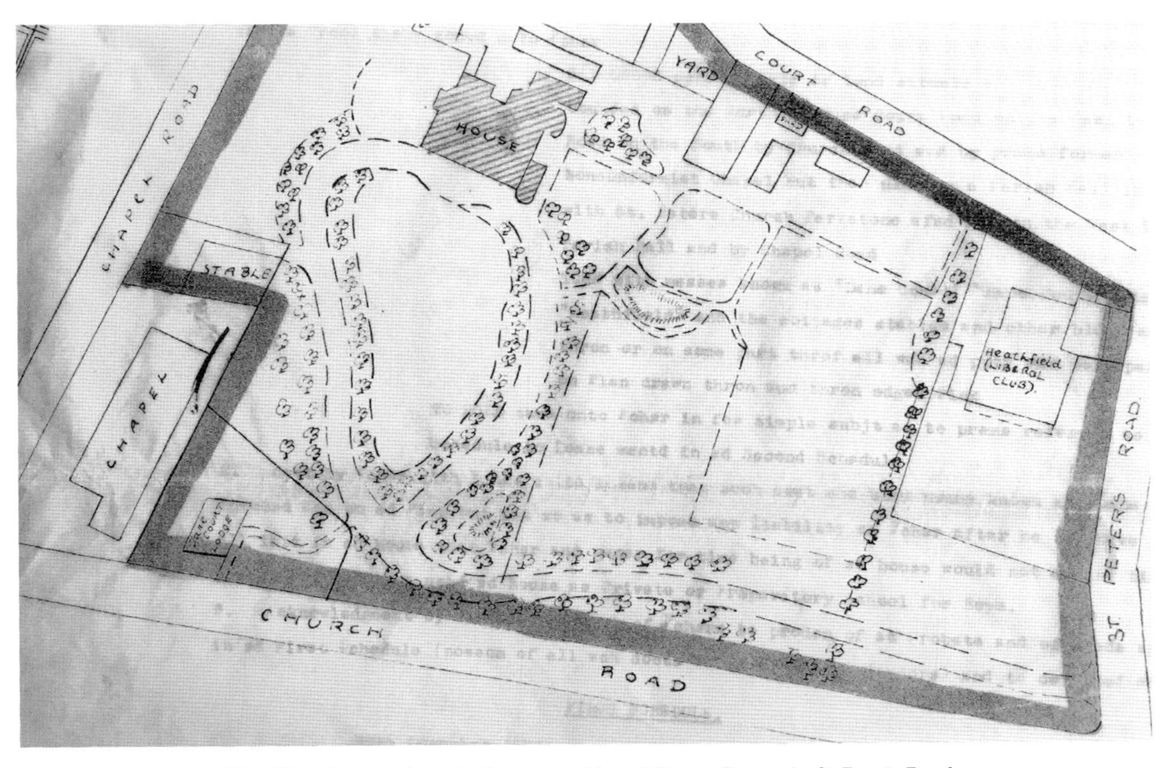

35. Plan showing the revised entrance drive of Dane Court *in St Peter's Road*

In 1898 George Jackson's business and the Maypole Dairy merged and at that point George and James Jackson retired, both with substantial fortunes. In April 1899, James' daughter Ada married the Managing Director of the merged Maypole Diary Company, Charles Jean Moosbrugger (known as 'Moss') at St George's Church in Hanover Square, London. A reception was held for 130 guests at the Hotel Victoria in London. They spent their honeymoon in Switzerland, Mr Moss being from Fribourg.

One day in June 1899, the bay horses in the stables at *Dane Court* pricked up their ears when a stranger's footsteps crunched the gravel on the drive. Unbeknown to them, an advertisement had appeared in *The Western Gazette* stating:

'Pair of Horses, Landau and Silver-Plated Harness for Sale. Quiet, sound and trustworthy horses at a moderate price. Apply to the owner'.

The owner was *'Mr James Jackson, Dane Court, Parkstone, who is shortly leaving the district'*. After they moved, the Jackson family continued to own the freehold of *Dane Court* (including *Dane Court Lodge* and *The Cottage*) until it was sold in early 1936. After 1900 it was leased to tenants.

Chapter 6

RIDER HAGGARD'S TUTOR

Early in 1900, *Dane Court* was a hive of activity. The Reverend Henry John Graham, then aged 60, had leased the property from James Jackson. He planned to move his boys' preparatory school, The Mount Lodge School in St Leonard's-on-Sea, to Parkstone at the start of the Summer Term in 1900. A Schoolroom and Boys' Changing Room were hastily erected, various internal changes made to the building and suitable furniture and dormitory beds moved in.

A later pupil, Hampden Fordham (known as 'Bim'), takes us on a tour of the house:

'an imposing gateway with stone pillars; a long drive dividing into two to encircle the tree-fringed lawn in front of the house. On the left of the drive, Charles the Gardener's cottage; on the left of the house a rough lawn and the Museum – a small timber building. On the right of the house the Tennis Court and a vast Kitchen Garden with pig sties. At the rear, the Playground or 'Gravel', at the bottom of which the famous huge beech tree 'Old Rum' flourished.

The house of Dane Court was of grey brick and ivy covered; it had three gables. It was lit entirely by gas, and not noticeably heated at all, except for fires or stoves in some of the rooms, but the Schoolroom was heated by a very efficient water radiator. The Dining Hall, T-shaped and extending from the front to the back of the house, was on the left of the front door'.

36. Dane Court *c1911*

'The back-stairs, through a loudly-banging self-closing door, led to the Junior Dormitory on the first floor, and the Senior Dormitories and Box Room on the second. I remember iron bedsteads, wash-stands with jugs and basins of Barnstable pottery – and the occasion during a hard winter, when the water was found to be frozen in the jugs one morning'.

37. The Dining Room on the west side of the house

38. Dormitory No.3 on the second floor

'At the back, a stone passage led to the Changing Room and the Schoolroom. The former was tile-floored and glass-roofed, with a bank of six wash basins in the middle. The Schoolroom (turn left out of the Changing Room) was a large wooden building sheathed in corrugated iron and painted brown. It could be divided into two sections by folding partitions. Leading off the Changing Room was The Cottage, containing quarters for the Matron and the Sick Room'.

39. The Boys' Changing Room

Pictured at the time of his retirement in the summer of 1911 when aged 71, the Reverend Graham had by then been Headmaster of the school he founded for 44 years. His first pupil in 1867, when a Curate at Hunstanton in Norfolk, was (Henry) Rider Haggard. Haggard became one of the most prolific Novelists of the Victorian and Edwardian eras being the Author of the best seller *King Solomon's Mines*. When Graham moved to become the Curate at Garsington in Oxfordshire later that year, Haggard followed him. In 1871, the Reverend Graham became the Vicar of Ashampstead and continued to tutor a few boys. In 1878 though, he decided to set up a fully-fledged school in St Leonards-on-Sea in a house called *Mount Lodge*, hence the name Mount Lodge School.

Arthur Graham Batterham, who attended Dane Court Preparatory School between 1908 and 1913, later recalled:

'the Reverend H J Graham (whom we always spoke of as "G") seemed to us to be a very old man; his bald head and wrinkled face were slightly brown; I can't recall his ever being ill and it never occurred to me that he would retire or that his rather grim school would ever be changed'.

'In G's time there were three dreaded punishments: the slipper, 'the plain pudding list' and lines. It must be explained that normally the first helping of pudding was a sweet such as jam tart or apple pie, but the second helping was milk pudding with a little brown sugar. If you were on the plain pudding list, you had milk pudding for your first

(compulsory) helping without sugar. Lines usually began: 'I must not...' When my brother Gordon bolted all three of the lavatory doors by climbing over the partitions, G told him to write a thousand lines:

"I must not play the giddy-goat with the water-closets" '.

While the episode probably caused great hilarity amongst the boys, clearly the Reverend Graham had to respond. One detects though in the wording that the hilarity of the prank was not entirely lost on him though he could not show it.

Arthur Graham Batterham was the youngest of four brothers who attended the school between 1902 and 1913: Douglas John (1902-1908); (Hugh) Willoughby (1904-1910), (Alexander) Gordon (1907-1912) and Arthur Graham Batterham (1908-1913). Their father was a Surgeon in St Leonard's-on-Sea where Graham had previously been. Dr Batterham could have sent his boys to any preparatory school in the country, but he chose the Reverend Graham's school. He seems to have rated him. The boys lost their mother in 1903 so it was particularly important that they were well looked after.

The discipline at *Dane Court* may be compared with Heathfield School next door. Herbert Carter OBE, a former Mayor of Poole, who attended the school in the late 1880s and early 1890s remembered that *'school discipline was of the strictest, though as far as I remember, no corporal punishment was inflicted. Punishment took the form of lines to be written, and ill-written lines did not pay the culprit, since they had to be written twice or thrice over'.*

To get a more rounded appreciation of the Reverend Graham, it is useful to review his earlier career. He had after all been tutoring schoolboys for 33 years when he arrived at *Dane Court.* The profile of the school changed considerably from his early years as a Tutor compared to the *Dane Court* era. Along the way Graham had suffered personal tragedies and his woes were to continue. It took a man of strong faith and dogged determination to start a new venture in Parkstone aged 60.

40. Rev H J Graham in 1911 on retirement

41. Arthur, Gordon and Willoughby

Henry John Graham (1840-1916) was born in Barrowgate, Penrith on 22 July 1840, the son of the Proprietor of a thriving grocery business, James and John Graham Limited. He had a younger brother Thomas Dawson Graham, who later became apprenticed in the business, and a younger sister, Rachel Ellen Graham who married a Surgeon. Henry Graham did well at Penrith Grammar School and then went to Queen's College, Oxford, which favoured applicants from Cumberland and Westmoreland at the time. He obtained a BA in Maths in 1862 and a MA in Law & Modern History in 1863. He became a Deacon in 1864 and was ordained as a Priest by the Bishop of Norwich in 1865.

His first position was as Curate of Hunstanton in Norfolk between 1864 and 1867. He married Jessie Janet Laura Fisher, a Solicitor's daughter, on 4 April 1866. While at Hunstanton, the couple had their first son, Kenneth James Cowper Graham, born on 26 March 1867.

It was in Hunstanton that Graham took in his first pupil, Rider Haggard. It was quite common for Clergymen to tutor a few boys. The Reverend Graham and his wife were friends of the Haggard family and Rider Haggard was initially taken in for the second half of the Summer Term in 1867 after some illness. In the summer of 1867, the Reverend Graham and his family moved to Garsington in Oxfordshire and Rider followed him there, where he would spend the next three years.

42. Garsington Rectory in Oxfordshire c1868

Rider Haggard would look back on his years with the Grahams at Garsington Rectory with great affection. He recalled the Rectory as *'long and low, and grey'* with a beautiful drawing room that *'looked upon a lawn with a big elm growing on it. Here we used to sit, in the hollow tree, and here this writer and a little fair-haired girl (Mrs Graham's small sister Blanche) once taught each other the rudiments of flirtation'.* Haggard wrote a piece *On Going Back* in *Longman's Magazine* in November 1887 after making a nostalgic visit to the area, though the old Rectory had by then long since gone. Haggard was treated as one of the family by the Grahams. His biographer D S Higgins quotes a letter from Jessie Graham recalling *'the little quiet gentle boy who used to drive with me about the Garsington lanes'*. Higgins also remarks: *'it is evident that Rider grew very fond of Mr Graham and this kindly Rector greatly influenced him'*. The Reverend Graham became the basis for Reverend Fraser in Haggard's early novel *Dawn* (1884). The fictional Reverend Fraser, imagined as aged 53, was described as follows:

'a tall and somewhat nervous looking man, with dark eyes, a sensitive mouth, and that peculiar stoop and pallor of complexion which those devoted to much study almost invariably acquire. He possessed academic abilities of a very high order and had in his youth distinguished himself greatly at college, both as a classical and mathematical scholar. When quite young, through the influence of a relation, he was appointed to his present living, where the income was good and the population very small indeed. Freed from all necessity for exertion, he shut himself up with his books, having his little round of parish work for relaxation'.

43. Rev H J Graham in the early 1880s

In a farewell conversation with his pupil Angela, who he had tutored for 10 years, the Reverend Fraser says: *'a classical education, properly understood, is the foundation of all learning. There is little worth saying which has not already been beautifully said by the ancients, little that is worthy of meditation on which they have not already profoundly reflected, save indeed, the one great subject of Christian meditation'.*

The Reverend Graham took in five other boys while he was at Garsington, most staying with him for one to two years. His third pupil William Bulwer (1869-1870), the son of Brigadier-General Lytton Bulwer from Norfolk, was with the Reverend Graham between 1869 and 1870. Haggard would later go to Natal between 1876 and 1880 with Bulwer's uncle, Sir Henry Bulwer, when the latter was Governor of Natal. Haggard's brother Edward Haggard was also tutored by the Reverend Graham between 1870 and 1871. Another of Graham's students at Garsington was Edward Elton (1871-1873), the son of the Reverend Edward Elton, Vicar of Wheatley in Oxfordshire. Over the years, Graham would tutor many sons of Clergymen so he must have been respected by his peers. Edward Elton was later to play a crucial role in the history of Dane Court Preparatory School. While at Garsington, the Reverend Graham and his wife had their second son, on 26 January 1869, named William Hope Machell Graham.

In mid-1871, the Reverend Graham became the Vicar of Ashampstead in Oxfordshire. He remained there until 1878. He continued to take in boys throughout this period, usually three or four at a time. A further 22 boys were tutored during this period, mostly staying for about two years although a few were with him for five to six years.

In the early years, Graham attracted quite a few pupils from overseas. For example, the President of the Bank of Hamilton in Ontario, Canada, Donald MacInnes, sent three of his sons

44. Rev. H J Graham's Coat of Arms

to the Reverend Graham between 1874 and 1878. Donald MacInnes was a very wealthy man living in an 18,000-square-foot, 40-room Italianate-style mansion called *Dundurn Park* in Hamilton, Ontario. Quite how a Clergyman in rural Oxfordshire came to tutor the sons of a wealthy executive in Ontario is a mystery. Presumably, MacInnes had received a strong recommendation. Some of the boys' parents worked for the Colonial Civil Service in India. Over the years this would provide a fertile source of pupils, with parents wanting to provide an English education for their sons while posted overseas.

On 1 November 1873, the Reverend Graham and his wife had a daughter, Margaret Graham Graham. The double use of the name Graham was to ensure that if she later married, she would always have Graham in her name, something important to the Reverend Graham as we shall see.

1878 was an important year for the Reverend Graham in several ways. On 31 July 1878, he was due to officiate at his sister's wedding in Penrith. Tragically their father, James Graham, died on the day before the wedding. It still went ahead though with the Reverend Graham officiating. He came into a small inheritance.

The Reverend Graham was proud of his Scottish ancestry. He had been avidly researching this. His great grandfather was James Graham of Westerkirk in the County of Dumfries. He had tried to establish genealogical links to various illustrious earlier Grahams.

He applied to the Lyon King of Arms in Edinburgh regarding a coat of arms. To his delight, *'Letters Patent from the Lyon King of Arms in favour of the Reverend Henry John Graham, Vicar of Ashampstead'*, were *'matriculated'* on 8 October 1878. The current Lyon Office has indicated that, as he bore the surname Graham, he was automatically a member of the Graham clan. The heraldic tradition in Scotland is that the arms for a member of a clan or family are based on those of the chief of the name and that was the case with the Reverend Graham's coat of arms.

Having come into a small inheritance, 1878 was also the year in which he established his fully-fledged school, The Mount Lodge School. *Mount Lodge*, which still exists as a listed building, dates from around 1870 and is attributed to the architect Decimus Burton who was responsible for several other properties in the area.

The Reverend Graham brought eight boys with him from Ashampstead, including the three MacInnes boys. Two further MacInnes sons joined the school when it opened in September 1878. In the early years, Graham continued to take in a significant proportion of boys whose parents were living overseas, especially Canada. For example, James Cameron Proctor's father is known to have been a business associate of Duncan MacInnes so presumably he came on MacInnes' recommendation.

Walter Ramsay (1880-1882) was also from Hamilton in Ontario. Further boys from Canada included Frederick Allan (1879-1881), the son of the Hon. George Allan, a lawyer and Mayor of Toronto (his father was born in Scotland and was later described as '*probably the wealthiest man in Canada in his day*'). The father of Henry Cawthra (1881-1883) was the Director and significant shareholder of the Bank of Toronto and several other companies.

45. Mount Lodge *on The Mount, St Leonard's-on-Sea*

46. Dalkenneth, *Lochearnhead*

Boys also came from South Africa, for example John Osborn (1879-1880) whose father Hon Melmouth Osborn was the Colonial Secretary in Pretoria. Parents who were working for the Indian Civil Service or Army also continued to send their boys to the school, for example Walter Knyvett (joined in 1881) whose father was the Superintendent of the Bombay Police. The

Reverend Graham also continued to attract the sons of Clergymen, for example the Burnside boys, Frederick, Walter and John Burnside (all attending between 1884-1887), whose father the Reverend Frederick Burnside was Rector of Hertingfordbury in Hertfordshire. The sons of senior Army personnel also featured. Gradually, the proportion of boys coming from a wider range of backgrounds in St Leonards-on-Sea and the southern counties increased.

Eighteen months after setting up The Mount Lodge School tragedy struck. Graham's eldest son, Kenneth Graham, died of phlebitis convulsions on 17 April 1880. The Reverend Graham was clearly much affected. Three years later when he had a beautiful holiday home built near Lochearnhead in Perthshire, he named it after his son, calling it *Dalkenneth.* In Gaelic, it means the plot of land belonging to Kenneth. The property still exists as a private house.

On 21 November 1882, the Reverend Graham and his wife had a third son, James Douglas Graham, known as 'Douglas'. In September 1891, he is recorded in the School Register as starting at the school. He would be tutored by his father until July 1897 when he left for Malvern College, aged 15. He did not like it there so transferred to Tonbridge School in 1898.

Around 150 boys attended The Mount Lodge School between 1878 and early 1900. The Reverend Graham would take on up to 10 new boys each year. While some stayed for just one or two years, the majority stayed for five or six years. It is not known for certain what prompted the move to *Dane Court.* It is possible that the lease on *Mount Lodge* was due to expire and/or that he was looking for a property with more accommodation and larger grounds.

However, there may have been another reason. His second son, William Graham died in Rhodesia on 9 January 1900, aged 30. He had been in the Transvaal since at least 1895 and died at Sebanga Port, Selukwe. This was a mining town. He was most likely involved in the industry. The cause of death is not known. Maybe this event triggered the move from *Mount Lodge*, the house where his first son Kenneth Graham had died and where William Graham had spent much of his childhood. His wife was also seriously ill with cancer, his daughter Margaret nursing her. Douglas was still away at Tonbridge School. Maybe it was time for a fresh start. The Reverend Graham took 16 boys with him to Parkstone, three of whom were in their final Term.

Sadly, his torrid times continued once he got to *Dane Court.* Less than a year after arriving, Jessie Graham died of breast cancer on 20 March 1901. His daughter Margaret had continued to care for her mother during her illness. The strain on Margaret was overwhelming. On 25 March 1901, she was admitted to the St Peter's Memorial Home in Woking. The Home's register recorded: *'debility after the illness and death of her mother'.* Fortunately, she was able to leave just over a month later, the register recording on 1 May 1901, *'quite recovered. Miss Graham is our Associate and a very nice girl'.*

This is the first mention that she had become an Associate. The Anglican Sisterhood of St Peter was founded in 1861 as a religious community devoted to nursing. The first homes run by the Sisters were in London, the St Peter's Home and Sisterhood in Mortimer Road, Kilburn being its London base. After acquiring land in Woking in 1883, the St Peter's Memorial Home was opened in 1885. It is not known whether Margaret became an Associate while at the Home or earlier, but it was most likely the former as there is no record of her being an Associate on admission. Maybe she was impressed by the work of the Sisters and her calling was revealed to her.

Susan Mumm in her study of the Anglican Sisterhoods indicates that *'there were between 3,000 and 4,000 members in 1900, living in around sixty communities'.* The Anglican Sisterhood movement had

47. St Peter's Memorial Home, Woking

48. One of the wards at St. Peter's Memorial Home in Woking

grown rapidly in the second half of the nineteenth century *'as sources of charitable relief and trained nurses to ameliorate the suffering of the poor'*. As regards Associates, Mumm remarks:

'Sister Associates were women who could not, or did not wish to, formally enter the community but who were interested in its work. Because communities often undertook more varieties of social work than their own sisters could staff, it was imperative to have large numbers of essentially leisured Associates in order to carry out their manifold projects. Being an Associate involved a significant level of commitment. In the early years of many Sisterhoods all Sister Associates were expected to devote six months of every year to the community, living and working with them and wearing the habit. By the end of the century the rule with regard to residence and active assistance had relaxed to the point where most Associates simply contributed financially to the work and followed their rule, although a sizeable number continued to offer direct assistance'.

The scale of Margaret's involvement at the time is not known. However, later events would demonstrate her commitment to the cause.

Meanwhile, the Reverend Graham had to get his school established in Parkstone. His existing contacts proved helpful, with boys whose parents were in the Indian Civil Service attending, such as the Geidt brothers, Edward, Frederick and Charles Geidt. Their father was a Judge in the High Court in Calcutta. Grant Rundle's father was the District Superintendent of Police in Lahore while Noel Rundle's father was a Surgeon with the Indian Medical Service.

Other countries represented in the school register included New Zealand. The Helmore brothers' father was a Barrister in Christchurch. Perhaps the most colourful parent was the Italian father of John Dracopoli (1902-1903) who was the Aide-de-Camp to the King of Montenegro. John's mother took a house in Parkstone, *Holmwood* on Castle Hill while John was at the school.

As regards boys with parents in the UK, the Reverend Graham had five of the Wodehouse brothers through his hands, the first two while at *Mount Lodge* and the other three after he moved to Parkstone. Their father was a Justice of the Peace and Gentleman Farmer, living at *Woolmer's Park*, a large mansion that would one day be purchased by the Queen's grandparents, the Earl and Countess of Strathmore. As noted earlier in the chapter, all four Batterham brothers were tutored by the Reverend Graham.

Graham also began to attract boys from the immediate locality, for example, Eric Moullin's father was a Civil Engineer living at *Fermain* nearby while Clive Gregory, whose father was a Clergyman, lived at *Melville* in St Peter's Road. Graham also attracted an increasing number of boys whose fathers were Merchants in the area, for example the Belben brothers, George (1905-1909), Thomas (1905-1910) and Stephen Belben (1909-1911), whose father had a long-established milling business in Poole.

The Reverend Graham did not list the school in the preparatory and public schools' bible, *Paton's List of Schools and Tutors*. Instead, he occasionally advertised in local and national newspapers, for example in the *Bournemouth Graphic*. The school also received regular local press coverage of annual sports days and prize-giving, and local and national listings of scholarship awards.

One might assume that the Reverend Graham always had a stream of privileged boys with no educational problems. However, this was certainly not the case. Soon after arriving in Parkstone, two brothers joined the school who would in various ways be challenging. The first he described in the School Register as *'very shy, very reserved, very painstaking, very simple-minded. Left-handed. A shocking dawdler'*. In fact, this boy had special needs. His brother on the other hand was described as *'very sharp, forward and quick of comprehension, rather indolent. Very upright and generous. Left-handed'*, but he also received the ultimate put down *'a shocking dawdler'*. The Reverend Graham was uncharacteristically short-tempered probably due to the stress he was under with his wife Jessie desperately ill. It is the only place in the Register where he shows such exasperation.

On another boy who joined a couple of years later aged 11, Graham wrote that he was *'not more than 8 years in attainment owing to neglect till nearly 7 years old'*. It is not known how this had come about. The boy was living with an aunt locally when he attended the school.

It is worth noting that the locality hosted hundreds of school children. The St Peter's School in Church Street (now Parr Street), which had been considerably enlarged, had an average attendance of 365 pupils in 1903 and 403 pupils by 1907. The British School in the old Buckland Chapel and Schoolroom had an average attendance of 208 pupils in 1903 and 165 pupils in 1907. In addition, there were around 30 pupils at Heathfield School next door. Parkstone School on Commercial Road would also open in 1908. The streets around *Dane Court* would therefore have been thronged with school children. The same was true in the 1960s when the Author was growing up there. Today all the schools have gone, the streets are quiet.

Regarding Heathfield School, the founder Walter Gill had died in 1893. His two sons continued the school, the elder son William then departing to set up his own school, leaving it to his brother Ernest Gill. They both ended up in the office of Carter Tiles in Poole. By 1907, Victor Guest and his wife Lavinia had acquired the school. When he died, his wife continued it for many years. It became a school for boys and girls and continued until the late 1920s after more than 70 years as a school.

Returning to the Reverend Graham, in 1905, as well as running Dane Court Preparatory School, he acted as Vicar at St Peter's Church for a time, presumably to cover a gap in clerical appointments at the Church.

The 1901 Census provides a snapshot of the staff and servants at *Dane Court* a year after the move to Parkstone. Assistant Masters would often only stay a year or two, using it as a stepping-stone to other things. William Atkins's father was a Clergyman in St. Leonards-on-Sea. He went to Clare College, Cambridge between 1896 and 1899 and presumably joined the Reverend Graham soon after he moved to Parkstone. By the 1911 Census he is recorded as Headmaster of a preparatory school with five boys boarding at Forest Hill near Sydenham. Kenneth Mayne, also recorded in the 1901 Census as an Assistant Master, later decided to become a Clergyman, becoming Rector of St. Mary's Church in Burgh St. Peter in Norfolk.

As regards the servants and visitors, Mary Gane stands out as she would remain at the school for most of the next 20 years in various roles, pictured in her Sunday best. She would feature in many later Annual School Photos. Agnes and Ella Baker were Kitchen Maid and Schoolroom Maid, respectively. They were from Parkstone and at the time of the 1891 Census were living with their grandfather, John Baker, a pottery moulder, in Lilliput. Alice Kail was a House Maid. She originated from Blandford where her father was a Gardener. The father of Fanny Paul, a Nurse Domestic, was also a Gardener. She came from Sydenham in Kent. Melinda Trowbridge was a House Maid from Okeford Fitzpaine in Dorset where her father was an Agricultural Labourer.

Concerning the teaching staff, Arthur Batterham later recalled that while Mary Gane and Charles Baker:

'went on for ever the teaching staff changed fairly often. When Mr Bellamy, the Senior Assistant Master was seen eating anything between meals we always assumed it was one of G Watkins's caramels, a large tin of which he had confiscated. It was Mr Jevons the Second Form Master who named me "Miserable Starkey" because I was so often in tears. He was the first Scout Master of the Dane Court Troop. When we enrolled, we each made our Promise standing before Mrs Murray-Scott who taught the first form. She held no rank in the movement, but because of the solemnity of the occasion I regarded her as some kind of High Priestess of Scouts.

Mr Bellamy was succeeded by Mr Cooper, a huge man with an alarming temper, who always wore a brown suit with a white pin stripe, even when playing hockey. Mr Jevons was succeeded by Mr Bazell who drew a map of the English coastline on the board showing each cape around the coast – the names of which we learned during term. That was Geography!'

49. Mary Gane in Sunday best

The Reverend Graham's son, Douglas, finished at Tonbridge School in 1901. He may then have lived at *Dane Court* for a couple of years as in 1903 he is recorded as playing hockey for Dorset. In 1904-5 he was ranching and mining in Colorado. He then went up to Trinity College Oxford obtaining an MA. He returned to *Dane Court* in 1908 and married Muriel Agnes Kavanagh Armstrong from Ireland at St Peter's Church, Parkstone. Later that year, on 7 November 1908, the couple had a son named James Kenneth Graham. They were still resident at *Dane Court*. Also in 1908, Douglas began working as a Political Secretary for Hastings Medhurst who was the Chairman of the Trade Union Tariff Reform Association.

Parkstone continued to develop during these early years, for example the introduction of a tram service in 1901 from Poole to County Gates via North Road. This was soon linked to the Bournemouth network. Traders in Ashley Cross initially objected to tramlines and overhead wires but later changed their minds when they saw how successful the service was. A second line was laid along Commercial Road in 1908. The trams are shown in the next two photos.

House building continued. On the right of the photo that follows houses are shown on both sides of the new section of North Road, between what is now Danecourt Road and Harbour View Road/St Peter's Road, constructed to facilitate the line of the tram. The two stages of the construction of St Peter's Church can be seen with the differently weathered sections of roof on the left. The next photo shows the completed St Peter's Church. The boys with their summer boaters may well be from *Dane Court*.

50. Ashley Cross c1910 with the tram service introduced in 1908.

51. Ashley Cross c1910 looking towards Parkstone Park

52. Constitution Hill Road with the playing field on right and development in North Road

53. Church Road looking west with the completed St Peter's Church and maybe Dane Court boys

Then as now loneliness could be an issue for boarders at preparatory schools, particularly if boys had lost a parent as in the case of the Batterhams. However, boys were able to send and receive letters and postcards to and from parents and relatives, as illustrated by the postcard dated 19 July 1907 received by Gordon Batterham from one of his relatives. Little did the relative know that as well as *'making lots of runs in cricket'*, Gordon would have an unrivalled ability in locking all the lavatory doors from the inside. Gordon Batterham had only recently joined the school in May 1907.

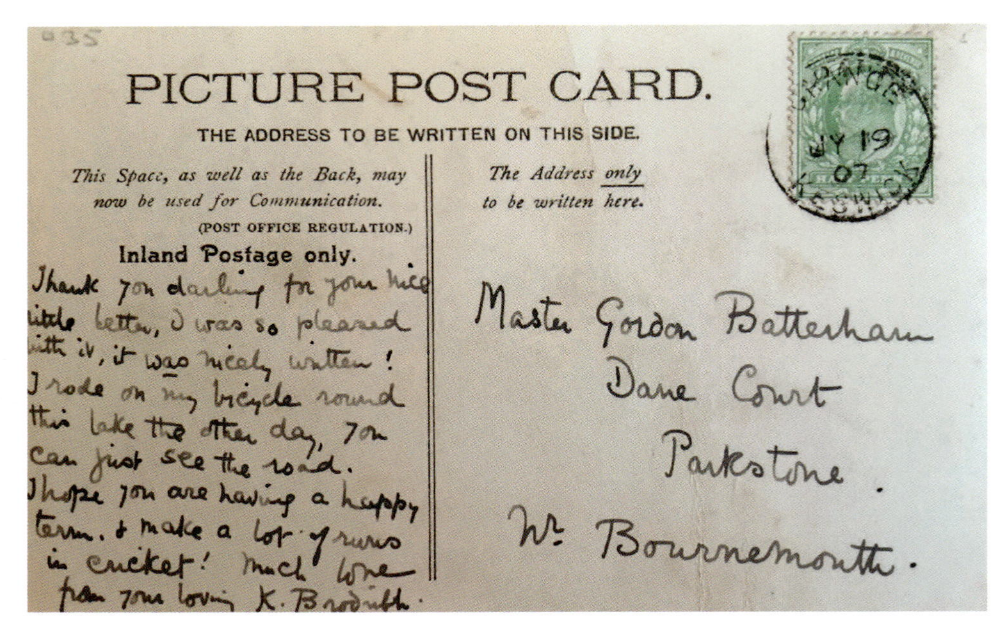

PICTURE POST CARD.

THE ADDRESS TO BE WRITTEN ON THIS SIDE.

This Space, as well as the Back, may now be used for Communication.
(POST OFFICE REGULATION.)

Inland Postage only.

Thank you darling for your nice little letter, I was so pleased with it, it was nicely written! I rode on my bicycle round this lake the other day, you can just see the road. I hope you are having a happy term, & make a lot of runs in cricket! Much love from your loving K. Brodribb.

The Address only to be written here.

Master Gordon Batterham
Dane Court
Parkstone.
Nr Bournemouth.

JY 19 07

54. Postcard received by Gordon Batterham dated 19 July 1907

In 1909, the Reverend Graham was looking to recruit an Assistant Master who would be interested in taking on the school when he wished to retire. Edward Elton, who had been one of Graham's earliest pupils at Garsington Rectory between 1871 and 1873 and who was then a Senior Master at Wellington College, recommended Hugh Francis Pooley. Pooley had been spending a year as an Assistant Master under Dr Pollock, who later became Bishop of Norwich.

Hugh Pooley later wrote:

'this possibility seemed to be just what I was looking for – perhaps I was swayed by the fact that the school was called Dane Court and I was already engaged to be married to a Danish girl – Michaela Krohn. So, I joined the staff of Dane Court under Graham at the princely salary of £80 a year resident. When we married in 1910 and lived in a little house of our own up the hill, the salary remained the same!'

The house was *Bourg-La-Reine* in North Road. It still exists as a private property though not called that now.

55. Bourg-La-Reine

Arthur Batterham would later recall: *'when Mr Pooley was on duty on a Sunday he took all nine boarders for a walk, ending for tea with*

56. Burnier G Batterham H F Pooley
Allen Hobson M Heathcote

Mrs Pooley (and doughnuts). After tea he read to us, mostly Kipling's stories'. At the time, Mrs Pooley was a Teacher of Modern Languages at the school.

Mr Pooley or his wife often seem to have had a camera available. They began to take photos of the boys and life at the school. Mr Pooley carefully recorded who was in each photo and after 1911 often the month and year that it was taken. This photo and the ones on the next few pages are from around 1910.

The mother of Richard Burnier (1908-1911) was a Teacher in St Leonards-on-Sea so may have already known the Reverend Graham. Francis Allen (1909-1912) was born in Bengal but at the time that he attended the school his parents were living at a house called *Sistina* in Ardmore Road, Parkstone. Frank Hobson (1910-1911) was also local, a ward of a Miss Norris. The father of Michael Heathcote (1908-1911) and his brother Geoffrey Heathcote (1908-9) was a Major in the Army, resident in Essex.

In the next photo, Richard Burnier is joined by Edmund Hodgson-Stevens (1907-1911) on Canford Cliffs beach around 1910. Edmund was born in Rio de Janeiro and his parents were still living there. The school's contact was his grandmother who lived in Hampstead.

57. Hodgson-Stevens and Burnier at Canford Cliffs c1910

58. Mrs Pooley with Hodgson-Stevens and John Barton c1910

Mrs Pooley was renowned for her amazing hats. John Barton's father worked for the Church Missionary Society, the family home being at *Crossways* in Wellington Road and later at 3 Belvedere Crescent. He attended the school for over six years, between 1906 and 1912 although he was unable to attend between 1908 and 1910.

John Barton later recalled:

'only a few weeks after my first meeting with Mr Pooley, he brought his newly-married bride Michaela from Denmark and within a month or so of her arrival she gave us a remarkable talk about her native country much of which I could still recall verbatim. Her first words were: "I want to tell you about the country, the country that I love . ." She went on to say that there were two things she missed in England – the sudden coming of Spring and the clear nights of the Summer months'.

In the next photo, we see the Mr Bazell, referred to earlier by Arthur Batterham. If he looks just out of school himself, this is because he was. Cuthbert Bazell was only about 16 or 17 at the time, the son of Charles Bazell, a Clergyman in Bridgwater, Somerset. He stayed a couple of years.

The parents of Cecil Fawkes (1906-1911) lived at *The White Lodge* in Parkstone, his father being Lieutenant-Colonel Montagu Fawkes. Charles Burn (1910-1912) and his brother George Burn (January 1911 – July 1912), shown in the following photo, were older than most boys when they joined, being 14 and 13, respectively. Their father was the Managing Director of the Barbados Light Railway. The family home was at *Pine Dene* in Mansfield Road.

59. *W Batterham* *Mr Bazell* *Fawkes* *C S Burn*
Not known *S J Belben* *I M Mack* *O'Shea* *Hoey* *Barton*

Stephen Belben (1909-1911), the youngest of the three Belben brothers mentioned earlier, is on the front row, being 8 years of age at the time. Ian Mack (1908-1910) next to him was a particularly interesting boy. His father was a Landowner and Farmer in St Kilda, Victoria in Australia but it was felt he and his elder brother Joseph Mack (1907-1910) needed an English education, so their mother was despatched to England with them. She initially lived at a house called *Airlie* in Kingsbridge Road, Parkstone then at *Craddock* in Balmoral Road.

Desmond O'Shea (1906-1913) had a particularly long innings at the school, although he had a gap of two years in the middle when he was not able to attend as a Boarder so went elsewhere. He was the son of the Reverend George O'Shea, who had the title The O'Shea of Kerry, living at *The Vicarage* in Canford Magna. Cedric Hoey (1910) was the son of Denys Hoey, a Clerk in Holy Orders who acted as the Diocesan Secretary of the Church of England Temperance Society. The contact in the School Register was his grandmother, a Mrs Welch who lived at *Montagu* in St Peter's Road.

The pupils on the back row of the next photo have already been mentioned, as have the Heathcote brothers, Hobson, Allen and O'Shea. James Erskine-Murray (1910-1911) was born in Edinburgh, his father being a Consulting Engineer. The family had moved to *The Oaks* opposite *Dane Court* in Church Road. The second of the Belben brothers, Thomas Belben (1905-1910) is on the front row. He tended to look rather sulky in photos. Robert Chesshire (1910-1914) on the far left of the front row had probably only recently arrived when this photo was taken. His father was a Captain in the Mercantile Marine Service.

60. Mr Bazell H F Pooley Fawkes G Batterham G F Burn
Norman Erskine-Murray G Heathcote Hobson Allen O'Shea
R Chesshire T A Belben - M Heathcote

Meanwhile, the Reverend Graham's son Douglas had become a Political Secretary for Major C B Levita in 1909-10. On 31 March 2010, Douglas and his wife had a second child at *Dane Court*, a daughter named Audrey Graham. At the time of the Census in April 1911, Douglas and his wife were lodging at 3 Royal Avenue in Chelsea, although their children are shown as still living with the Reverend Graham at *Dane Court*.

The Reverend Graham's daughter Margaret had become a Sister of Mercy at the St Peter's Home and Sisterhood in Mortimer Road, Kilburn by the time of the 1911 Census. It is not known when she became a Sister of Mercy although it may have been some years before as there was a lengthy process involved. Despite the Reverend Graham's best laid plans to always have Graham in her name, she was henceforth known as Sister Margaret O'Syth, as Sisters adopted the name of a Saint.

61. St Peter's Home and Sisterhood, Mortimer Road, Kilburn

On 15 March 1910, the Reverend Graham and Hugh Francis Pooley entered into an agreement where Pooley would take an assignment of the Lease on *Dane Court* and the Lease on the Cricket Field on 18 October 1911, unless the parties fixed an earlier date, but on a date no later than 28 April 1913. In summary, Pooley would pay to the Reverend Graham an amount equal to one and half times the net profits of the school, based on an average of the three years ended on 31 December 1910. In addition, Pooley would pay £150 for the iron and wood Schoolroom, £100 for school furniture, £100 for the baths, lavatory and heating apparatus and £12 10s for the Cricket Pavilion. The Pavilion is shown below in a rare photo looking towards the viewpoint on Constitutional Hill. Hugh Pooley's father guaranteed due performance of the agreement by his son.

In the event, the handover happened at the Prize Giving at the end of the Summer Term in 1911. Pooley later recalled that the Reverend Graham retired to an adjoining cottage that belonged to him. This is believed to have been the cottage on the triangular plot between Chapel Lane (now called Chapel Road) and North Road having renamed it *Westerkirk*, in memory of his great grandfather who lived in Westerkirk in the County of Dumfries. The plot can be seen on the 1890 Ordnance Survey Map reproduced in illustration 6 in the Prologue.

62. Dane Court School Playing Field and Cricket Pavilion

Arthur Batterham remembered:

'G publicly handed over the school to Mr and Mrs Pooley at the Prize Giving on the lawn in front of the house at the end of the Summer Term 1911, and they moved into Dane Court after a Summer of energetic re-arranging'.

Chapter 7

SUNRISE

The new arrangements suited the boys very well. Batterham continued:

'we boys were delighted about the 'change-over' and all the pleasant surprises that awaited us in September 1911. The ground floor room on the right which had been G's Drawing Room was now the Boy's Room – a pleasant sitting room with comfortable chairs, a large table and the much-augmented library. This made a great difference to us, for in G's time we had lived in the large Schoolroom and the Changing Room. Matron's Room had become a Classroom and the Dormitory above the Boys' Room was now the Pooley's Drawing Room'.

63. The Boys' Room, formerly the Reverend Graham's Drawing Room

He recalled:

'one of the new delights of the Pooleys' Dane Court was our freedom to enjoy a wider extent of gardens – its lawns, the Mound, the paths and many fine trees – the chicken run was removed giving access to the giant beech tree which we called Old Rum'.

64. The Schoolroom

65. The First Form Room in the Conservatory

66. The Workshop in the Greenhouse

67. The Tennis Lawn and the Mound with Dane Court *in the background*

68. The Front Lawn of Dane Court

Hugh Francis Pooley was the second son of a Barrister who worked at the Board of Education, Henry Pooley, resident at 48 Well Walk in Hampstead. Hugh attended Rugby School between 1897 and 1902, then University College, Oxford. As already noted, he became an Assistant Master at Wellington College prior to being appointed by the Reverend Graham at *Dane Court* in 1909.

He married Michaela Kobke Krohn in 1910. She was born in 1884, the daughter of Pietro Kobke Krohn. From 1893 he was the director of the Danish Museum of Art & Design (Kunstindustrimuseet) in Copenhagen. He had studied painting at the Royal Danish Academy of Fine Art in the 1860s and worked as an illustrator. He later became interested in other art forms and between 1880 and 1893 was a costume designer at the Royal Danish Theatre where he also directed opera. Over the years he spent time in Germany, France and Holland.

As well as her illustrious father, Michaela Krohn's great uncle on her mother's side of the family was Christen Schiellerup Kobke (1810-1848), one of the finest artists of the Golden Age of Danish Painting. Amongst the family's contacts was the Finnish Painter Albert Edelfelt who produced a fine drawing of Michaela Krohn aged 16 in 1902, reproduced below.

Sydney Levey (1918-1920) later wrote in his unpublished book *The Fires Are Burning Low*:

'by any standards Hugh Pooley was a fine teacher, a born leader and a man with the most amazing insight into the mind of a small boy. He was strict but humane, respected but not feared. He had the entire confidence of every one of the boys in the school, which was more than just a cold scholastic establishment. There was a homelike warmth about it, made even more patent by the fact that his young family were either babies or small children there in

my time. Hugh Pooley was keen on games and I duly learned to play cricket, soccer, hockey and tennis. Technically, he was a very good coach at all these games'.

'Michaela Pooley (we all called her "Mor") was an absolute gem . . . she inherited a sense of the artistic from her father. Her dress sense was incredible, for only she could wear the vivid combinations of russets, browns and oranges in which she clothed herself with aplomb. Very often we would see some of the school curtains dismantled and turned into dresses. Her hats were unbelievable'.

'She introduced many delightful Danish customs, such as Almond-in-the-Pudding (the only time I ever willingly ate rice pudding which I detested) and the Cat-in-the-Barrel. The annual school play was invariably an adaption by Mor of one of Hans Christian Andersen's fairy tales, such as The Emperor's New Clothes or The Ugly Duckling or sometimes a story from the Bible. She would read Kim and The Jungle Book to us at bedtime'.

'It was a wonderful partnership between a typical Englishman, educated at Rugby and Oxford, a devoted Schoolmaster and conventional sportsman, and an almost zany Dane with all the flair and imagination of her heritage'.

69. Michaela Krohn aged 16 by Edelfelt

'Mor' is Danish for 'Mum'. The boys never called her 'Mor' to her face. It is nevertheless how she was known to them.

Hugh and Michaela Pooley are shown below in the first of many Annual School Photos. Most of the boys' names have been erased from the edges of the photo over time by much handling. Those that can be identified are noted in the caption overleaf.

The boys are wearing the revised school uniform with caps bearing the school's new Sunrise symbol. Mr Pooley later recalled that the russet colour of the uniform was based on one of Mrs Pooley's dresses and the school motto came from Seneca in her Latin primer: *'non scholae sed vitae' (discimus)*, meaning *'we do not learn for school but for life'*.

70. Annual School Photo July 1911. Top Row: A G Batterham (second left), C Burn (fourth left) G Burn (fifth left), Baker (first right). Middle Row: Hodgson-Stevens (first left), G Batterham (second left), Mr Pritchard (third left), O'Shea (first right). Front Row: Scott (first left), Norman (third left)

For the School Years 1911 to 1915, Mr Pooley prepared informative and entertaining Annual Reports for parents on activities at the school. Together with the photos, the record of activities for this period is therefore particularly vivid.

In the Winter Term 1911, he recorded that there were 19 boys at the school: 9 Boarders and 10 Day Boy. As regards the Curriculum, Pooley highlights that a few changes had been made:

'the Curriculum has in all essentials remained the same, though in accordance with the recommendations of the Headmasters' Conference, none but the more exceptional boys at the head of the School are encouraged to begin Greek until they have reached their Public School. We have further introduced Drawing as a Compulsory Subject once a week and Carpentering in the Christmas and Easter Terms, as being both of them invaluable for the scientific training of hand and eye in combination and also as giving a boy a better understanding of the skill involved in advanced manual labour. A systematic, if elementary, Study of History of the World, apart from the History of England, is being carried on all through the School. Instruction is also given in Natural History to the younger boys, and one period a week is allotted to Nature Study at the top of the School'.

He added that *The Daily Graphic* and *The Illustrated London News* were taken throughout the year. As regards the grounds, he noted that the enlargement of the playground by half of its original size, in the Christmas holidays:

'gave a ground on which it was possible to organise regular games on doubtful afternoons; while a levelled and turfed cricket pitch proved very useful in the Summer, for practice in breaks and short intervals'.

71. Boarders at dinner with Mr & Mrs Pooley at Dane Court *September 1911*

Of the six new joiners in the School Year 1911-12, four came as Day Boys, two as Boarders. The Day Boys came from a range of backgrounds and family circumstances. Wilfrid Fuller joined the school unusually late, aged 15, and only stayed three months. He lived with his mother at *Nilgiri Lodge* in Alexandra Road. Sadly, his father had died in San Francisco earlier that year, being an Artist for a British newspaper out there. Campbell Greenlees (1911-1912) was the son of a Retired Distiller, his parents living at *Danaverty* in Ardmore Road. He was withdrawn after a year as his parents wanted to find a cure for his stammering. Gilbert Beal (1912-1913) lived with his parents at *Dophcot* in Highmoor Road, his father being a retired Barrister, while David Ingram (1912-1916) was the son of an Electrical Supply Engineer, living with his parents at a house called *Caldicott* in Birchwood Road. David lost no time in making friends with a furry friend.

72. David Ingram with a pet rabbit

73. Eric Lassen

Eric Lassen (1911-1915) was one of two Danish boys to join the school that year as a Boarder, his father being a manufacturer in the engineering sector. The other Danish boy who arrived in July 1912 was Tage Hagelstam, of whom more shortly. He was officially part of the intake for the School Year 1912-13 as he only started at the school in September 1912. Having arrived early though, he was included in the July 1912 Annual School Photo. The other Boarder of the 1911-12 intake was Edward Ormerod (1911-1914). His father was a Doctor. The next photos are of Francis Scott (1911-1913), who had recently arrived when the Pooleys took over, and John Barton (1906-1912), pictured in the last chapter, who was awarded a History Scholarship at Harrow in April 1912. He sent the photo to Mr Pooley from Harrow the following year.

As well as noting the various sporting fixtures and results during the year, Pooley remarked that there were two half-day holidays during the Winter Term 1911, on 2 October and 9 November 1911 *'in honour of the birthdays of Mr and Mrs Pooley'*. On the first date a picnic was held in Branksome Woods and on the second a bonfire was lit in the garden of *Dane Court* with a *"Guy", 'both made by the boys'.*

Winter Prize Giving took place on 18 December 1911 in the Schoolroom, which had been decorated by the boys with holly and evergreens. Over the platform hung the school flag. The programme included passages from Euripedes *Alcestis* acted in the original Greek by the boys of the Fourth Form, who had been reading it during the Term. There were also some French 'costume songs', rendered by the First and Second Forms. On the last day of Term, there was a Christmas Tree in the Dining Room of *Dane Court: 'for weeks previously the boys had made boxes of paper and cardboard, and anything they could think of, for the Tree. There was some carol singing and games of various kinds'.*

74. Francis Scott

75. John Barton

On 16 January 1912, the Pooleys' first son, Peter Krohn Pooley, was born. Extra half-day holidays were given on 16 February and on two later occasions *'in honour of his christening and to commemorate the winning of a Bell Scholarship at Cambridge by an old boy of the school'.* At the end of March, the Dane Court Scout Troop was *'informally inspected'* by Captain Grewing, Chief Commissioner from London. *'Some scouting was done in his presence on Constitutional Hill and a dispatch was run to* Dane Court'.

On 30 March 1912, the School Sports Day was held on the School Playing Field, attended by several parents. In the Obstacle Race boys appear to have had to take a bite out of suspended apples. Milner excelled in the 100 yards Race for Under 12s, with Arthur Batterham second.

On Whit Monday 1912, the school had a picnic at Shell Bay, *'ferrying across the mouth of the harbour, and taking both dinner and tea with us'.* Mr Pooley also wrote that *'we were able to get a great deal of bathing in June and July, three times a week being the general rule. On Sunday afternoons we usually walked to the bathing place, with such of the Day Boys as cared to come'.*

76. The Dane Court Scout Troop 1912

77. Obstacle Race during Sports Day in March 1912 on the Dane Court *Playing Field*

78. Under 12's 100 yards Race March 1912 – 1st Milner, 2nd A G Batterham and 3rd R Chesshire

79. 'Ferrying across the mouth of the harbour . . .'

80. Walking to the beach at Sandbanks - Summer 1912

81. Another photo a little further on at Sandbanks - Summer 1912

82. Picnic at Sandbanks - Summer 1912

83. Bathing at Sandbanks - Summer 1912

Richard Salmon, who joined some years later, recalled the following about bathing: *'one thing that definitely sticks out in the mind is Mor's extreme kindness and sympathy to small boys in all their little problems. I remember my absolute fear of first going in the sea and Mor making it clear to me that there was no need for me to do so if I did not wish it, yet, at the same time convincing me that my choice in the matter would not cause any loss of face . . . and behind all these early recollections the feeling of her ever-present benign influence over all that went on at* Dane Court'.

Summer Prize Giving was held on 29 July 1912. The Reverend Graham, the former Headmaster, gave out the prizes and in his speech *'said many things about the school which were much appreciated by us'*. After tea, scenes from the life of *Joan of Arc* were performed, *'Batterham Minor as "Joan" being particularly effective. The dresses were designed and made almost entirely at home. We have to thank both the boys and the parents for much kind co-operation'*

Michaela Pooley's cousin, Emily Berry Malthe-Bruun, known as *'Mrs Bruun',* arrived in the Spring Term of 1912 to act as Lady Matron during *'Mrs' Pooley's indisposition'* while she was having her first child. Mrs Bruun, who was from Denmark, was a divorcée with three children; it is believed that they remained there. She is pictured outside *The Cottage* (formerly called *Brunswick* or *Brontë Cottage*) with an Assistant Master called Mr Bassett-Smith. This was Dudley William Bassett-Smith, then aged 22, who had graduated from Oxford University a year or two earlier and was probably in his first teaching post. He joined the school in September 1912.

The second photo looks out of the front door towards Chapel Lane (now Chapel Road). The Reverend Graham's retirement cottage *Westerkirk* is believed to be glimpsed through the trees, on the other side of the road. This was previously called *Fir Tree Cottage*. The 1911 Census shows Charles Baker, the Gardener, and his wife living there. The cottage may have been owned by the Reverend Graham and rented out to Charles Baker. Baker later transferred to *Dane Court*

84. Joan of Arc *school play in the grounds of* Dane Court *on 29 July 1912*

85. A G Batterham, G F Burn, O'Shea and C S Burn in front of The Mound 29 July 1912

86. Dudley Bassett-Smith, Emily Bruun and Hugh Pooley in 1913 outside The Cottage

87. Annual School Photo – July 1912. Back Row: G Batterham, Baker, not known, C S Burn, Hagelstam, A G Batterham. Middle Row: D Ingram, O'Shea, Mrs Pooley and Peter, Mr Pooley, Mr Pritchard, G F Burn, not known. Front Row: R Chesshire, Scott, Ormerod, Lassen, Norman

Lodge on the left of the circular carriage drive, as noted by Fordham at the beginning of the previous chapter.

On other staff matters, David Pritchard left at the end of Winter Term 1912 owing to ill health but was able to return on a part-time basis in the Summer Term of 1913. Hugh Pooley also noted that a Mr Blaylock taught Drawing and Serjeant-Major T Kelly was responsible for Drill: he taught the boys to march and turn. In the Spring and Summer Terms 1913, Madame Gantier, *'who is well-known in the Bournemouth Schools'*, took a course in French conversation once a week for the more advanced boys. This was Berthe Gantier, a widowed Professor of French, who lived in Bournemouth at the time.

Elspie Pridden taught the boys Music. She was the daughter of a retired Schoolmaster, Frederick Pridden, the Sheriff of Poole. The family lived at *Chevington Croft* in Mount Road at the top of what is now North Road. There was an orphanage called St Faith's Home run by two German spinsters a few doors away where Elspie provided lessons free of charge. One of the children at the Home, Edna Wright (née Wheway), later wrote:

88. Looking from The Cottage *towards the Rev Graham's cottage* Westerkirk

'Miss Elspie, as we called her, came voluntarily once or twice a week to teach us singing and dancing. How our ancient piano must have frayed her nerves to say nothing of the efforts of girls like myself who simply cannot sing'.

Edna Wheway continued: *'Miss Elspie was gentle, kind and forbearing, and would provide any girl who had throat trouble or other minor ailments with lozenges or cough medicine. One day the piano sounded even worse than usual and seemed to have something wrong inside: the notes were flat and muffled. On opening the top and peering into the works, Miss Elspie found several bright pink capsules stuffed down among the wires'.*

One evening Elspie Pridden happened to be passing the garden of *St. Peter's Vicarage* and, hearing children's voices thought how good the choir sounded. Edna recalled:

'she went in to see who was singing with the idea of congratulating them. To her astonishment it was 'her' girls from St Faith's. Somehow the powers-that-be had slipped up and Miss Elspie had not been consulted to ask if we might appear and sing before the public'.

They were due to sing in a series of tableaux depicting stories from the Bible. Elspie Pridden was also involved in forming a Girl Guide Troop at the Home. Another member of the Pridden family, a Miss C Pridden, believed to be a relative of Elspie's rather than one of her sisters, was also involved at *Dane Court* for a period, assisting Emily Bruun as Lady Matron.

Mr Pooley noted that the Reverend Graham took weekly Catechism classes, with the Reverend J A Mackonochie, a Curate at St Peter's Church, taking over later in the School Year, possibly due to the Reverend Graham's failing health.

89. Elspie Pridden in a studio photo c1905

90. Elspie at Dane Court *c1913*

91. Mickbird the mystery lady

92. Possibly Agnes Baker c1912

The 1911 Census provides a snapshot of the other staff and servants at *Dane Court*, three months before the Pooleys took over. Presumably, many staff stayed on for a while. As well as the Assistant Master Cuthbert Bazell, there was also a Governess called Cordelia Gertrude Lavinia Howard White recorded as a *'Teacher'*. She is not mentioned by Pooley in his First Annual Report so maybe she left soon afterwards.

Mary Gane was still at the school, with the title Housekeeper, aged 39, as was Agnes Baker the Cook, then aged 25. Other servants were Mary Moran, a Nurse aged 36, Emily Rendell, a House Maid aged 22, Rosina Bailey, a House Maid aged 22 and Clara Dunford, a Kitchen Maid aged 17. Another member of staff who was probably an Assistant Matron or the Nurse Mary Moran was a lady noted on photographs as *'Mickbird'*. It is not known whether this was a nickname or her real name. She appears in most of the Annual School Photos and in several others. The photo on the right above of one of the servants was taken around 1910/11. Unusually, Mr Pooley did not record who it was. It may be Agnes Baker as she had been at *Dane Court* for at least 10 years.

Mr Pooley reported that the School Museum had been re-organised and *'housed in the Old Aviary'*. It contained some bizarre items:

'from G F and C S Burn (old Dane Court boys) a crocodile, two weeks old; crocodile three days old, sharp-nosed; snake, water tortoise, a quantity of shells, sugar cane and mahogany seeds, Barbados; tea seeds and many others; fossilised wood, volcanic dust, water from the Dead Sea, some birds' skulls and animals' tusks and teeth; stones from the Mount of Olives, the Pyramids, the Dead Sea, Mount Vesuvius, Nile, Thebes, Mount Hor, etc, a piece of tessellated pavement from the Judgement Hall, fossilised bone from Lancashire. From Batterham: sea urchin and teeth; from Wilson – slow worm; from Chesshire, a collection of shells; from Milner, caterpillars; on loan from Hagelstam, a collection of Japanese butterflies; from Milner, a collection of English butterflies; a piece of gold quartz'.

In the next photo, Charles Baker, the Gardener an odd-job man who taught the boys Carpentry is pictured with Robin John. He was one of five brothers to join in the Winter Term 1912, sons of the Painter Augustus John: David (10), Caspar (9), Robin (8), Edwin (7) and Romilly (6). They lived at *Alderney Manor* on Ringwood Road. This was described by Ted Ward in his book on the manor as *'a curious low, pink building - an elongated bungalow with Gothic windows and a fantastic castellated parapet'*. The bungalow, a studio and a cottage for visitors, were set in 50 to 60 acres of heathland with an abundance of trees and shrubs.

93. Charles Baker and Robin John

Augustus John married a fellow student from the Slade School of Fine Art, Ida Nettleton, in 1900. They had the five boys who attended the school. She died in 1907. Later Augustus John's mistress, Dorelia McNeill, took the role of stepmother. She was referred to by the Pooleys as *'Mrs John'*.

Michael Holroyd in his biography of Augustus John quotes a letter received from Michaela Pooley recalling the day that Dorelia first arrived at *Dane Court* with the children:

'from our stand by the window we saw a green Governess cart drawn by a pony approaching up the drive. A queer square cart – later named "The Marmalade Box" by the boys in the school – and out stepped a lady in a cloak with a large hat and hair cut short... After her a couple of boys tumbled out, their hair cut likewise, and they wore coloured tunics. For a moment we thought they were girls... It was soon fixed that the three boys aged 8, 9 and 10 should come as Day Boys. When Mrs John was going, she turned at the door and said: "I think there are two more at home, who might as well come"'.

Hugh Pooley breezily remarked:

'in 1912 the school was enlarged and enlivened by the arrival of the five sons of Augustus John – their long hair

and tunic shirts were certainly picturesque and did not seem to worry anybody very much'.

After their first term, Pooley recommended that David, Casper and Robin became Boarders, mindful of the bohemian lifestyle at *Alderney Manor*.

94. Woman Smiling 1908-9 by Augustus John

Dorelia McNeill posed as the model in Augustus John's painting *Women Smiling* (now in the Tate Gallery), having made the high-waisted, gypsy style dress herself, typical of the clothes that she wore at the time. Augustus John painted several paintings of her and the family in gypsy-style clothes.

Romilly John later wrote:

'I was especially afraid that one of my brothers would let out some frightful detail of our life at Alderney and thus ruin us for ever, a needless alarm as they were all older and warier than I. I contracted a habit of inserting secretly after the Lord's Prayer a little clause to the effect that Dorelia might be brought by divine intervention to wear proper clothes; I used also to pray that she and John might not be tempted by the invitation sent to all parents to appear at the School Sports'.

Rebecca John in her biography of Caspar John quotes her father:

'we were enrolled as weekly boarders and entered our first experience of orderly living away from the family . . . I wondered what was in store for us. By reason of our long hair, strange clothing and relatively outlandish habits, we became known as The Persians. We completed the blotting of our copybook by being able to speak French – not a good thing in 1912. But we shone on the Playing Field and won many games of cricket and football for the school – without short-pitched bowling or bad temper. Augustus once scored a goal – palpably offside – playing for the parents and Old Boys. Unhappily, I was the goalkeeper and was accused of deliberately letting the ball into the net. Physical prowess in English sports being more important than knowledge of a foreign language, we were forgiven our strange ways'.

95. H Everett Caspar Hagelstam O'Shea Norman
Romilly Robin Edwin P Pooley Wilson

Another 1912-13 joiner, pictured in the above photograph, was Henry Everett, also the son of a Painter. His father was Herbert Barnard John Everett, who publicly went by the name 'John Everett' from the time of his marriage in 1901. His son Henryt had joined in January 1914. Mrs Everett, who like her husband had studied at the Slade School of Fine Art, was friendly with the Johns. She had been responsible for finding *Alderney Manor*. As already noted, Tage Hagelstam from Denmark had arrived in July 1912. At the time his mother was living in Paris. O'Shea and Norman were referred to earlier. Lyell Wilson had just joined. He was born in Australia and at the time his father was a Mining Engineer in Tarquah, South-West Ghana.

Pooley's Annual Report contained the usual details of sporting fixtures and results. The boys played some away matches, for example at Durlston Court School, Swanage. Half-day holidays were given on 2 October and 9 November *'in honour of Mr and Mrs Pooley's birthdays'*. On the first date, *'we tried roller-skating in the Schoolroom'*. On the second, there was a bonfire with a guy made by the boys. The year rounded off with Winter Prize Giving and the annual Christmas Tree in the Dining Room with home-made decorations. The last evening of the Winter Term *'ended with some riotous dancing'*.

Many afternoons in the Spring Term 1913 were devoted to Scouting. O'Shea and A G Batterham were patrol leaders. The Poole Lifeboat was visited during the Term and *'one afternoon we had a full fire-escape practice from the dormitory windows'*. Further half-holidays were given in honour of Peter Pooley's

96. Looking at the sea at Sandbanks June 1913

97. The Pooleys' donkey-cart c1913

birthday and O'Shea obtaining a Scholarship to Marlborough School. A full day's Scouting took place in the grounds of *Alderney Manor*, where *'Mr and Mrs John entertained us all to tea'*.

An annual picnic at Shell Bay was held on Whit Monday and there were several trips to Sandbanks. Hugh Pooley later wrote: *'we acquired a patch of sand at Sandbanks, on which Charles (our marvellous Gardener and Handyman) and I erected a large wooden hut. The school used to drive down to bathe at least twice a week in a two-horse waggonette – which for a while I was allowed by the liveryman to drive myself. A donkey-cart also did duty for ourselves and the children'*.

Also in the Summer Term 1913, Mr and Mrs Everett invited everyone to Broadstone, *'where we all enjoyed climbing on the scaffolding of their new house, and a splendid tea in the open'*. This was *Prospect*, later called *Broadstone House*, of which Katherine Everett had designed and supervised the building. The family had moved in before it was complete.

Annual Prize Giving took place in the garden of *Dane Court* on 28 July 1913. The Reverend O'Shea gave away the prizes. Tea was served on the Tennis Lawn, *'an innovation which proved popular'*. *The Crusaders* was the school play: *'the success of the costumes was largely due to the fact that Mrs John kindly lent us many silks and velvets'*.

There were several changes in staffing during the 1913-1914 School Year. The big news was that David Pritchard and Mrs Bruun were engaged to be married. Mr Bassett-Smith left in December 1913 *'to take up educational work in Natal'*. Edward Hewett Williams joined the staff. He was born in Jamaica, the son of a Missionary, and by 1891 was attending the School for the Sons of Missionaries in Lewisham. He had become an Assistant Master at the Mission School in

98. Summer *by Henry Tonks 1908 which featured Katherine Everett and her son Tony*

Blackheath Village by 1901 and at a grammar school near Midhurst by 1911. He was 36 or 37 when he joined Dane Court Preparatory School. Mrs Bruun's duties as Lady Matron were taken over by Miss C Pridden. Mrs Ida Brennand joined: *'she has many years' experience with small children and her extreme care and thoroughness have worked wonders with the First Form'*, sharing the work with Mrs Pooley. She had previously run a small school near Blandford where she was the sole Mistress. Her father-in-law, William E Brennand, a Solicitor and Newspaper Proprietor, had funded the building of Parkstone School on Commercial Road which opened in 1908. Iris Morris has told the full story of that school in her book on Ashley Cross.

Pooley reported that 8 new boys joined. *'The most gratifying feature regarding our numbers was that at the end of the year we had 12 Boarders as opposed to 9 in 1913 and 6 in 1912. Of the 5 boys who left us during the year both Batterham and Milner passed very creditably into Aldenham and Epsom, respectively'.*

Mrs Brennand's son, Arthur Brennand (1913-1917), joined the school as a Day Boy aged 9 in September 1913. Other local boys who came as Day Boys around that time reflected the widening social backgrounds of pupils. While on the one hand, the father of George Watts (1913-1914) was an Army Captain, his mother living at *The Golf Club* Broadstone, and John Olivey (1913-1919) was the son of a Doctor in Poole, on the other hand Charles Taylor (1913-1920) was the son of a Master Butcher and Farmer, the family home being *Denby Lodge* in Fernside Road, while the father of Godfrey Ellis (1914-1916) was a Bank Cashier, living at *Birklands* in Penn Hill Avenue.

Two other boys started as Boarders in January 1914, both aged 9: Francis Buller (1914-1916), whose parents lived on their own means at *Purbeck Lodge* in Parkstone and Henry Everett's younger brother, Tony Everett (1914 only). Katherine Everett and her son Tony, then aged 2, had modelled in 1908 for a painting by her Slade School friend, Henry Tonks, called *Summer*. It was painted at their previous property, an old mill house near Corfe Castle called *Arfleet*. They had to move out when nearby ball clay mining operations threatened to cause subsidence.

There was the usual round-up of sporting fixtures and results. The football team lost 9, won one and drew one. Pooley observed: *'the chief fault of the team was that it was usually asleep for the first 20 minutes of the game and allowed the enemy to establish his superiority before waking up'*. Other events and half-holidays followed a similar pattern to previous years.

Pooley continued to have his camera at the ready, picturing Tage Hagelstam with Petricia (sic) the donkey near the side gates which opened on to Chapel Lane (where number 12 Chapel Road is now). Tage and Eric Lassen were pictured on the same bicycle. The two Danish boys struck up a close friendship. The Assistant Matron or Nurse 'Mickbird' was also pictured on her bicycle riding round the carriage drive. David John (1912-1916) practiced his batting stroke in the nets, near the north wall and top gate opening on to Danecourt Road. Pooley commented: *'each boy had two periods of ten minutes batting regularly per week for the greater part of the Summer Term. A small matting pitch was bought'.*

99. Tage Hagelstam with Petricia (sic)

100. Mickbird

101. Hagelstam and Lassen

102. David John

On the 12 March 1914 there was a half-holiday to commemorate the wedding of Mr Pritchard and Mrs Bruun. The Pooleys' second son Ole Krohn Pooley was born on 13 March 1914 and a whole day holiday was spent by the Boarders at *Alderney Manor, 'by the very kind invitation of Mrs John'.*

During the Spring Term, the boys spent *'several afternoons doing various repairs to the Playing Field, weeding, rolling and mending the Pavilion fence'*. Two picnics at Shell Bay were held and one afternoon a week was spent at Sandbanks.

Annual Prize Giving was held on 28 July. Pooley reported: *'unfortunately, it poured with rain just as proceedings were going to begin in the garden, but we were able to have the play out of doors as arranged after tea'*. Ingram's father, Mr Edgar Ingram, presented the prizes, assisted by Captain Chesshire, Mrs Everett and Mrs Pooley (senior).

The history of the First World War has been covered extensively elsewhere. The impact on the local area was described by M A Edgington in his book *Bournemouth and the First World War* and Rodney Legg in *Dorset in the First World War*. This chapter focuses on how the war affected those at *Dane Court*.

103. Cricket on the Playing Field c1914

104. Picnic at Shell Bay Whit Monday 1914

105. Mr and Mrs Pooley and staff at Shell Bay Whit Monday 1914

106. Caspar John and John Olivey at Shell Bay

Mr Pooley overriding objective was to ensure that the boys' education continued as normal. In his Annual Report dated November 1914 he wrote:

'the close of our Third School Year finds the country engaged in a stupendous and all-engrossing struggle; if however, there is one subject which still deserves its usual share of attention, it is that of the training of the future generation whose task it will be to repair the damage done during these terrible months'.

There were immediate staffing issues. In November 1914 Edward Williams left the school to enlist in the Warwickshire Regiment Territorial

107. Annual School Photo – July 1914. Back Row: not known, H Everett, Norman, Caspar John, Brennand, R Chesshire, D Ingram, Lassen. Middle Row: Buller, D John, Mary Gane, Mrs Pooley and Ole, Mr Pooley and Peter, Mrs Brennand, Mr Williams, Hagelstam. Front Row: T Everett, Romilly John, A G Batterham, B Ingram, not known, Taylor, not known, E John, R John

Force. He was promoted to Sergeant, and then obtained a commission in the Lancashire Fusiliers. The school continued until Christmas without an Assistant Master.

In January 1915, Mr Pritchard *'once more came to our help'*. In the Summer Term, the Reverend A R Fernsby, a Curate at St Peter's Church, *'very kindly coached the boys in cricket twice a week until at the end he was called to Egypt as a Military Chaplain. We were indebted to Mr Knapp for his Arithmetic lessons and to George F Burn (a Dane Court old boy) for helping with Preparation and so on. All these measures were rendered necessary by the impossibility of obtaining a suitable resident master of the right age. Mrs Brennand was also able to materially assist us by giving her full time'*.

Hagelstam and Lassen were both in Denmark at the outbreak of hostilities and their parents decided that it was better to leave them there.

The Headmaster attempted to give the boys in the school *'a connected idea of the happenings of the year, and with that purpose twice a week the elder ones have had half an hour's War Lesson. They have shown great interest in them and in some cases developed considerable knowledge'*.

Pooley continued: *'during the Winter Term we turned out a number of knitted articles – mufflers and mittens – made by the boys instead of their usual knick-knacks for their Christmas tree. Most of them were given to Mr Williams for the men of his company. We also collected in the Spring and Summer Terms quite a nice sum of money amounting in all to more than 30 shillings for a tobacco fund and the Poole Motor Ambulance'*.

108. E H Williams

In the Winter Term, a Belgian refugee from Antwerp came daily to the school, but soon returned home with his father. In the Spring Term, two further Belgian boys were at the school, the first for a few weeks, the second for the greater part of the Term.

Pooley gave an update on two old boys (since 1911 when he took over): Wilfrid Fuller was a Lieutenant in the Dorset Regiment and Charles Burn had gained a commission in the Seaforth Highlanders.

In other respects, Pooley continued the boys' education and the usual programme of sporting fixtures and excursions. The football team struggled, only winning two of their ten matches. Half-day holidays were granted for Mr and Mrs Pooley's birthdays: on the first, a picnic was held in Branksome Woods, at which *'many fires were lit and potatoes baked'*. On the second half-holiday, there was a fine display of fireworks at *Alderney Manor*. There was a school concert on 17 December 1914 and a French play: *'the acting of all was quite good and the pronunciation really first class, with one exception'*. Tactfully, Mr Pooley did not mention the boy's name.

On the last night of Term, *'we had a small Christmas Tree and a successful concert, at which Willoughby*

Batterham, O'Shea and the Burns (all old boys) were present, as well as Mr Williams who came expressly from Birmingham'.

Meanwhile at the Everett household, all was not well. Mrs Everett later wrote in her memoirs:

'the national calamity was temporarily overshadowed for me by a personal one, for at the start of the war my marriage foundered. In the past if things had been uncomfortable, as for instance directly after my babies were born, Herbert went away, perhaps to Paris or Cornwall, or I might not know where he was. This time he informed me that his disappearance was to be final . . . . he made no effort to see or interfere with the children and from then onwards I looked after them exclusively'.

Apparently, Tony Everett was being difficult at school which was not surprising given the wretched home circumstances. Pooley had to deal with the issue. He wrote in the School Register that Tony Everett *'finally left'* in December 1914: *'his mother asked if he could return to* Dane Court, *but he was altogether subversive of discipline and fellowship among his mates'.*

Young Tony, then aged 8, went to Durlston School in Swanage instead. His brother Henry, who was three years older, stayed on at *Dane Court* until the following Summer. He then joined his brother at Durlston School: Pooley noting his mother's words *'to get better air and to get away from the Johns'.*

New Day Boys in 1914-15 whose parents lived in Parkstone were Richard Eyre Lloyd (1914-1916), the son of an Army Colonel, living at *Vernon* in Sandecotes Road; Raymond Margrie (1915-1921), the son of Thomas Margrie, a Bank Clerk who lived at *Reca* in Glenair Avenue; and Maurice Dixey (1915-1916), who was born in India, son of Albert Dixey, a Clergyman then living at *Ravenhurst* in Parkstone Road. The Walford brothers, John Neville (1915-1917) and William Neville (1915-1918), came as Boarders with their fees paid at a special rate by the Professional Classes War Relief Council. Their parents lived in Surrey.

Pooley accepted Georges Metophis in January 1915. His father, Victor Metophis was a Lieutenant in the Belgian Army and had come to Poole Hospital badly-wounded. Georges entered the school free of charge until September 1915, after which his father paid *'10 shillings a week for his keep'*. In 1916, his father was transferred to a post in France and mother and son left for Le Havre. Georges sent this photo of himself to Mr Pooley a couple of years later.

109. Georges Metophis

In the Spring Term, Pooley reported that a great deal of time was devoted to Scouting, the troop organised into two patrols, Ravens and Kangaroos with Caspar John and David John being the patrol leaders. Caspar John later observed: *'we had many a battle in the nearby woods with wooden staves and rubber balls. Honours were probably even, and we retained some brotherly love'*. He also commented:

'conversations at school and at Alderney Manor frequently turned to the achievements of the Army, the Navy and the Royal Flying Corps'.

The School Sports Day was held on 29 March 1915 even though there was some snow. The prizes were distributed by Edward Williams, *'who again came down to our breaking up, this time from Lancashire'*. In the Summer Term, a full list of fixtures was played including away matches at Wychwood and Old Ride Schools and locally against Parkstone School. Pooley reported that there were two successful picnics at Shell Bay, *'taking both dinner and tea. We bathed regularly from 7 June until the end of July'*. Annual Prize Giving was held on 27 July, but no pageant play was produced. Miss C Pridden continued as Matron, Mr Blaylock on Drawing and Elspie Pridden on Music. Sergeant-Major T Kelly continued to drill the boys.

110. Edwin, Robin, Caspar and David John – Summer 1915

Annual Reports appear not to have been prepared after November 1915, the last report being for the School Year 1914-15. It is possible that they were mislaid but it is more likely that it became too difficult for Mr Pooley to write these breezy reports as news came in of more and more old boys being killed in the conflict.

In 1915, several of the Reverend Graham's former pupils were killed. From the *Mount Lodge* days, James Silcock (1894-1897) was killed in action aged 31 at Ypres on 8 May 1915 while his elder brother Claude Silcock (who also attended between 1894 and 1897) died aged 32 on *SS Falaba* which had been torpedoed off the southern Irish coast on 28 March 1915. From the Reverend Graham's *Dane Court* days, Noel Rundle (1904-1907) was killed in action aged 31 on 19 June 1915 at Gallipoli leading his platoon.

The following year, three more of Reverend Graham's former pupils were killed. James Landale, who attended *Mount Lodge* for five months in 1889, died on 9 March 1916 aged 34 from wounds received during the Battle of El Singh. Godfrey Philpot (1899-1905) was killed on 1 September 1916 aged 17 on the Somme by a shell while acting as a Front Observing Officer (his father Henry Philpot was one of Graham's first pupils at *Mount Lodge*). John Carpenter (1904-1907) was killed in action aged 32 on the Somme on 15 September 1916.

In 1917 more of the Reverend Graham's former pupils were killed. Louis Robinson (1904-1907) from *Dane Court* days was missing believed killed in action aged 23 on 25 May 1917 in

111. Annual School Photo – July 1915. Back Row T Fletcher, H Everett, C John, not known, Brennand, Robin John, Dixey, Buller; Middle Row D John, Mrs Brennand, Mrs Pooley and Ole, Mr Pooley and Peter, Mary Gane, Mr G F Burn, D Ingram; Front Row: W Walford, R Fletcher, Silley, not known, B Ingram, not known, Taylor, E John, Eyre Lloyd, not known.

France. Thomas MacGregor (1904-1909), who joined the Royal Flying Corps, was killed by an air shell aged 19 on 8 June 1917. Ernest Helmore, who attended *Dane Court* for a couple of months in 1905, died of his war wounds at Arras in France on 1 January 1917 aged 20.

In 1918, the first new pupil who joined Reverend Graham at *Mount Lodge*, Duncan MacInnes (1878-1883), one of the five MacInnes brothers from Hamilton in Ontario, was killed on the front in France aged 47 on 23 May 1918, possibly due to his work on mines. Charles Geidt who attended *Dane Court* between 1903 and 1904 was accidentally killed on 10 April 1918 aged 23 while flying with his squadron at a flying school near Alexandria in Egypt. Also in 1918, Charles Robinson (1904-1907) who was an Air Mechanic died in hospital abroad following an accident in service. On 27 October1919, one of the boys Graham brought with him from *Mount Lodge* to *Dane Court*, Frederick Armstrong (1896-1901), attached to 1/69th Punjabis on the North-West Frontier, died of his wounds in hospital aged 31 at Kohat in Pakistan.

Joseph Mack (1907-1910) was someone who both the Reverend Graham and Hugh Pooley would have known well as he attended during Pooley's first two years at *Dane Court.* He was killed on 31 May 1916 aged 20 on the Royal Navy ship *HMS Defence* at the Battle of Jutland. Unfortunately, there are no photographs of any of the above boys in the school albums.

112. Charles Burn

113. Richard Burnier

Charles Burn was invalided in India with cholera and dysentery in 1916 then killed in action in Mesopotamia on 3 November 1917 aged 21. Richard Burnier, who overlapped with Charles Burn at *Dane Court,* died of his wounds in France aged 20 on 21 February 1918. The two photos above were taken in 1912 and 1911, respectively, when they were still at *Dane Court.*

On 25 September 1916, the Reverend Graham who had been ill for some time, died at *Westerkirk*. A requiem was held at St Peter's Church followed by interment at Parkstone Cemetery. The chief mourners were his daughter Sister Margaret O'Syth and son Douglas Graham.

Amidst all this gloom, Mr Pooley had to keep his boys' spirits up and continue their education, not least because some of them would go to the Royal Military College and the Royal Naval College and become soldiers or sailors themselves. Caspar John (1912-1916), having received *Jane's Fighting Ships* as a school prize, and after much discussion between his father and Mr Pooley, decided to join the Royal Naval College in July 1916, aged 13½. David Ingram (1912-1916) left the school in December 1916, joining the Royal Naval College at Osborne House, also aged 13½.

The profile of the school changed considerably during the later war years, both as regards the number of pupils attending and their social backgrounds. In the School Years 1901 to 1914, between 6 and 8 boys would join each year with an even mix of Boarders and Day Boys. In the School Years commencing September 1915 and 1916, 15 and 16 boys, respectively, joined, still evenly split between Boarders and Days Boys.

114. Caspar John

115. David Ingram

116. Annual School Photo – July 1916. Top row: Buller, Douglas, J Crockett, Robin John, Dixey, Brennand, J Walford, B Routledge, D Ingram, Fordham, W Walford, T Fletcher and Romilly John. Middle Row: David John, Casper John. Front Row: Edwin John, R Fletcher, B Ingram, Scutt, M van Namen, G Yeatman, Hearder, Taylor, J Braithwaite, Silley, Selous. Absent: Olivey, Cope, Dawson

However, in the School Years commencing September 1917, 1918 and 1919, 24, 20 and 17 boys, respectively, joined, two thirds of them as Day Boys. The numbers of boys in the Annual School Photos in July each year increased to 33, 43, 51 and 45 in 1917, 1918, 1919 and 1920, respectively. Presumably, the higher numbers were due to the increasing population of Parkstone, a wish by parents during wartime to send their children to a local school as Day Boys rather than as Boarders further afield and the growing reputation of the Pooleys' school.

Several local boys joining as Day Boys in the School Year 1915-1916 were sons of Merchants, for example, Graham Yeatman was the son of Neville Yeatman, Proprietor of W H Yeatman & Sons, Corn Merchants at the Victoria Steam Flour Mills near Poole Quay. Melville Scutt was the son of Homer Scutt, Proprietor of Scutt & Sons, Corn and Seed Merchants on West Quay Road in Poole. Maxwell Van Namen was the son of a Diamond Merchant, his mother living in *Harbour View* in Parkstone Road.

The other boys came from the more traditional family backgrounds: Hampden Fordham (known as 'Bim') (a Boarder 1915-1919) was the son of a Barrister; John Crockett (1915-1919) the son of a Clergyman; David Cope (1916-1921) and Richard Fletcher (1916-1920), the sons of Chartered Accountants; Reginald Dawson (1916-1918), the son of a Royal Navy Commander; Joseph Braithwaite (1916-1921) the son of an Army Major; and Edric Selous (1916-1923) the son of a Retired Surgeon. Robin Hearder (1916-1919) was born in Australia, his father being a Major in the Australian Imperial Force.

Fordham is shown with Mrs Pooley on the front doorstep of *Dane Court* in 1916 with the youngest of Augustus John's sons, Romilly and Edwin. Having arrived in 1912, they would only leave in 1918 and 1919, respectively, spending six years or so as Boarders at *Dane Court*.

117. Romilly John, Fordham, Mrs Pooley and Edwin John in 1916

In his memoirs, Melville Scutt, pictured on the left of the group photograph below, dispels any impression that *Dane Court* boys never misbehaved. One of the many pranks Scutt used to play was tying together adjacent front door knockers, so that when one door was opened from the inside, there was a clatter on the other door. Scutt also related an incident where after a 2nd XI football match he was awarded his Colours only to be deprived of them a week later when he managed not to touch the ball at any time during the match. On another occasion, he was captaining a side when he told his rival Edric Selous that he could take the next goal kick, but when the time arrived asked another boy. Selous fought back: *"Liar! Liar! You said I could take the next behind!"*

118. Edric Selous

This was not an auspicious start for Scutt who later became a Clergyman. He was also not a fan of Mrs Pooley's famous Almond-in-the Pudding, served on the last day of the Christmas Term. He explained: *'a stodgy rice pudding was served for lunch strict instructions being given that no boy should start eating before all had been served. Then there was a mad rush, not because we liked the pudding, but for the simple reason that concealed in the rice was an almond, the finder being presented with the coveted prize of a diary for the following year'.*

119. Scutt Crockett Walford Salmon Douglas R Fletcher R John E John Browne-Poole Silley Routledge Byers

Bathing at Sandbanks continued, Pooley pictured below with the school in July 1917.

120. At Sandbanks July 1917

121. Pritchard, R Fletcher and Hearder on The Wreck at the Haven

122. Salmon Pritchard Hearder E John R Fletcher

The Annual School Plays also continued to be produced. In the Summer of 1917, it was a production called *Saxons* and *Normans*.

123. Saxons and Normans production 1917

124. Lobley, Yeatman, Dawson, Christie and Hearder

John Lobley (1917 only) on the left of the photo was the son of the Painter John Hodgson Lobley, best known for his work as an Official War Artist for the Royal Army Medical Corps during the First World War, producing around 120 paintings in that role. The family lived at *Westland House* in Poole but also had a London address. Unfortunately, Lobley had to leave the school after six months in November 1917 due to a medical issue. Christie was a Boarder, the son of a Civil Engineer in Surrey.

The Dane Court Scout Troop remained very active, in 1918 divided into three patrols: Kangaroos, Ravens and Wood Pigeons. As Romilly and Edwin John were still at the school in 1918/9, the Troop still received invitations to *Alderney Manor*.

125. Kangaroos, Ravens and Wood Pigeons

126 Annual School Photo – July 1917. Back Row: Christie, Scutt, B Ingram, Lobley, Olivey, Browne-Poole, Silley, Yeatman, E John, Braithwaite, Dry. Next Row: Crockett, Salmon, Douglas, Walford, T Fletcher, Fordham, Wills, Taylor, R Fletcher, Romilly John. Staff Row: Brennand, Routledge, R John. Front Row: Cope, Hearder, Dawson, Chronander, P Pooley, Mairis, Linklater, Van Namen, Phillips. Absent: Byers, Sitwell, Selous.

127. Dane Court Scout Troop in the woodland at Alderney Manor 1918

The following photo dates from 1918, taken near the gate in the north wall facing Danecourt Road.

128. Philps Salmon Olivey R John R Fletcher E John Taylor Scutt
Christie Wiggins Linklater G Yeatman Pritchard Dawson Not known M Van Namen

Of the boys not so far mentioned, the father of Seymour Philps (1918-1920), Francis Philps, was the Editor of *The Financial Times*. The family home was in Radlett, Hertfordshire. Seymour came as a Boarder. Charles Pritchard (1917-1922), born in Manildra in New South Wales, Australia, also came as a Boarder.

129. Silley (upper) and Philps (lower)

130. Tom and Richard Fletcher

131. Braithwaite Selous Yeatman Browne-Poole

132. Christie Pritchard Cope M Levey

Edward Browne-Poole (1916-1919) came as a Boarder, his mother living in Blackheath. In the right-hand photo, Maurice Levey (1918-1923) was the younger brother of Sydney Levey, from whom we heard in the opening pages of the chapter. They were the sons of Lieutenant Colonel Joseph Henry Levey who lived in London. They therefore both came as Boarders.

Fordham and Romilly John were both photographed on the front doorstep of *Dane Court*. This is around the time that Romilly John left in May 1918, .

A bonfire was held on 11 November 1918 to celebrate the Armistice, with Little Willie and Big Willie placed on top. These names were used by the press to describe the German Imperial Crown Prince Wilhelm and his father Emperor Wilhelm II. They were also used as names for two models of tank.

133. Fordham

134. Romilly John

135. Armistice Bonfire 11 November 1918 - with Little Willie and Big Willie

136. Peace Day 19 July 1919: picnic in the New Forest

A picnic was held in the New Forest to celebrate the Peace, presumably on or around 19 July 1919 following the Treaty of Versailles.

As the Annual School Photos show, the school had grown to more than three times the size of the 1912 Annual School Photo. It was obvious that the school was outgrowing *Dane Court*. Mr Pooley reflected:

'all the time we were aware that Parkstone was not the right place for us – nor the Bournemouth area a good one for our sons to grow up in. Our hope had always been to build a school of our own to our own ideas – but when the end of the war came this was financially impossible for us – so we spent a long time looking for a suitable spot, North, South, and West London'.

Having grown up in London himself, Pooley obviously thought that his sons would be better off nearer the capital.

137. Annual School Photo – July 1918. Back Row: Phillips, P Carter, M Levey, Christie, Pritchard, Cope, G Yeatman, J Deekers, Gerfalk, Hearder, Selous, M Van Namen, Dry, Wiggins, Dawson. Next Row: Browne-Poole, Taylor, Crockett, Olivey, Romilly John, J Braithwaite, E John, Fletcher, Burbury, W Walford, S Levey. Staff Row: Fordham, R John, Salmon, Philps. Front Row: Jones, D Braithwaite, C Deekers, B Van Namen, D Carter, P Pooley, not known, M Yeatman, Phiby, West, G Chesshire, Chronander, Penrose. Absent: Silley, Scutt, Lawton.

138. Annual School Photo – July 1919. Back Row: B Van Namen, P Carter, Jones, Cope, M Levey, Evans, Hawkins, Selous, M Braithwaite. Next Row: G Chesshire, M Van Namen, D Fletcher, Hearder, Christie, Pritchard, Scutt, Bell, Lewis, Phillips, Tarver, D Salmon. Next Row: Taylor, J Braithwaite, Philps, S Levey, R Fletcher, J Crockett, Olivey, Burbury, Clark, Tolson, Crokaert, Egremont, G Yeatman, Lawton. Staff Row: Flemmich, E John, G Salmon, Silley. Front Row: Le Good, M Yeatman, H Crockett, Pope, D Carter, O Pooley, P Pooley, J Chesshire, West, Philby, Shipp, P Field-Richards.

139. Annual School Photo - July 1920. Top Row: Wiggins, Barton, Dry, Gervis, Fletcher, M Van Namen, Selous, not known, M Swatman. Next Row: Cope, Ship, B Hamilton, P Field-Richards, P Pooley, J Margrie, Chesshire, West, M Braithwaite. Next Row: R Margrie, M Levey, Smith, Christie, S Levey, G Yeatman Tolson, Scutt, Hearder, Philip Swatman, Thomas, G Egremont, Salmon, Pritchard. Staff Row: Burbery, Philps, J Braithwaite. Front Row: H Egremont, Le Good, Philby, T Hamilton, O Pooley, P Swatman, D Evans, M Yeatman, M Field-Richards, C Van Namen. Absent: F Bell, N Bell, Jones, Lewis, Pope, Crockett, Budge.

140. The Emperor's New Clothes *July 1920*

The boys lined up for what would be their final Summer production in July 1920, *The Emperor's New Clothes*, in an adaption of Hans Christian Andersen's tale by Mrs Pooley. A pensive Sydney Levey, standing second from the right, would later reflect:

'the Pooleys were the most significant influence in my life then and later. I imbibed more about the tenets of decent living and good citizenship, of honest endeavour, of unselfishness and the value of teamwork, than at any other period of my life'.

There was however one thing that he wanted to clear up about his prize marble which one day fell through a knot hole in the Schoolroom floor:

'in the floor was a large knot hole and into it, one day, went my prize marble, a glass alley. How to get it out was the problem. I thought I could solve it by coating a fishing sinker in chewing gum on the end of some string and letting nature take its course. Light was the difficulty, so I lit matches and tied them on the string also. What I didn't realise was that the rubbish of ages, papers and otherwise, was under the floor. After the resultant blaze, which was put out with difficulty by Charles Baker, the gardener, pig slaughterer and general handyman, who tried to teach us woodwork, the Schoolroom was uninhabitable for the next few days. This made me the most popular boy in the school, but I would rather have had my marble back. In the event, I did the only sensible thing. I reported sick and spent the rest of the week in the seclusion of the sick-bay'.

Forty-seven years later, Sydney would write to the school magazine *Sunrise* from Port Elizabeth in South Africa:

'I spend many happy hours daydreaming about Parkstone, the embryo of us all'.

Chapter 8

ARCHANGEL TO DANE COURT

The next *Dane Court* Headmaster, Paul Campbell Phipps, had a very different kind of war to his predecessor. Having joined the Gordon Highlanders in July 1915, he was involved on the Somme in France three times, then near Poperinghe and Ypres in Belgium. In April 1918, he obtained a commission with the 18th London Regiment (the London Irish Rifles) and was soon assigned to the Allied Intervention in northern Russia at Archangel.

Seated on the left in the photograph, he was at the time a Cipher Officer at the General Headquarters of the North Russia Expeditionary Force at Archangel. Coincidentally, the aunt of Ambrose Sturdy, seated second from the right, was Eleanor Sturdy the wife of Laurence Pike mentioned in Chapter 4 who took charge of Pike Bros when his father died.

141. Paul Campbell Phipps in Archangel North Russia in 1918 or 1919

Phipps brought different life experiences to *Dane Court* compared to previous Headmasters. His wartime service is therefore set out in some detail below. Many of his wartime drawings have survived. They communicate better than any words the character and humour of the man.

Paul Campbell Phipps was born in Clewer Village in Berkshire on 24 October 1886, the son of Gerald Edward Phipps, a Stockbroker, and Emily Campbell. He had an elder sister Geraldine Nina Phipps and two brothers Harold Edward and Christopher Leckonby Phipps. The family moved to *The Laurels* in Bricket Road, St.Albans a few years later. Between 1893 and 1900 Phipps attended Doon House Preparatory School in Westgate-on-Sea. He then went to Radley College between 1900 and 1905 before going up to Keble College, Oxford where he obtained his BA. While at Oxford he was a member of the Voluntary Reserve Corps.

142. Doon House Preparatory School in Westgate-on-Sea

After university, he returned to Doon House Preparatory School as an Assistant Master for several years. In the 1911 Census he is shown as lodging at *Eastbourne Lodge*, a boarding house in Westgate-on-Sea, along with three other Schoolmasters.

Phipps' wartime experiences set out below are based on records at the National Archives and information and documents provided by the Gordon Highlanders Museum ('the GHM') in Aberdeen and the Phipps family. The general history of the Gordon Highlanders in the First World War has been covered by Cyril Falls.

Paul Phipps enlisted in the 7th Battalion (Territorial Force) of the Gordon Highlanders on 31 July 1915 at Cricklewood. Seven days later he was in Scone at the Highland Division Territorial Training Camp where he received around 14 weeks training. This was followed by two weeks pre-embarkation leave.

On 29 November 1915, he joined the British Expeditionary Force, embarking at Southampton, and arrived at the Infantry Base Depot at Etaples, 27 kilometres south of Boulogne, on 12 December 1915. He joined his Battalion on 17 December 1915 in the trenches at Authuille near Albert on the Somme. According to the GHM, the Battalion had *'a hard and dismal time of it during the winter of 1915/16 which was very wet. The requirement for more substantial accommodation, once out of the front-line, was not met and men suffered real hardship, despite little contact with the enemy'.*

Following the winter in the trenches, Phipps was invalided home on 2 March 1916 suffering from trench foot. This was a debilitating fungal infection of the feet resulting from prolonged exposure to damp, cold conditions allied to poor environmental hygiene. Such was the severity of the condition that Phipps was admitted to the Duchess of Connaught, Canadian Red Cross Hospital in Taplow, Buckinghamshire and remained there for five weeks until 8 April 1916.

After his discharge, his next movements are not documented but the GHM believes that he was most likely sent to the 7th Battalion Gordon Highlanders' base at Witton Hall near Durham. He received further treatment at the Workhouse Military Hospital, Newcastle-upon-Tyne, during July 1916.

On 2 October 1916, he re-joined the British Expeditionary Force, sailing from Folkstone to Boulogne. He arrived at the Infantry Base Depot at Etaples on the next day. He remained there for further training and fitness sessions until he was re-assigned to the 4th Battalion of the Gordon Highlanders. He joined the Battalion in the trenches at Mailly Wood, which lay 8 kilometres north of Albert on the outskirts of the village of Mailly-Maillet, on 5 November 1916. The 4th Battalion was one of several battalions involved in the Battle of Ancre.

He was again on the casualty list. He suffered severe barbed wire injuries to both hands and his right leg. According to the GHM, the war diary for 17 November records that *'the Battalion was employed on salvaging material from the first and second German lines'*. The GHM continues: *'it is likely that it was during this work that Paul became badly entangled in German wire and suffered significant injuries. His records confusingly also refer to a gunshot wound ('GSW') in his leg but this is likely to be simply a clerical error as the war diary indicates no contact with the enemy on the day of his wounding'*. However, the Phipps family has the original official notification recording admission to the General Hospital in Boulogne suffering from *'a gunshot wound in the left leg'*. The National Archives records are inconsistent regarding the date of wounding: in one place they indicate 18 November, in another 19 November, when according to Cyril Falls, there was engagement with the enemy. His son Robin recalls his father saying that *'in order to initially clean the gunshot wound, they connected a hose to the water tap in the yard at the field service station and passed water through his leg from one side to the other'*.

He was transferred from Boulogne to the 2nd Western General Hospital in Manchester on 26 November 1916. He remained there for over four months until 6 April 1917. It was while he was in hospital that Phipps produced several sketches, included in a sketch book dated January 1917, called *Happy Days in France*. Some may have been drawn at an earlier date. Six of the sketches are reproduced below.

143. Fall out for 10 minutes

144. *Going In*

145. *Over the bags in 5 minutes*

146. *Types of Hideous Huns*

147. *The price of keeping warm*

148. They say there's a war on. Na, Na. It's only a rumour

On 23 May 1917, Phipps returned to France and in Etaples was posted to the 7th Battalion Gordon Highlanders at Arras. On 9 June, the Battalion was withdrawn from the line for rest and training. At this point Phipps was transferred back to the 4th Battalion.

The GHM indicates that *'following the fighting around Arras, the 51st Highland Division, of which the 4th Battalion was part, was moved north into Belgium to the area around Poperinghe where throughout July and August they were in the trenches and were in continual touch with the enemy taking numerous casualties primarily from gas and artillery attacks'.*

Paul Phipps' sister used to relate that her brother received shrapnel injuries to his thigh during this period and rescued a wounded officer from 'no man's land' despite being wounded himself, although for some reason the details were not noted in his war service record.

The GHM continues: *'at the end of July, Paul was promoted to Lance Corporal following the loss of large numbers of experienced men. He had obviously been recognised as an individual who was well-educated and motivated with potential for leadership'.* He left the Battalion at Poperinghe on 27 September 1917 following the arrival of 115 reinforcements. He returned to the UK to attend the No.9 Officer Cadet Battalion at Gailes in Ayrshire, one of 25 such establishments for training officers with No. 9 and 10 Battalions taking men from Scottish regiments. The training course lasted for four and a half months at the end of which time, on 30 April 1918, he was commissioned as a 2nd Lieutenant in the 18th London Regiment (the London Irish Rifles).

Paul Phipps probably never actually served with the 18th London Regiment as his records show that he was soon deployed to Archangel in northern Russia as a Cipher Officer. The GHM adds: *'to be assigned as a Cipher Officer he would almost certainly have been trained by naval cryptographers at Room 40 which was the room in the Admiralty which was the original location of the British cryptography effort during the First World War. It was established shortly after the start of the war in October 1914 and retained its informal name when it expanded during the war, later moving into other offices'.*

The background to the Allied Intervention in Russia is complex and has been covered in detail elsewhere. In essence, the Allied operation was designed to support Russian forces. After the Treaty of Brest Litovsk between Russia and Germany in March 1918, the Allies were concerned that the treaty enabled German entry into Finland from which it could approach the Russian ports of Murmansk and Archangel where large stockpiles of the Allies' military supplies were kept. They were also concerned that German U-boat bases might be established on the North Cape. While the new Bolshevik government initially welcomed the Allied troop landings, relations deteriorated so in August 1918 Archangel was seized by British and French troops. The Allied force at Archangel was then enlarged by three American battalions.

As noted, Paul Phipps was a Cipher Officer in the General Headquarters of the North Russia Expeditionary Force at Archangel. His role presumably involved supervising the encryption and decoding of communications sent and received. He was acting as a 'temporary Captain' during this period.

The General Armistice on the Western Front on 11 November 1918 removed the anti-German rationale for the campaign. British troops were eventually withdrawn at the end of September 1919. He was allowed to relinquish his appointment as Cipher Officer with effect from 6 October 1919. He sailed to Liverpool on the *SS Czaritsa* and reported to Knotty Ash Camp from where he returned home. On his return to England, he was rewarded by being promoted to Lieutenant on 1 November 1919. For his service, he was awarded the 1914/15 Star, the War Medal, Victory Medal and an MBE (military).

Several drawings from this period have survived. One drawing wonderfully captures a comical scene of troops mounting guard at GHQ Archangel. The second is a cartoon of his comrades dated 1918 as though they are only going to leave Archangel in 1999! It is known by the Phipps family who each of the characters is: Ambrose Sturdy is second from the left and Paul Phipps is on the far right, the last to disembark. The captions are written in the respective languages of the seven men in the cartoon. The Phipps family also has an intriguing collection of 150 photographs taken by Paul Phipps during his time in Archangel and the camera with which he took them.

149. Mounting Guard GHQ Archangel

150. 1999 or Return of the Archangels! (Cipher Section GHQ NREF)

On his return to civilian life, Paul Phipps was briefly a Master at Wychwood School in Bournemouth. Then in 1922, he obtained a lease on *Dane Court* and, aged 36, set up his own preparatory school, initially in partnership with a Mr H W Turner. Phipps became the sole Principal from around 1925.

151. Dane Court *by Paul Phipps 1925*

It is fascinating that one of the surviving unfinished drawings by Phipps from his *Dane Court* period focuses on the Chapel. One can see the chimney faintly, confirming that it was heated. It is possible that the Chapel had been converted into upstairs and downstairs rooms in 1900 when the Reverend Graham moved there, if not long before. The Chapel is never mentioned by Mr Pooley or any of his schoolboys in their detailed reminiscences of the house.

Dane Court had at long last been converted to electric lighting. It had also had a lick of paint, probably arranged by the landlord between

152. Dane Court in Paton's List of Schools and Tutors

April 1921 and the date in 1922 when Phipps moved in. A large number of trees and some garden features, such as The Mound, were removed on the eastern half of the site in order to provide a full-size cricket pitch within the grounds of *Dane Court.* The photo and advertisement are taken from *Paton's List of Schools and Tutors* for 1929.

Sadly, the School Registers for the years 1922 to 1933 have not survived. Presumably, they were passed on to the next incumbent when he took over the school. Only one Annual School Photo has been handed down included at the end of the chapter, probably dating from 1930 or 1931. At the time of the photo, there were 42 boys at the school. It shows Paul Phipps with to the left of him his wife Flora Phipps (née Gruning). They had married in June 1929. Her sister, Lilian Gruning, married Graham Yeatman mentioned in the previous chapter. To the left of them is Paul Phipps's sister, (Geraldine) Nina Tasker, and her husband Maurice Tasker who were both Assistant Teachers at the school.

DANE COURT, PARKSTONE DORSET
PREPARATORY TO THE PUBLIC SCHOOLS AND NAVY

Principal – Paul C Phipps, MBE, BA, Keble College Oxford

Assisted by M B Tasker, MA Camb, late of RNC Dartmouth, and efficient Staff

Boys are admitted at the age of 7 years and are not allowed to remain after the term in which they reach 14.

Dane Court stands in its own grounds of 4 acres, including fruit and vegetable gardens and tennis court. The rooms, most which face south, are lofty and well-ventilated, and lighted by electric light.

The school playing field is in the grounds and there is every facility in the neighbourhood for riding, boating, bathing and nature study. Sea-bathing nearly every day in the Summer.

The course of instruction includes all subjects necessary for Public School Common Entrance. Scholarships are frequently won, and boys are specially coached (not crammed) for these, if desirable.

The domestic arrangements are in the hands of Mrs Phipps, assisted by a fully qualified Matron. There is a well-equipped changing room, with hot and cold shower baths. Private laundry in the school premises.

Entire charge taken of boys whose parents are abroad. Prospectus and full particulars on application to the Principal.

Source: 1929 edition of Paton's List of Schools and Tutors

In 1933, Paul Phipps decided to sell the goodwill of the school to a Mr Cecil William Ayerst. The lease on *Dane Court* would have been assigned to Ayerst as the house remained in the ownership of the Jackson family.

Cecil William Ayerst continued the school for a couple of years in 1934 and 1935. He was born in 1910, the son of the Reverend Cecil Francis Ayerst. Cecil William Ayerst had only obtained his BA at Queen's College, Cambridge in 1931. He was aged 23 when he took over the school. It was ambitious to take on a school as Principal with so little experience. Most preparatory school Headmasters, such as Hugh Pooley and Paul Phipps, had several years' experience as an Assistant Master or a Master before taking on a role as Principal.

Early in 1936 *Dane Court* was advertised for sale. The Jackson family put the freeholds of *Dane Court* and *Heathfield* on the market. Both were purchased by the surveyor Edward Fox, later of Fox & Sons, for £5,950 in January 1936, with a view to selling off the *Dane Court* site as building plots. Later in the Spring of 1936 *Dane Court* was demolished.

153. Annual School Photo of Dane Court Preparatory School c1930

Chapter 9

LATER YEARS

Over 300 people are known to have lived or spent significant time at *Dane Court* as residents, servants, teachers, schoolboys, visitors or the developer, Alfred Crabb. This chapter reveals what became of them in later years.

Alfred Crabb (Chapter 1)

In October 1864, Alfred Crabb no doubt breathed a sigh of relief as he entered *Pelham House* in Poole, discharged from bankruptcy and free to continue his practice as a Surgeon. He died just 10 years later though aged 61. Maybe the bankruptcy took its toll. On his death, his wife Mary Crabb removed to *Glenquaich* in Alum Chine Road Bournemouth with her daughters, where she lived for the next 36 years until her death in 1911, the bankruptcy hopefully a distant memory.

Elizabeth and Lucy Robinson Humfrey (Chapter 2)

We left Elizabeth Humfrey in a dreadful state following the suicide of her husband, Richard Morgan Humfrey. Fortunately, her devoted niece Lucy Robinson Humfrey came to the rescue. She was to remain her constant companion. In October 1871, they moved to *Little Tew Cottage* in Enstone, Oxfordshire where they lived until Elizabeth's death in 1882. Little is known of Lucy's later years. She ended her days at Hyde Park Mansions in London where she died in 1901 aged 52.

Richard Humfrey's Coachman, George Masterman, moved from *Brontë House* to a cottage in Parkstone Road where he worked for another Master locally. He continued to be a Coachman in the Parkstone and Bournemouth areas for a few decades and was still a Cabman in 1911 aged 70. He died aged 94 in 1935. It is not known what became of the Humfreys' Cook, Fanny Legg.

Richard and Caroline Ley (Chapter 3)

The auctioneer of the Leys' house contents remarked that the Reverend Richard Ley was *'removing to a distance'*. Indeed, he was. In the 1881 Census he was living on *The Green* in his birthplace Maker on the Rame Peninsula in Devon (now in Cornwall). He clearly wanted to return to his roots. He no doubt visited Rame Church where he had funded the beautiful east window in honour of his father nearly a decade earlier. There was no sign of Mrs Ley in Maker though. She was living on the other side of Plymouth Sound at 39 George Street with two servants. Allowing for house renumbering, this may have been the *Port Admiral's House*, now called *Hamoaze House*, in which she may have had lodgings, as a base for good works in the community. Otherwise, she

154. St Barnabas Hospital in Saltash

would have had to walk from Maker on the Rame Peninsula to the Cremill Ferry each day and cross Plymouth Sound to Plymouth and back.

Despite appearing estranged, the Leys were in fact a devoted couple. For the first few years after they moved from *Brontë House* in 1874, they lived in a waterfront property at Kingsand on the Rame Peninsula. Records of happy visits to *'Uncle Dick and Aunt Carrie'* feature in the diaries of their niece, Lucy Du Buisson. In 1881, the Reverend Ley agreed to donate £200 to the Alexandra Hospital, in lieu of the £18 per annum rent he had been contributing, to help the hospital purchase *Eldon Lodge* in West Hill Road, Bournemouth. This opened as a convalescent branch of the Alexandra Hospital in March 1881 and was renamed as the Helen Branch the following year. Eventually, in the mid-1880s the Leys moved to a house called *Claremont* in Higher Port View, Saltash, with panoramic views of the River Tamar. The Reverend Richard Ley died there on 11 November 1886.

Caroline Ley's finest works were yet to come. After her husband's death, she financed the building of the St Barnabas Hospital and Convalescent Home in Saltash in loving memory of her husband. In common with the National Sanatorium in Bournemouth, and their previous homes, *Stewarton Lodge* and *Brontë House*, the hospital had a large Chapel on the back of it, as shown in the above photo. A stone altar slab is inscribed: *'To the Honour and Glory of God and in Loving Memory of Richard Ley, Priest, this building is erected by his widow, A.D. 1887-88'*.

The hospital was originally intended *'for the benefit of people of both sexes residing within a radius of*

155. The garden of St. Barnabas Hospital overlooking the River Tamar

15 miles of Saltash who may be suffering from accident or non-contagious diseases, or were convalescing from illness, especially those who were discharged from hospital but were not sufficiently strong to resume work'.

It was vested in Trustees and managed by the Sisters of St Mary's Home, Wantage who were involved until 1893. Towards the end of that year their Mother Superior gave notice that the staff were required for a new hospital in Worthing, so its operation was transferred by Mrs Ley to the community of St. Margaret's, East Grinstead. They operated St Barnabas Hospital until the mid-1950s, the National Health Service having taken the hospital under its wing in 1948. St Barnabas is still operating as a hospital today over 130 years after it was built. In 1927, the hospital purchased the Leys' former house *Claremont* next door and it became part of the hospital connected by a covered walkway.

Caroline Ley had one further surprise. In her 60s, after her husband's death, she adopted a daughter, Rose Ellen Gemmer. In the 1881 Census, Rose Ellen Gemmer, the daughter of an actor Frederick Gemmer, was in All Hallows Orphanage, in Ditchingham, Norfolk aged six. The All Hallows Sisters' House of Mercy was initially formed for prostitutes and girls in need of care, providing rescue, training and rehabilitation. All Hallows School was established in 1862. The girls at the school were mostly orphaned girls of middle-class origin. At some point between 1886 and 1891, Mrs Ley adopted Rose. How she came to have contact with the All Hallows Sisters and to adopt Rose Gemmer is a mystery.

By the 1891 Census, Rose Gemmer was boarding at Cambridge Place, Albany Road in Falmouth with a Professor of Music, Charles Robinson, and his wife Louisa, a Headmistress of a High School, and their family. Rose was then aged 16. Meanwhile, Caroline Ley was staying at The Vicarage in Sellack, Herefordshire, where her nephew Augustin Ley was the Vicar. Augustin was a widower, having married his cousin Lucy Du Buisson who had sadly died soon after they were married. Later Caroline Ley moved to 55 James Street, Cowley Road, Oxford. She attended the wedding of her adopted daughter in Oxford on 21 January 1896 to Edward Lindsell Hunt.

Two years later, on 13 April 1898, Caroline Ley died while staying at a boarding house called *Strathnairn* in Florence Road, Boscombe. She was 72.

William Joseph Pike's family (Chapter 4)

William Joseph Pike's three spinster daughters, Anne, Katherine and Marion Pike, inherited *Leymore* and its contents when he died in November 1884. However, they moved out early in 1885 having sold the contents. The youngest daughter, Marion, married an Army Captain in 1892 and later lived in Marnhull near Shaftesbury. Little is known of the whereabouts of Katherine and Anna for most of the twenty-five years after 1885. At the time of the 1891 Census all three sisters were staying at a hotel in Cork Street, London while in 1901 Anna and Katherine were staying at a hotel in Churt near Frensham in Surrey. Maybe they travelled and/or lived abroad. Some of their brothers and cousins had done so. By 1911, the sisters had bought a large house called *East Down* near Winterborne Whitechurch in Dorset where they were to remain for the rest of their lives. Anna died in 1941, Katherine ten years later in 1951.

Laurence Pike, who lived at *Leymore* for about two and a half years from December 1874 until he married Eleanor Sturdy on 30 April 1877, took charge of Pike Bros after his father's death in 1884. He and his wife Eleanor moved into *Furzebrook House*, near to the Furzebrook clay mines. Tragically he died aged 51 on 30 August 1900 after a sudden illness. As well as being a Justice of the Peace and Vice Chairman of the Harbour Commissioners, his obituary noted that he and his wife had a strong interest in animal welfare. His cousin Leonard Gaskell Pike, who had previously worked as a Barrister in London, took charge of the Pike Bros business. Arnold Pike, who had been left a share of the business by his father, had little involvement in it. Pike Bros merged with B Fayle & Co Ltd in 1949, becoming known as Pike Bros Fayle & Co Ltd and subsequently the business was acquired by English China Clays, which in turn became part of Imerys Ltd. The later history of the Pike Bros clay mining business and railway is covered in the definitive book on the subject by Chris Legg.

Evelyn Pike, who also lived at *Leymore* for about two and a half years from December 1874 had married Walter Squire on 26 July 1877. She is believed to have spent most of her life in Chile with her merchant husband.

William Lewison Pike resided at *Leymore* for three and a half years until he married Jessie Aldridge Durrell on 19 June 1878 at St Peter's Church, Parkstone. As noted in Chapter 4, the couple lived at *Mayfield* on Sloop Hill, then at *Windholm* in Mount Road, Parkstone in the early 1880s. Tragically, he died within eighteen months of his brother Laurence, aged 55, in December 1901. William Lewison had retired from the clay business in his late 30s, soon after his father's death, and removed to the rather grand *Richmond House* in Appledore in Devon with his family to live the life of a country squire. At the time of his death, he had recently moved to *Westleigh House* in Bideford. In his obituary, he was described as *'a very genial gentleman, a liberal supporter to every good cause and willing to extend a hand wherever needful'*.

As regards the Pikes' various servants at *Leymore*, Mary Dowland from Swanage, the Pike's Parlour Maid, died aged 31 in April 1884 while William Joseph Pike was still at *Leymore*. Their widowed Cook, Ellen Sherwood, did not remarry and died in Poole in 1923. By 1891, their Kitchen Maid, Mary Selby from Church Knowle was a servant at a house called *Savernake* in Pokesdown, Boscombe. It is not known what became of her sister Annie Selby, the Housemaid. By 1891, William Pike's Coachman, George Roe, who came with the Pikes from Wareham, living at *Leymore Lodge* with his wife and family, had moved to 5 Archway Terrace in Salterns Road, Parkstone, then employed as a Gardener aged 66. By 1901, Thomas Best, the Pikes' Gardener, who in the 1881 Census lived with his wife and family at *Brunswick Cottage* (recorded under its original name), was living in Westport in Wareham in business as a Market Gardener. He died in Wareham in 1906, described as a Nurseryman and Florist.

James and Ada Jackson and family (Chapter 5)

When we left James Jackson at *Dane Court*, he was selling his two bay horses and landau, *'shortly to leave the district'*. As noted, he retained the freehold of *Dane Court* leasing it out thereafter. The house remained in the ownership of the Jackson family until 1936. James and Ada Jackson moved to an impressive property called *Kingscote* in Palace Road, East Molesey, near Hampton Court. The property still exists. It was situated quite close to his married sister, Catherine Ratcliffe, who lived at *Coniston* in Dukes Avenue, New Malden.

Tragically, James and his brother George Jackson died within 12 days of each other in August 1906, not long after the photo in Betws-y-Coed was taken with the Lanchester Landaulette. James Jackson left around £102,000, or about £6 million in today's money. It is not known how long Ada Jackson and her sons remained at *Kingscote*. She died on Christmas Day 1922 aged 68. James and Ada Jackson are buried in Hampstead Cemetery.

As regards their daughter, Ada Jackson (1879-1966), her marriage to Charles Jean Moosbrugger (1870-1916), the managing director of the Maypole Diary Co Ltd, ended sadly. A high-profile divorce case featured in the national press for about 10 days in 1913. James Jackson's first son, James Jackson (1880-1951) became a *'Director of a Provision Merchant'*, living at *Sunridge* in Dukes Avenue, New Malden, the street where Catherine Ratcliffe and her family lived. His second son, Vincent Jackson (1881-1964), is recorded in the 1939 Register as being a *'Retired Butter Taster'*. His youngest son, Alfred Jackson (1884-1953), trained as an Electrical Engineer and worked as a Charge Engineer at the original Bankside Power Station in London for nearly 40 years (the power station that preceded the one that currently houses Tate Modern). As noted in Chapter 5, nothing is known of the Jacksons' servants as the Jacksons arrived at *Dane Court* after the 1891 Census and left before the 1901 Census.

Margaret and Douglas Graham (Chapter 6)

The Reverend Graham's final years were covered in Chapter 7 as he lived nearby and continued to have some involvement in the Dane Court Preparatory School. Before the First World War, his youngest son Douglas trained as an Engineer, working for Messrs Hans Renold in Manchester for a few years. The company was involved in mechanical and motor engineering. He then became a Schoolmaster. In July 1917 he joined the Royal Flying Corps as a Second Lieutenant, acting as an Equipment Officer. His engineering skills were soon required in the Aeronautical Supply Branch on urgent work concerning aircraft engines and materials.

After the war, Douglas Graham arranged the sale of his father's former holiday home *Dalkenneth* in Lochearnhead and its contents were sold. Douglas returned to being a Schoolmaster. He was last recorded in Kensington where he died from tuberculosis aged 49 in 1932. Sister Margaret O'Syth from the St Peter's Home and Sisterhood was present at his death. She remained at the St Peter's Home and Sisterhood in Kilburn for many years. Much later, the Sisterhood moved to the St Peter's Memorial Home in Woking, where Margaret had spent a month convalescing in April 1901. She remained a Sister of Mercy there until her death in 1953.

Hugh and Michaela Pooley (Chapter 7)

We left Hugh and Michaela Pooley busily searching for a new school at the end of Chapter 7. Eventually they found a purpose-built school in Pyrford, near Woking, called Dean Court. Mr Pooley later remembered: *'a simple transposition of the 'e' soon brought the two schools together. A number of our boys came with us from Parkstone, and we took on about twenty from the former Headmaster, Mr H E Kingford'.*

Hugh Pooley continued as Headmaster for another 40 years finally retiring in 1961. Dane Court Preparatory School had only had two headmasters in 94 years. Sir Caspar John, who had a remarkable naval career having become First Sea Lord by 1961, made the presentation. Although he planned to attend in civilian clothes, driving an old Volkswagen Beetle, Mr Pooley was keen that he wore his impressive naval uniform. There was no better way of showing boys what they could achieve if they aimed high.

At the time of Mr Pooley's retirement there were 55 boys at the Boarding School and 70 at the Day School. In his retirement speech he reflected: *'the boys of today are not really more tiresome than when I was a boy. Boys are very much the same. They still pinch the fruit'.* He said that *'there was a great need for an all-round education rather than concentration on either Science or the Arts'.* He emphasised that two people do not make a school: *'it is the earnest endeavour of every member of a school that makes it what it is'.* Mrs Pooley said that the years she had spent working with her husband had been the realisation of a dream she had while a girl to help run a boarding school: *'we work together in absolute agreement on the major parts and urging each other on by the disagreements in the minor'.*

Their youngest son Robin Pooley, born soon after the move to Pyrford, took over as Headmaster. In 1967, at the time of the school's centenary, 156 boys were on the books. Numbers grew further over the next fourteen years. There were separate Boarding and Day Schools. The school eventually closed in July 1981 after an unsuccessful search for suitable premises to merge the Boarding and Day Schools. The Old Dane Court Society continued to thrive for many years thereafter.

Dane Court staff 1900 to 1921 (Chapters 6 and 7)

As regards the staff listed in the 1901 Census, the Assistant Master **Crofton Atkins** served in the Royal Army Service Corps in the First World War. Later he became a member of the Senate at Cambridge University. **Kenneth Mayne**, who was also an Assistant Master in 1901, became Rector of St Mary's Church, Burgh St Peter in Norfolk.

Cuthbert Bazell, who featured in a few of the early school photographs, subsequently enlisted in the Somerset Light Infantry. He later joined the RAF becoming a Flight Lieutenant, then Group Captain. After the Second World War, he was a Flight Instructor at Cranwell, the Officer Training School. Sadly, little is known of what became of **Elspie Pridden,** the much-loved Music Mistress. She did not marry. She died in Bridport in 1962.

156. Retirement presentation to Hugh Pooley by Sir Caspar John in 1961

157. Hugh and Michaela Pooley in the 1960s after they had retired

As regards **Dudley Bassett-Smith**, who was last seen sitting on the front doorstep of *The Cottage* with Emily Bruun in 1912, he left *Dane Court* in December 1913 to take up an appointment at Hilton College in Natal. He remained there for the next 35 years, teaching Science. He improvised in and then improved the school's Science laboratories. In 1932 he was appointed as the Second Master to the Headmaster and was Acting Headmaster on four occasions. He was one of the first people in Natal to get a driving licence, motoring in an early 'Tin Lizzie'. He had a passion for mountaineering with several first ascents of the Drakensberg peaks being credited to him. At the time of his retirement in 1947, his first Headmaster William Falcon wrote:

'Bassett-Smith is the last of that small band of long-service masters who, differing widely from one another in character, disposition and interests, but bound by the common tie of love for Hilton, kept her in the forefront in every sphere of school activities throughout those critical years when the ability of private schools to retain their place in the South African system of education hung in the balance'.

We left the newly married **David Pritchard** in the Spring Term of 1914 as he helped to cover staffing shortages after the enlisting of Mr Williams. **Pritchard** had wed Michaela Pooley's cousin, **Emily Bruun**. The couple later settled in Nymindegab in Denmark where they lived for over 40 years. When Emily died in 1960, David returned to live in St Leonards-on-Sea, sadly dying there the following year.

Edward Williams, later known as *'Old Willie'* by Mr Pooley, returned to *Dane Court* in 1920. He moved with the Pooleys to Pyrford and got married there in 1921. He taught at Pyrford for several years before the Second World War. He later lived at *Pine Hill* in St Ives near Ringwood. He died in 1954.

Turning to the household staff at *Dane Court* in 1901, **Mary Gane** remained at *Dane Court* as Housekeeper or Matron for most of the next 20 years. She appears in several of the Annual School Photos. It is not known what became of her after she left *Dane Court*. **Agnes Baker** who was a Kitchen Maid aged 15 at the time of the 1901 Census, stayed at least another 10 years. It is not known when she left. She did not marry. She lived to the ripe old age of 94 in Parkstone. Her sister **Ella Baker**, who was a Schoolroom Maid at *Dane Court* in 1901, left some time before 1911. In that year she was a cook at *Holmwood Vicarage* in Dorking, looking after the Reverend Charles Inge. She met her future husband in the area, William Henry Tuppen, a Gardener, marrying him at St Peter's Church, Parkstone in 1913.

Alice Kail, who was a Housemaid at *Dane Court* in 1901, married Alfred Smith, a Lamplighter for Bournemouth Gas and Water Company, in 1908. **Fanny Paul**, who was recorded as a Nurse Domestic at *Dane Court* in1901, married Thomas Williams in February 1902. They had a daughter and two sons. In 1913, the family emigrated to Canada and by 1921 were resident in Ontario. It is believed that they stayed there. **Melinda Trowbridge**, a Housemaid in 1901, married one of the uncles of Agnes and Ella Baker, Bertie Baker, a House Painter, in October 1901. By 1911 they were living at 2 Allington Cottages in Lilliput with two sons. All three women married in St Peter's Church, Parkstone.

Dane Court Preparatory School boys 1900 to 1921 (Chapters 6 and 7)

Over 240 boys attended the school while it was at *Dane Court* between 1900 and 1921.They are central to the history of the house. Many were there for several years. For most they were their formative years. The Supplement to this book sets out details of all boys to the extent known by the Author. A number are highlighted below.

Firstly, we should remember four old boys who tragically lost their lives in the Second World War; those killed in the First World War were remembered in Chapter 7. **George Devereux Belben** (1905-1909), the eldest of the three Belben brothers from Poole, had a distinguished naval career. He was awarded the DSO in 1918. He became Captain of the armed merchant cruiser *HMS Canton* and the light cruiser *HMS Penelope* in the Second World War. He was drowned at sea in 1944 when *HMS Penelope* was torpedoed. He was posthumously awarded the DSC. His posthumous citation for the Albert Medal read: *'Captain Belben lost his life from ultimate exhaustion as a result of his outstanding bravery and self-sacrifice in directing the rescue of survivors from the water'*.

Godfrey Ellis (1914-1916) became a Serjeant in the Royal Artillery in WWII. He was killed in 1941. **Edward Ormerod** (1911-1914) later became a 2nd Lieutenant attached to 2 Field Regiment of the Royal Indian Artillery. He died in 1942 in one of the campaigns. **Edric Selous** (1916-1923) subsequently worked in Sarawak as the Secretary for Chinese Affairs in the Sarawak Civil Service. He died while interned by the Japanese in Sarawak in 1945.

We should also remember those boys who had their lives cut short due to other causes. **Willoughby Batterham** (1904-1910), the second son of Dr Batterham, the surgeon from St Leonards-on-Sea, attended the Royal Naval College at Dartmouth and became a Lieutenant Commander in the Royal Navy. He died in July 1931, aged just 34. His younger brother **Gordon Batterham** (1907-1912), who played the glorious prank with the lavatory doors described in Chapter 6, became ill soon after the First World War. His health gradually deteriorated over subsequent years. He died from tuberculosis in 1931, aged 32, just two months after his brother. **Hector MacLeod** from Australia (1906-1908) tragically drowned in an accident in St Helier in Jersey in 1925.

Ian Mack (1908-1910), the second son of Mrs Mack from Victoria in Australia, was speared by natives in Upper Rama, New Guinea in 1933 while acting as a District Patrol Officer. The full background to this tragedy is covered in Chapter 6 of Naomi McPherson's book *In Colonial New Guinea: Anthropological Perspectives*. His Patrol Reports have also been published. **Bernard Ingram** (1913-1917) sadly died of pneumonia while at St John's School Leatherhead in 1922. **John Crockett**, (1915-1919) was killed in a motorcycle accident near Poole in 1924.

In addition to George Belben and the other boys mentioned above, several other boys had distinguished careers in the armed services. **Sir Caspar John** has already been mentioned in connection with Mr Pooley's retirement. In 1962 he became Admiral of the Fleet. His daughter wrote a full-length biography of her father. **Joseph Braithwaite** (1916-1921), pictured below, studied mechanical sciences at Cambridge and subsequently became a torpedo specialist. He joined the RAF in 1929. In 1946 he was awarded the CBE and later became Air Vice-Marshal Joseph Braithwaite. He was Commander in charge of Singapore. Tragically, he was killed in a solo air accident on the Indonesian island of Palau Batam in 1956. **Norman Gwatkin**, also pictured below, who came to the school in 1907, had a distinguished career in the Army and later became the Extra Equerry to King George VI and had the same role in the household of Queen Elizabeth II. He was knighted becoming known as Brigadier Sir Norman Wilmhurst Gwatkin.

Another old boy who had a distinguished military career was **Richard Eyre Lloyd** (1914-1916), who was seen seated on the front row of the 1915 Annual School Photo. His career included being Chief of Staff for the Middle East Land Forces in 1957. He became Major-General Richard Eyre Lloyd and received the honour of Companion of the Order of the Bath in 1959. The

National Portrait Gallery photo dates from 1960. **David Ingram** (1912-1916), who we last saw departing for the Royal Naval College in December 1916, had a distinguished career in the submarine service being awarded the Distinguished Service Cross and the CBE. He was Chief of Intelligence Staff in the Middle East in 1948-1950 and Deputy Director of Naval Intelligence in 1952-3. **Charles Tarver**, who attended the school in 1919, reached the rank of Brigadier in the Indian Army and later became Major-General Charles Herbert Tarver CB CBE DSO. **Vincent Budge** (1920-1924), who spent a year at *Dane Court* before moving with the Pooleys to Pyrford, became a Brigadier in the Grenadier Guards and was awarded the CBE and MVO. While the number of boys with parents serving in the Indian Army and the Colonial Service gradually reduced over time, several boys still had careers there. **Shirley Burroughs** (1897-1901), **Basil Jones** (1898-1903), **Edward Geidt** (1900-1904), **Charles Stevens** (1900-1903), **Grant Rundle** (1901-1907), **Thomas Belben** (1905-1910), **Gilbert Beal** (1912-1913) and **Hugh Linklater** (1917-1918) all had careers in the Indian Army.

Several other boys pursued careers in the Colonial Service or in other disciplines overseas. **Clarmont Skrine** (1896-1900), who came with the Reverend Graham to *Dane Court* in April 1900 for his final Term, had a fascinating career as a Consul and Political Agent. He wrote three

158. Air Vice-Marshal Braithwaite
© National Portrait Gallery

159. Sir Norman Gwatkin
© National Portrait Gallery

160. Major-General Richard Eyre Lloyd
© National Portrait Gallery

161. Major-General Charles Tarver
© National Portrait Gallery

books, including *Chinese Central Asia* in 1926 and *World War in Iran* in 1962. He was knighted, becoming Sir Clarmont Percival Skrine. **Kenneth Dobson**, who attended *Dane Court* briefly in 1918, worked for the Colonial Service of Tanganyika from 1930 to 1957. His daughter Julia Tugendhat has described her father's work in her book *My Colonial Childhood in Tanganyika*. **Guy Barton** became a Civil Servant in Nigeria during the 1930s. He was then Assistant Colonial Secretary and later the Chief Colonial Secretary in Barbados. He was awarded the CMG and the OBE. He wrote a book called *The Prehistory of Barbados* in 1953.

Other boys who embarked on careers in the Colonial Service or in similar occupations include **Sydney Lukis** (1897-1902) who became a Civil Engineer in India, being involved in the Immingham Dock Construction in 1910-1911 and the Sara Bridge construction in 1911-1913. **Claude Child** (1908-1909) was a Mechanical Engineer who trained at the Albion Motor Car Company in Glasgow between 1930 and 1932 and then resided in India and Ceylon. From 1946 he was the Assistant Director of Mechanical Engineering for the British Commonwealth Occupation Forces in Japan. **Melvin Tracy** (1908-1909) and **George Rogerson** (1908) became Surveyors in Kenya and the Gold Coast, respectively. **Graeme Lawton** (1920-1921) became Registrar of the High Court in Northern Rhodesia and then in Kenya.

162. Barton in 1937

163. Bishop Phillips

Several old *Dane Court* boys became Clergymen including **Francis Allen** (1909-1911), **Edwin Gargery** (1911-1912) and **Melville Scutt** (1916-1921). **John Barton** (1906-1912) became Canon of Westminster Cathedral in 1971 and **John Phillips** (1916-1919) was the Bishop of Portsmouth between 1960 and 1975 and a member of the House of Lords from 1967. Hugh Pooley enjoyed ribbing the Bishop in *Sunrise* at the time of the wedding of his daughter, writing that he was *'the first old boy to be pictured in* The Times *kissing his daughter'*.

The medical profession was well served. **Douglas Batterham** (1902-1908), the eldest of the four Batterham brothers, trained at Bartholomew's Hospital, becoming a Fellow of the Royal College of Surgeons in 1923. He was a Surgical Specialist in the Rhine Army in 1924 and in Burma in 1927. In World War II he was a Surgical Specialist in France, Northern Ireland and West Africa. He later practiced in Newton Abbott. **Seymour Philps** (1918-1920) became an Ophthalmic Surgeon. He was made a Fellow of the Royal College of Surgeons in 1931. He mainly worked at St. Bartholomew's Hospital. He wrote a book called *Ophthalmic Operations*, illustrated with his own drawings and photographs. Others who entered the medical profession included **Albert Drew** (1901-1905), **Cyril Politeyan** (1910) and **Maurice Dixey** (1915-1916).

Old boys in other professions and academia included **Eric Moullin**, attending under the Reverend Graham in 1902, who became a Professor of Electrical Engineering at Cambridge University. He wrote several books including *The Principles of Electromagnetism* and *Electomagnetic*

Principles of the Dynamo. He was also responsible for several important inventions. Another clever boy was **Clive Gregory**, who became a Lecturer in Astronomy at University College, London, setting up the Observatory at Mill Hill in 1929. Although he only attended the school briefly in 1903, six years before the Pooleys arrived, he recognised Mrs Pooley 50 years later when travelling on a train in 1954. There was much to talk about. **Heathcote Helmore** was articled to the Architect Sir Edwin Lutyens for two years, later returning to his native New Zealand to become Senior Partner of the important architectural practice, Helmore and Cottrell in Christchurch.

Media and the Arts were well represented. **Thomas Woodroofe** (1906-1910) became a Commentator on the BBC between 1936 and 1939. He wrote several naval stories including *Naval Odyssey* and *River of Golden Sand*. **Peter Pooley** also worked for the BBC between 1939 and 1947, being the Founder and first Editor of the BBC's Radio Newsreel and an Associate Producer with the Crown Film Unit between 1947 and 1951. He later worked for NATO and was awarded the OBE in 1977.

164. Thomas Woodroofe at the BBC

John Dracopoli, whose father was the Aide-de-Camp to the King of Montenegro, later became a Sculptor and Painter of Synchromist paintings. **Sidney Rogerson**, who attended *Dane Court* briefly in 1903 became an important Author concerning the First World War. He wrote seven books including *Twelve Days* (1933), *Last of the Ebb* (1937) and *Propaganda for the Next War* (1958). **Ole Pooley**, later known as 'Olaf', worked at Pinewood Studios before the war and had a wide-ranging career as an Actor in supporting roles on stage, TV and in films. He was also a Script Writer and Painter.

David John (1912-1916) studied Music and was in the BBC Orchestra in Belfast for a time. Later *Sunrise* reported that he worked at the Head Office of the GPO. **Romilly John** became an Author and Poet (1912-1918), publishing a volume of poems in 1931 and writing an autobiography called *The Seventh Child* in 1932 with some reminiscences of his time at *Dane Court*. In *Sunrise*, Hugh Pooley wrote tactfully: *'we beg leave to differ from the Author in a statement he makes about Eton suits'*. In the School Register he was more direct: *'mention of Dane Court is largely inaccurate'*. Romilly's brother **Edwin John** (1912-1919) became a noted Watercolourist. According to his obituary, having inherited the estate of his aunt, the Painter Gwen John, he did much to restore her posthumous reputation.

As one would expect many boys entered the commercial field. Of particular interest were **Peter Swatman** (1920-1921) who became a Director of the SU Carburettor Company. **Carl Chronander** (1917-1918) became an Aviation Engineer. In the July 1936 edition of *Sunrise* he was reported as working on *'stresses and strains with the Fairey Aviation Company'*. Later that year he was reported in the same magazine to have *'designed and built with two other people an all-metal low-wing monoplane called the CWA Cygnet'*. He then worked for General Aircraft Ltd who had acquired the rights for the monoplane. **Derek Saben** (1915-1922) became an Electrical Engineer involved in radio and television development. He later wrote two books on the Saben family. **Pierre Crokaert** (1919), whose father was a Diamond Cutting Merchant, joined the family business in Antwerp. Later he was a Director of De Beers for several years. **Graham Yeatman** initially joined the family flour milling business in Poole. He later became an Army Major and in 1978 was appointed as High Sheriff of Dorset.

Several boys entered the legal profession including **Giles Woodgate** (1895-1900), **Edgar Anthony** (1901-1903), **Henry Everett** (1913-1915), **Charles Kite** (1916) and **Maurice Yeatman** (1918-1925). A few joined accountancy firms including **Thomas Fletcher** (1914-1918), **David Cope** (1916-1921) and **Richard Salmon** (1918-1922).

Some old boys became Schoolmasters such as **Cecil Fawkes** (1906-1911), **Stephen Belben** (1909-1911), **Charles Taylor** (1913-1920), **Anthony Hamilton** (1919-1927) and **Donald Christie** (1916-1922). As noted in the previous chapter, in the April 1933 edition of *Sunrise* Christie was recorded as *'taking up residence at old Dane Court Parkstone as Modern Language Master'*. This was probably the final term of Paul Phipps' period at *Dane Court*. He later seems to have moved with Phipps as he turns up in the 1934 edition of *Sunrise* at The Old Ride School in Branksome Park, to which Paul Phipps had moved. Christie wrote several books including one called *While the World Revolves*, a couple of books on French usage and practice, and some travel books. He also wrote a book called *Andy Was Eight* about which he commented: *'there are incidents which are based on my own memories, where necessary altered to fit the circumstances. I think the overall picture of prep school life of the time is accurate and those who were at Dane Court in those days may recognise some of the incidents'*.

A few personalities do not readily fit into any category. The gentle giant from Denmark, **Tage Hagelstam**, had not been seen for nearly 20 years by 1933 so some old boys set off for deepest France in search of him. They wrote in *Sunrise*:

'after an injunction to the driver to "rouler lentement", we followed one of those marvellous French roads which climb and wind in and up and around the mountains. An old peasant woman assured us that "Monsieur Hagelstam et sa mère" had just passed in their "auto". It transpired that had really been about two hours before ... And there was Tage, looking just the same, if a little larger. There is a photo of him in the old Dane Court book standing by a donkey: you could recognise him from that. And here he works and lives on the side of this marvellous hill near Vence, overlooking valleys and hills and overlooked by mountains... we had some of his own red wine... he grows oranges, mandarins, lemons, olives, peaches, artichokes, tomatoes and every kind of vegetable'.

Michael Silley had a tough time in the Second World War. By 1929 he was in the Malay Police, then became a 2nd Lieutenant in the Royal Army Service Corps. He was wounded and captured as a prisoner in Thailand in 1942 and remained in prison until 1945. Having survived, he later became a Racing Correspondent.

Last but by no means least, we find out what happened to the three boys who have illuminated this book so admirably with their eloquent reminiscences: **Arthur Batterham** (1908-1913), **Hampden Fordham** (1915-1919) and **Sydney Levey** (1918-1920).

Arthur Batterham became an Assistant Master at Dane Court Preparatory School in Pyrford between 1922 and 1930, after service in the armed forces. He then entered RADA in

1931 and toured in Repertory for a time before returning to the school in 1934. Hugh Pooley wrote in *Sunrise*: *'by great good fortune we were able to persuade Mr Batterham to join us again. He has been connected with Dane Court for so many years of its existence that the place never seems quite right without him'*. He was to remain at the school for a further 20 years, known by the Pooleys as *'our beloved Batty'*. The photo below is a studio photo taken in his acting days.

165. Batterham c1931

166. Fordham in 1967

Hampden Fordham (1915-1919) became a Commander in the Royal Navy. He was second in command of the London Fire Brigade during the Second World War. His obituary in *The Times* noted that he *'had a great reputation as an energetic and fearless leader during the air raids in London'*. After the war he became the Chief Fire Officer of Kent and was awarded the CBE.

167. Levey in 1936

Sydney Levey (1918-1920), after attending Westminster School, became a preparatory Schoolmaster in 1926. He then went to Canada aged 21 in 1928 with the intention of going into farming. By 1934 he had returned to England, pictured here in a 1936 cricket team photo. He later moved to Port Elizabeth in South Africa where he became an Insurance Underwriter. He was also a cricket commentator and pundit, often heard on the South African Broadcasting Corporation. He was a regular contributor to *Sunrise* and helped to organise football and cricket matches of the Old Dane Court Society when in the UK. He wrote two books: the unpublished work, *The Fires are Burning Low*, quoted in this book, and a history of the Port Elizabeth cricket club.

Paul Campbell Phipps (Chapter 8)

Paul Phipps moved to The Old Ride School in Branksome Park in 1934. He went into partnership with the Reverend T H Flynn as Joint Headmasters. However, it did not work out and the family moved to St. Albans in 1935. It is not known where he was employed between 1935 and 1938.

168. The Old Ride School in Branksome Park

In 1939, he bought Pembroke House School in Hampton and he became the Headmaster. During the war it was evacuated to the Ravenswood School near Tiverton. Phipps' drawing of *Pembroke House* is included opposite.

He continued as Headmaster until he was 69 in 1956 when he was unexpectedly taken ill while on holiday in Majorca. He died soon afterwards on 1 September 1956. His wife Flora Phipps died in a Parkstone nursing home later that month.

Cecil William Ayerst (Chapter 8)

As noted in the previous chapter, Cecil William Ayerst only remained at *Dane Court* for a couple of years. He then changed direction, obtaining his MA from Queens College Cambridge in 1935. He became a Deacon in 1938 and was ordained as a Priest in 1939. He was a Curate at St Matthew's Church in Bayswater in 1938-1939, then held an appointment in Dr Barnardo's Homes for the West of England in 1939-1940. During the war he was an Assistant Master at Wallington School from 1942 to 1944, at Alleyn's School in Dulwich in 1944, then at Mitcham Grammar School from 1945. From 1949 he became Rector of Titsey in the Diocese of Southwark. He died in 1952, aged 42.

It is sad that the records of the Dane Court Preparatory School that existed between 1922 and 1935 under Paul Phipps and Cecil Ayerst have not survived. Another 200 boys probably attended *Dane Court* during these years. A few are mentioned in press notices of scholarship awards or in a

169. Drawing of Pembroke House by Paul Phipps

few Sports-Day reports. However, the 1921 Census when available will not list any of the pupils as they only started to arrive the following year. The records for the 1931 Census have been destroyed. Published public school registers do not record the preparatory school that boys attended.

Between 1937 and 1939, a gentleman called Gordon Holligan was shown as principal of a Dane Court School at 12 St. Peter's Road. It is not known whether this had any connection with the former Dane Court Preparatory School or whether he was just using the name. The house used to be on the corner of St Peter's Road and Charmouth Grove (the block of flats now on the site is also called *Dane Court*). Holligan's wife died in 1938 and the school closed in 1939.

170. Sydney Levey (1918-1920)

Many of those who lived at *Dane Court* probably never returned. It was just a distant memory. For many others though it was a special place, full of treasured memories, perhaps none more so than Sydney Henry Wilfred Levey.

In the Spring of 1936, he drove 100 miles from his home near Barnet to Parkstone to see the derelict house for one last time. His haunting words form the Epilogue.

Epilogue

'The gate creaked on its broken hinges as we lifted it. We drove the car through to where once there was a sweeping drive. Across the overgrown field we bumped, a field which had started life as a kitchen garden tended so carefully by Charles, now a jungle.

The front porch was broken down, the windows blown in or discoloured; even the ivy drooped as though the walls were too feeble to bear their weight. An owl hooted dismally as if in keeping with our thoughts.

We opened the familiar front door. As we stood in the old, tiled hallway the mists of time seemed to lift again and the old house to rattle once more. Ghosts, everywhere, ghosts.

The Boys' Room but no boys – unless that brown shadow in the corner is one in a corduroy coat. But it was only a shadow. The little Conservatory that was the First Form Room; we looked through those dingy broken windows again to where there used to be The Mound.

The Dining Room was much the same; almost we could hear again the clatter of the plates, the hum of piping voices: shades of Buck Teas, Almonds in the Pudding, and war-time margarine in saucers, each with its greasy little label, came crowding in one after another.

It is a curious thing how the inhibitions of youth are always with us; we hesitated a little outside the Study door and felt as though we ought to knock.

More ghosts here too, some of them rather painful, others foundations upon which we built our lives.

Dormitories. They are merely so many rooms now with the wallpaper discoloured and hanging in strips. Gone are the trim little beds, and gone, too, forever are the children who had such adventurous battles with one eye on the foe and the other on the door.

And so, through the green baize door which after nearly twenty years still shuts with the same echoing noise, and down the dim back stairs with ghosts following hotfoot all the way in the echo of tiny footsteps grown to manhood. Down the passage to the Changing Room: more desolation here, the footbath filled with rubble, the Sea of Galilee even fuller of dead leaves, the showers looking about as large as coffins.

And up above it all, the old bell hung mute and limp, its string broken and flapping idly in the breeze, its familiar note stilled for ever. A symbol.

The Schoolroom, just a shed today, hollow and echoing. Steaming radiators, boxing tournaments, French verbs, dramatic societies, a knot-hole in the floor and a certain fire . . . . gone.

Old Rum and The Gravel, or what was The Gravel. A pigmy of a tree in reality. Deeply scored into its gnarled old bark are the initials of half-forgotten children who are now men. Time marches on, only the initials remain.

The sun had nearly set as we came away, each busy with his own thoughts. It was a watery sun with a hopelessness about it like the shell of the house we had just left. We closed the creaky gate, almost reverently, as if in the presence of the dead.

SUPPLEMENT: DANE COURT BOYS 1900-1921

This Supplement provides further details of all boys who lived or spent significant time at Dane Court Preparatory School between April 1900 and April 1921. The notes are not intended to be comprehensive biographies. They provide in a consistent format the following information, where known, for each boy:

- when and where born;
- their father's name and profession;
- where their parents lived;
- how long they were at *Dane Court* and whether as a Boarder or a Day Boy;
- their later education;
- key elements of their careers and any significant awards;
- any books written by or about them;
- details of any obituaries in national newspapers;
- their dates; and
- references to relevant picture numbers in this book.

Where the further education or details of careers of any boys are missing, this is usually because they are not known to the Author. In some cases, certain career details are excluded in the interests of brevity as they are included in the published obituaries referred to or in books by or about the individuals.

An alphabetical list of boys is provided on the next page to enable readers to look up the biographies of boys pictured and/or mentioned in the book. The list is cross-referenced to the boys' joining dates as shown in the main part of the Supplement. The potted biographies are set out in the order in which boys joined the school. This makes it easier to track the changing profile of the school when reading the Supplement as a whole and for any descendants of boys to see who their contemporaries were and what became of them. It also enables the potted biographies of the boys in any of the Annual School Photos to be looked up in the same few pages of the listing.

The Supplement begins with the 16 boys who came to *Dane Court* with the Reverend Graham in April 1900, followed by the four boys who joined in the Summer Term of 1900. Thereafter, the boys joining in each School Year, starting in September, are listed. The months of joining and leaving are indicated in the following way: 1916.10 means October 1916, 1918.9 means September 1918.

Alphabetical Index to Supplement: *Dane Court* boys 1900-1921

Name	Joined
Allen, Francis Lechampion	1909.9
Anthony, Edgar Holden Hollis	1901.5
Armstrong, Frederick Edmund John	1896.9
Baker, Samuel	1909.9
Barker, Norman George	1904.9
Barton, Guy Trayton	1920.5
Barton, John Mackintosh Tilney	1906.1
Batterham, (Alexander) Gordon	1907.5
Batterham, Arthur Graham	1908.9
Batterham, Douglas John	1902.9
Batterham, Hugh Willoughby	1904.5
Beal, Gilbert Roger Wallis	1912.5
Belben, George Devereux	1905.9
Belben, Stephen James	1909.6
Belben, Thomas Alan	1905.9
Bell, Francis Graham	1918.9
Bell, Neil Graham	1920.1
Braithwaite, (Francis) Joseph	1916.5
Braithwaite, John Duncan	1918.5
Braithwaite, Michael Robert	1918.1
Brennand, Arthur Fynes	1913.9
Browne-Poole, Edward Gerald	1916.9
Budge, Vincent Alexander Prideaux	1920.5
Buller, Francis Warwick	1914.1
Burbury, Thomas Evelyn Thornley	1917.9
Burn, Charles Scott	1910.6
Burn, George Frank	1911.1
Burnier, Richard	1908.1
Burroughs, Geoffrey Herbert Gore	1897.9
Burroughs, Shirley Victor Gore	1897.9
Byers, Jack	1917.5
Carpenter, John Philip Morton	1904.5
Carter, (John) David Armishall	1918.5
Carter, (William Henry Charles) Philip	1918.5
Chesshire, George Pountney Peregrine	1918.1
Chesshire, John Barnabas	1918.1
Chesshire, Robert Humphrey Hooper	1910.9
Child, Claude Herbert	1908.9
Christie, Donald Drayton	1916.9
Chronander, Carl Robert	1917.1
Clark, Roger Land	1918.9
Clarke, Arthur Christopher Lancelot	1894.1
Coleridge, Reginald Ernest	1907.9
Cope, (Alfred Arthur) David	1916.1
Cowie, (Kenneth) David	1920.9
Cowie, Samuel Richard	1920.9
Crockett, Hugh	1919.5
Crockett, John Oliver	1915.11
Crokaert, Pierre Jacques Leopold	1919.1
Davenport, John Forbes	1902.6
Dawson, Reginald Arthur	1916.1
Deekers, Christian	1918.5
Deekers, Jacques	1918.5
De Woolfson, Robert St. John Green	1920.9
Dixey, Maurice Boxwell Duncan	1915.5
Dobson, Kenneth Blair Austin	1918.9
Douglas, Kenneth Christie	1916.1
Dracopoli, John Chance	1902.6
Drew, Albert John Kingman	1901.2
Drew, Vincent	1902.9
Dry, Edward Nelson	1916.9
Druitt, Charles Edward Hobart	1902.1
Dupret, George Henri	1918.9
Dupret, Jean	1918.9

Alphabetical Index to Supplement: *Dane Court* boys 1900-1921 (continued)

Name	Joined	Name	Joined
Dupret, Robert	1918.9	Gregory, Christopher Clive Langton	1903.5
Edsell, George Lynton	1899.9	Gwatkin, Norman Wilmhurst	1907.9
Egremont, (Alan) Godfrey	1919.1	Hagelstam, Tage	1912.9
Egremont, Humphrey	1920.5	Hamilton, Anthony Norris	1919.7
Ellis, Godfrey Newell	1914.1	Hamilton, Benjamin Charles	1919.9
Erskine-Murray, James Alistair	1910.5	Harington, Hubert Lionel	1906.9
Evans, David	1920.5	Harper, Austin Byers	1915.9
Evans, Frederick	1921.1	Hawkins, Raymond Summerfield	1919.3
Evans, John Edward	1918.9	Hearder, Robin Dixon	1916.6
Everett, Anthony Blaze	1914.1	Heathcote, Geoffrey Arthur Unwin	1908.9
Everett, Henry	1913.1	Heathcote, Michael Arthur Unwin	1908.5
Fanner, Henry Lewis	1901.5	Helmore, Ernest Cresswell	1905.5
Fawkes, Cecil Wentworth	1906.1	Helmore, Heathcote George	1905.5
Field-Richards, Michael Jackson	1920.5	Hobson, Frank Martin Carrington	1910.6
Field-Richards, Peter John	1916.9	Hodgson-Stevens, Edmund James	1907.5
Flemmich, Peter Max Davy	1919.5	Hoey, Cedric Clinton	1910.2
Fletcher, David	1919.5	Howes, Basil Edward	1904.5
Fletcher, Richard	1916.5	Ingram, Bernard James	1913.2
Fletcher, Thomas Simon	1914.5	Ingram, David Caldicott	1912.1
Fordham, (John) Hampden	1915.9	John, Caspar	1912.10
Freeman, John Horace Evans	1914.10	John, David Anthony Honore Nettleship	1912.10
French, Arthur Cecil	1905.5	John, Edwin	1912.10
Fuller, Wilfred Robert	1911.9	John, Robin Thornton	1912.10
Gargery, Edwin John	1911.3	John, Romilly	1912.10
Geidt, Charles Uppleby	1903.1	Jones, Basil Ivor	1898.5
Geidt, Edward Wollaston	1900.9	Jones, Charles Allen Foulkes	1911.6
Geidt, Frederick Bernard	1903.1	Jones, (John) Russell	1918.5
Gerfalk, Ole Bernth	1918.5	Kite, Charles Macadam Bagehot	1916.9
Gervis, Geoffrey Rawlinson	1920.5	Kite, Edward de Cheveley	1916.10
Gorst, Edmund Rann Kennedy	1904.1	Lassen, Eric	1911.9
Gorst, Harold John	1908.5	Lawton, Graeme Monk	1920.9
Greenlees, Campbell Glencairn	1911.9	Lawton, Patrick Herbert	1917.11

Alphabetical Index to Supplement: *Dane Court* boys 1900-1921 (continued)

Name	Joined
Leir, John Russell Charles Vernon	1900.9
Leonard, John Marius Ronald	1907.1
Le Good, Dennis Ivan	1918.9
Levey, Maurice Emmanuel	1918.1
Levey, Sydney Henry Wilfred	1918.1
Lewis, Norman Kingsbury	1918.9
Linklater, Robert Hugh	1917.1
Lloyd, Richard Eyre	1914.9
Lobley, John Oliver Hargreaves	1917.5
Logan, Reginald Francis Arthur	1915.9
Luff, Cyril Edgar Evelyn	1910.9
Lukis, Sydney	1897.9
MacGregor, Thomas Charles Stuart	1904.9
Mack, Ian MacCallum	1908.10
Mack, Joseph	1907.1
MacLaurin, Robert Hall	1920.11
MacLaurin, Stuart Glare	1920.11
MacLeod, Hector John Roderick	1906.5
Mairis, Henry Shuckbrugh	1916.9
Margrie, James David	1919.9
Margrie, Raymond John	1915.1
Maxwell, Reginald	1902.6
May, Peter	1920.1
Mercier, Amadee	1900.6
Mercier, Pascal	1900.6
Metophis, Georges	1915.1
Milner, Guy Sommerville	1908.9
Moullin, Eric Balliol	1902.9
Morley, Vincent Streatfield	1902.5
Norman, Hallion Addison	1911.1
Oakley, Edwin Herbert	1921.1
Oakley, Philip John Bowen	1902.9
Oakley, William Edward Bowen	1907.9
Olivey, John Richard	1913.9
Ormerod, Edward Tyssen	1911.9
O'Shea, Desmond Gerald	1906.1
Parry-Burnett, John Edward	1899.9
Parish, Arthur Basil Okes	1903.5
Penrose, Derek John	1918.5
Philby, Frank Montague	1918.5
Phillips, Henry Walter	1904.1
Phillips, John Henry Lawrence	1916.9
Phillips, Walter Seymour	1902.1
Philpot, Godrey	1899.5
Philpot, Reginal Henry	1902.5
Philps, (Alan) Seymour	1918.1
Pillans, Albert Nelson	1906.5
Pillans, James Pritchard Scarth	1905.9
Pitman, Alan Theodore	1898.11
Politeyan, Cyril Dunhelm	1910.6
Pooley, Ole Krohn	1920.5
Pooley, (Henry) Peter Krohn	1917.9
Pooley, Richard Warner	1920.9
Pooley, Thomas Brooke	1920.9
Pope, Norman William	1919.1
Pritchard, Charles Arthur	1917.9
Rawlins, Jocelyn Charles	1901.5
Robinson, Charles William	1904.7
Robinson, Frederick Roland	1904.7
Robinson, Louis Francis	1904.7
Rogerson, George Carroll	1908.1
Rogerson, Sidney	1903.6
Rosenberg, David John	1920.9
Routledge, Bryan Howard	1916.1

Alphabetical Index to Supplement: *Dane Court* boys 1900-1921 (continued)

Name	Joined
Rundle, Cubitt Archer Grant	1901.5
Rundle, (Cubitt) Noel	1904.9
Saben, Derek Russell	1917.5
Salmon, Geoffrey Fitzjohn	1917.1
Salmon, Richard Henry	1918.9
Scott, John Bodley	1902.5
Scott, (John) Francis Robson	1911.5
Scutt, (John) Melville	1916.5
Selous, Edric Medley	1916.5
Shedden, John Lewis Le Hunte	1900.7
Ship, Dudley Stuart	1919.5
Silley, Michael Leeson	1915.1
Sitwell, Isla William Hurt	1916.9
Skrine, Clarmont Percival	1896.4
Smith, William Josef Maurice	1920.1
Stern, Michael Leopold	1901.7
Stevens, Cecil James Duff	1903.1
Stevens, Charles Francis	1900.9
Strange, John Clement	1917.9
Sunderland, Harcourt Kingsley	1904.9
Swatman, Michael Raigersfeld	1920.1
Swatman Peter Phillimore	1920.1
Swatman, Philip Stenning	1920.1
Tarver, Charles Herbert	1919.1
Tayler, Noel	1903.9
Taylor, Charles John	1913.9
Tennent, Hugh Patrick Lorraine	1906.6
Thomas, Lewis George Alfred	1919.9
Tolson, Richard Frederick Herman	1919.6
Tracy, Melvin Maxwell Carew	1908.1
Turner, George Henry	1897.9
Van Namen, Claude Dudgeon	1918.5
Van Namen, Maxwell Newton	1915.11
Walford, John Neville	1915.1
Walford, William Neville	1915.1
Watts, George Miles	1913.9
West, John Andrews Stallon	1918.5
Wiggins, Henry Desmond	1917.11
Willmott, Percy Greville	1898.4
Willmott, (Walter) Greville	1898.4
Wills, Phillip Francis James	1917.1
Wilson, Lyall Alexander Winder Otway	1913.5
Wodehouse, Charles Reid	1901.5
Wodehouse, Francis Oakley	1895.9
Wodehouse, Frederick Guy de Picquigny	1904.5
Wodehouse, Percy George	1900.5
Woodgate, Giles Musgrave Gordon	1895.3
Woodroofe, Thomas Borries Ralph	1906.9
Yeatman, Graham Neville	1915.9
Yeatman, Maurice	1918.5

Boys who came to Dane Court with the Reverend Graham in April 1900

1894.1 – 1900.8 Clarke, Arthur Christopher Lancelot (1886-1983)

Arthur Christopher Lancelot (known as 'Kit') Clarke was born in Brighton, the son of Ronald Stanley Clarke, a Solicitor, who lived in St Leonards-on-Sea. Spent 6 years at Mount Lodge School. Came to *Dane Court* for his final term as a Boarder. Attended Winchester College from 1900 to 1905 and University College, Oxford. Served in the 2nd Battalion Cameronians (Scottish Rifles) in 1909, promoted to Captain in 1915, commanding the 10th Battalion in 1916. Awarded the DSO with Bar. Awarded the French Légion d' Honneur and Croix de Guerre. Instructor at Royal Military College, Sandhurst from 1922 to 1925. Chief Instructor in Hythe 1929. Lieutenant-Colonel, commanding 1st Battalion of the Royal Scots Fusiliers in 1931. Assistant Commandant at the Netheravon Wing of the Small Arms School in 1934. Commanding 154th (Argyll and Sutherland) Infantry Brigade in the Territorial Army in 1937. He later added the name Stanley to his name. Became known as Brigadier Kit Stanley-Clarke DSO. Died in Ireland in 1983.

1895.3 – 1900.8 Woodgate, Giles Musgrave Gordon (1886-1963)

Giles Woodgate was born in Cambridge, the third son of the Reverend Gordon Woodgate of Wisbech. Spent five years at Mount Lodge School. Came to *Dane Court* for his final Term as a Boarder. Gained a Foundation Scholarship to Tonbridge School which he attended from 1900 to 1904. Later education not known. Admitted as a Solicitor in 1909. Became a Partner in Messrs Fraser, Woodgate & Beall of Wisbech. Served in WW1. In the Home Guard from 1940 to 1945. Died in Cambridgeshire in 1963.

1895.9 – 1901.4 Wodehouse, Francis Oakley (1886-1978)

Francis Wodehouse was born in Hertingfordbury in Hertfordshire, the third of six sons of Charles Edward Wodehouse, a Justice of the Peace and Gentleman Farmer, to be taught by the Reverend Graham. His parents and grandfather lived at *Woolmer's Park* in Hertingfordbury, a large mansion later purchased by the Queen's grandparents, the Earl and Countess of Strathmore. Spent 4½ years at *Mount Lodge* and a year at *Dane Court* as a Boarder. Attended Malvern College from 1901 to 1902. By 1911, he worked on the Great Northern Railway. In 1930, he was a Salesman in bonds in the USA. Listed as a Broker in New Jersey in the 1940 US Census. Died in the USA in 1978.

1896.4 – 1900.8 Skrine, Clarmont Percival (1888-1974)

Clarmont Percival Skrine was born in Calcutta, the son of Francis Henry Bennett Skrine, the Commissioner of Chittagong, Calcutta, in the Indian Civil Service. His maternal grandfather acted as guardian, Colonel Stewart of Ardrorlich, Lochearnhead in Perthshire. Spent 4 years at *Mount Lodge* and his final term at *Dane Court* as a Boarder. Attended Winchester College from 1901 to 1906, then New College, Oxford. In the Foreign and Political Department in 1915. Then Vice-Consul for South Persia. In the Political Office of South Persia Rifles from 1916 to 1918. Consul at Kerman from 1918 to 1919. A political agent in Quetta in 1921. Consul-General Chinese in Turkestan from 1922 to 1924. Under-Secretary for Consul Sistan and Kain from 1927 to 1929. Political agent in Sibi from 1929 to 1931. Several other posts as detailed in his obituary. *The Times* covered his 1925 expedition to *Chinese Central Asia* in detail. He wrote three books including *Chinese Central Asia* (1926), which covered his expedition more fully, and *World War in Iran* (1962). Awarded an OBE in 1935. Knighted, becoming Sir Clarmont Percival Skrine. Died in London in 1974. Further details of his life and work are included in *The Times* obituary dated 23 September 1974.

1896.9 – 1901.12 **Armstrong, Frederick Edmund John (1888-1919)**

Frederick Armstrong was born in Littlehampton in Sussex, the son of Montagu Fullerton Armstrong who lived on his own means in London. Spent 3½ years at *Mount Lodge* followed by one year and four months at *Dane Court* as a Boarder. Attended Harrow. Later became a Lieutenant in the Indian Army 181st Pioneer Regiment. Attached to the 1/69th Punjabis on the North-West Frontier. Died of his wounds in hospital at Kohat, 27 October 1919.

1897.9 - 1900.8 **Turner, George Henry (1884-1952)**

George Turner was born in Battersea, the son of a Solicitor who lived in Ewell in Surrey. Joined when he was 13. Spent 2½ years at *Mount Lodge* and came to *Dane Court* for his final term as a Boarder. Died in 1952.

1897.9 – 1901.7 **Burroughs, Shirley Victor Gore (1887-1963)**

Shirley Burroughs was born in Chatham in Kent, the first son of the Reverend William Gore Burroughs who was resident in Cheshire. Spent 2½ years at *Mount Lodge* and one year and three months at *Dane Court* as a Boarder. Attended Lancing College from 1901 to 1904, then the Royal Military College, Sandhurst. Became a 2nd Lieutenant in the Worcester Regiment in 1906. In the Indian Army 4th PAV Rajputs in 1909. Became a Lieutentant in the Indian Army in 1912. In East Africa attached to the 13th Rajputs from 1914 to 1915. In Mesopotamia with the 4th Rajputs from 1915 to 1918. Involved in the 3rd Afghan War and Waziristan. Attached to the 1/150th Indian Infantry from 1919 to 1921. Retired as a Major in 1925. Tea planter in Ceylon 1934. Died in Essex in 1963.

1897.9 – 1902.7 **Burroughs, Geoffrey Herbert Gore (1888-1972)**

Geoffrey Burroughs was born in Southsea in Hampshire, the second son of the Reverend William Gore Burroughs who was resident in Cheshire. Spent 2½ years at *Mount Lodge* and 2¼ years at *Dane Court* as a Boarder. Gained an Open Exhibition at Lancing College which he attended from 1902 to 1904. Became a Lieutenant in the Indian Army. Served in Mesopotamia. Prisoner at Kut-al-Amara in Turkey April 1916. Later an agent for the Mercantile Bank of India in Kandy, Ceylon. Died in Suffolk 1972.

1897.9 – 1902.7 **Lukis, Sydney (1887-1963)**

Sydney Lukis was born in Lahore, India, the son of Lieutenant General Sir Charles Pardey Lukis FRCS, a Civil Surgeon in the Indian Medical Service. Spent 2½ years at *Mount Lodge* and 2¼ years at *Dane Court* as a Boarder. Attended Dulwich College from 1902 to 1906, then Caius College Cambridge. Became a Civil Engineer in India. Involved in the Immingham Dock construction from 1910 to 1911 and the Sara Bridge Construction from 1911 to 1913. Then an Assistant Engineer at the Bengal Nagpur Railway. Became a 2nd Lieutenant in the 36th Bengal Nagpur Railway Battalion in the First World War. Died in Surrey in 1963.

1898.4 – 1901.4 **Willmott, Percy Greville (1883-1951)**

Percy Willmott was born in Mortlake in Surrey, the first son of William A Willmott, a Manager in the Wine Trade who lived in Mersham, Surrey. Spent 2 years at *Mount Lodge* and a year at *Dane Court* as a Boarder. Became a Director of an Insurance Broking business. Died in Brighton in 1951.

1898.4 – 1901.12 **Willmott, (Walter) Greville (1886-1956)**

Greville Willmott was born in Mortlake in Surrey, the second son of William A Willmott, a Manager in the wine trade who lived in Mersham in Surrey. Spent 2 years at *Mount Lodge* and one year and eight months at *Dane Court* as a Boarder. Joined the Army Service Corps and was incapacitated in WWI. Died in Shropshire in 1956.

1898.5 – 1903.5 **Jones, Basil Ivor (1889-1958)**

Basil Jones was born in Lahore, India, the son of A E Jones, a Dental Surgeon in the Indian Medical Service. Spent 2 years at *Mount Lodge* and 3 years at *Dane Court* as a Boarder. He was in 2/ Regiment Irish Fusiliers, then a Captain in the Indian Army. Then in the 8th Punjab Regiment of the Indian Army. Became known as Lieutenant Colonel Basil Jones, DSO with Bar, MC. Died in Kent in 1958.

1898.11 – 1904.7 **Pitman, Alan Theodore (1891-1970)**

Alan Pitman was born in Whitwell in Yorkshire, the son of the Reverend Arthur Pitman who lived in St Leonards-on-Sea and later in Bramley near Guildford. Spent one and a half years at *Mount Lodge* probably as a Day Boy and 3¼ years at *Dane Court* as a Boarder. He became a 2nd Lieutenant in the Yorkshire Light Infantry. Wounded in 1918. Later he entered the Bank of England. Died in London in 1970.

1899.5 – 1905.8 **Philpot, Godfrey (1891-1916)**

Godfrey Philpot was born in Kingston in Surrey, the first son of Henry John Philpot, a member of the Stock Exchange, who had himself been one of the Reverend Graham's early pupils at Mount Lodge. Godfrey attended *Mount Lodge* for a year and then spent 5¼ years at *Dane Court* as a Boarder. Attended Cheltenham College from 1905 to 1910, then the Royal Military Academy in Woolwich. Became a 2nd Lieutenant in the Royal Garrison Artillery in 1912. Served in Gibraltar in 1913. Became a Lieutenant in 1915. Involved in the British Expeditionary Force in France with a Heavy Battery. Killed in action at the Somme by a shell while acting as a Front Observing Officer on 1 September 1916.

1899.9 – 1901.12 **Parry-Burnett, John Edward** (1889-1961)

John Parry-Burnett was born in London, the son of the Reverend Frederick Parry-Burnett who lived in Colnbrook in Buckinghamshire. Spent 6 months at *Mount Lodge* and one year and four months at *Dane Court* as a Boarder. Died in Chelmsford in Essex in 1961.

1899.9 – 1900.12 **Edsell, George Lynton** (1888-1962)

George Edsell was born in Thame in Oxfordshire, the son of Dr C A Edsell, a Surgeon. He was 12 years of age when he joined the school. His parents continued to live in Thame. Spent 6 months at *Mount Lodge* then 8 months at *Dane Court* as a Boarder. Attended Lord Williams' Grammar School in Thame. Became 2nd Lieutenant in the 1st Battalion of the Hampshire Regiment in 1911. Wounded in 1914. Promoted to Captain in 1915. Eventually reached the rank of Major. Died in Hampshire in 1962.

Boys joining after the move to Dane Court 1900.4 – 1900.7

1900.5 – 1903.4 **Wodehouse, Percy George** (1888-1940)

Percy Wodehouse was born in Hertingfordbury in Hertfordshire, the fourth son of Charles Edward Wodehouse, a Justice of the Peace and Gentleman Farmer, to be taught by the Reverend Graham. His parents and grandfather lived at *Woolmer's Park* in Hertingfordbury, a large mansion later purchased by the Queen's grandparents, the Earl and Countess of Strathmore. Spent 3 years at *Dane Court* as a Boarder. Attended Malvern College from 1903 to 1905. He later qualified as a Motor Engineer. In the First World War he was involved in the Mechanical Transport side of the Army Service Corps. Died in Kent in 1940.

1900.6 – 1901.7 **Mercier, Pascal** (1888-1972)

Pascal Mercier was born in Letchworth Heath in Hertfordshire, the first son of Frank Mercier, a Stockbroker. Spent just over a year at *Dane Court* as a Day Boy. Parents lived at *Delors Lodge* in Parkstone. Also had a London address. Later a resident at the Royal Earlswood Institution in Reigate which catered for people with developmental disabilities. Died in Surrey in 1972.

1900.6 – 1901.7 **Mercier, Amadeé** (1889-1936)

Amadeé Mercier was born in Gunnersbury in Middlesex, the second son of Frank Mercier, a Stockbroker. Spent just over a year at *Dane Court* as a Day Boy. Parents lived at *Delors Lodge* in Parkstone. Also had a London address. Became a 2nd Lieutenant, then Lieutenant in the Royal Sussex Regiment, then a Captain in the Railway Transport Establishment. Clerk on the Stock Exchange in 1921. Died in Purley in 1936.

1900.7 – 1904.7 Shedden, John Lewis Le Hunte (1889-1955)

John Shedden was born in Boldre near Lymington, the son of Lewis Shedden who was of private means. His parents continued to live in Boldre. Attended *Dane Court* as a Boarder for 4 years. Attended Repton School from 1904 to 1907. Became a 2nd Lieutenant 12th Reserve Regiment of Cavalry. Obtained a Royal Aero Club Aviator's Certificate on 9 January 1916. Died in London in 1955.

School Year 1900 – 1901

1900.9 – 1904.4 Geidt, Edward Wollaston (1891-1961)

Edward Geidt was born in Calcutta, the first son of Justice Bernard George Geidt, a High Court Judge in Calcutta. His mother had died in 1894 when he was three. Spent 3½ years at *Dane Court* as a Boarder. Attended Wellington College from 1906 to 1910, then the Royal Military College in Sandhurst from 1910 to 1911. Enlisted in the 107th Pioneers in 1912 as a 2nd Lieutenant rising to Captain in 1914. Involved in the Indian Expeditionary Force in France in 1914. In Mesopotamia in 1915. In the North-West Front in India in 1917. In North-East Persia in 1918. North-West Persia in 1920 as Assistant Political Officer. Retired from the Army in 1923. Died in Oxford in 1961.

1900.9 – 1903.12 Stevens, Charles Francis Linnaeus (1892-1968)

Charles Stevens was born in Darjeeling, India, the son of Captain Cecil Robert Stevens, a Captain in the Royal Engineers. Spent 3 years and 4 months at *Dane Court* as a Boarder. Gained a Foundation Scholarship to Wellington College which he attended from 1904 to 1905. Enlisted in the 10th DCO Lancers in 1912. In France from 1915 to 1918. Involved in the Egyptian Expeditionary Force in 1918. Awarded the Military Cross. Graduate of the Army Staff College 1928. Major 1928. DAAG Lucknow District from 1934 to 1936. Lieutenant-Colonel Commandant Hodgson's Horse in 1937. Awarded the OBE in 1943. Died in the Isle of Wight in 1968.

1900.9 – 1903.12 Leir, John Russell Charles Vernon (1889-1962)

John Leir was born in Perkelly, Breconshire, the son of Frank William Leir who lived on his own means. His parents lived at *Stanley Court* in Longfleet, Poole. Spent 3 years and 4 months at *Dane Court* probably attending as a Day Boy. Attended Bedford Grammar School later. Was a Member of the Institute of Mechanical Engineers from 1929 to 1940. Worked as a Locomotive Engineering Draughtsman. Later became a Farmer. Died in Essex in 1962.

1901.2 – 1905.4 Drew, Albert John Kingman (1889-1961)

Albert Drew was born in Wareham, Dorset, the son of John Albert Drew, a Coal and Iron Merchant. His parents continued to live in Wareham. Spent just over 4 years at *Dane Court* probably as a Boarder. Later qualified as MRCS and LRCP. He was a Medical Practitioner in Ramsgate, Kent in 1939. Died in Kent in 1961.

1901.5 – 1903.6 Anthony, Edgar Holden Hollis (1891-1975)

Edgar Anthony was born in Lydgate, Yorkshire, the son of the Reverend Edgar Polly Anthony. His parents lived at *Almondbury* in Parkstone Road, Longfleet, Poole. Spent 2 years at *Dane Court* as a Day Boy. Attended Lincoln College, Oxford. Second Lieutenant in the Norfolk Regiment from 1916 to 1919. By 1939 he was a Solicitor. Died in West Sussex in 1975.

1901.5 – 1905.12 Wodehouse, Charles Reid (1890-1971)

Charles Wodehouse was born in Hertingfordbury in Hertfordshire, the fifth son of Charles Edward Wodehouse, a Justice of the Peace and gentleman farmer, to be taught by the Reverend Graham. As already noted, his parents and grandfather lived at *Woolmer's Park* in Hertingfordbury, a large mansion later purchased by the Queen's grandparents, the Earl and Countess of Strathmore. Spent just over 4½ years at *Dane Court* as a Boarder. Attended Malvern College from 1906 to 1908. Enlisted in the 1/5th Bedford Regiment by October 1915. Then became a Lieutenant in then Bedfordshire Regiment. By 1939 he was working as a Hall Porter. Died in London in 1971.

1901.5 – 1905.8 Fanner, Henry Lewis (1890-1959)

Henry Fanner was born in Islington, the son of Harry Fanner a Distillers' Clerk. His parents lived in Port Elizabeth in South Africa. Only spent three months at *Dane Court* as a Boarder. Attended Repton School briefly until 1906. Apprenticed in the explosives trade by 1911. By 1939 he was a Travelling Salesman in the non-ferrous metal industry in Hendon. Died in Croydon in 1959.

1901.5 – 1903.7 Rawlins, Jocelyn Charles Penrose (1887-1946)

Jocelyn Rawlins was born in Wimborne, Dorset, the son of Thomas Rawlins, a Solicitor. His parents lived at *The Brackens* on Bournemouth Road in Parkstone. Spent just over 2 years at *Dane Court* as a Day Boy. Qualified as a Second Mate of a foreign-going ship in the Merchant Service in 1908. Emigrated to India in 1908 and became a Marine Pilot in the Bengal Pilot Service. Stayed in India until at least 1931. Had returned to Kingsbridge in Devon by 1939. In the Royal Naval Volunteer Reserve in 1940. Died in Dorset in 1946.

1901.5 - 1907.3 Rundle, (Cubitt Archer) Grant (1893-1979)

Grant Rundle was born in Amritsar in the Punjab, the first son of Gunton Archer Rundle, the District Superintendent of Police in Lahore. His parents still lived in India. He was care of a Miss Hastell of 1 Belvedere Crescent in Parkstone. Spent nearly 6 years at *Dane Court*, most likely as a Day Boy. Attended Blundell's School in Tiverton from 1907 to 1910 and the Royal Military College in Sandhurst in 1911. Became a Lieutenant then a Captain in the 128th Pioneers in the Indian Army 1916. Awarded the Military Cross. Mentioned in Despatches. Had become a Major in the Indian Army by 1939 and later a Lieutenant-Colonel. Died in Devon in 1979.

1901.7 – 1901.9 Stern, Michael Leopold (1887-not known)

Michael Stern was most likely born in Romania, the son of Dr H Stern, a Medical Practitioner based in Bucharest, Romania. He only stayed 2 months at *Dane Court*. No other details.

School Year 1901-1902

1902.1 – 1905.12 Phillips, Walter Seymour (1890-1940)

Walter Phillips was born in Brecon, the son of Colonel Henry Phillips. His parents lived in Exeter. Spent nearly 4 years at *Dane Court* as a Boarder. Later emigrated to Nigeria becoming a Treasury Accountant in the Nigerian Civil Service in Lagos from at least 1915. Died in Gloucestershire in 1940.

1902.1 – 1905.8 Druitt, Charles Edward Hobart (1892-1965)

Charles Druitt was born in Whitchurch Canonicorum, Dorset, the son of the Reverend Charles Druitt. His father had died by the time his son arrived at *Dane Court*. The family home was in Exeter. Spent three years at the school as a Boarder. Gained a Mathematical Scholarship at Blundell's School in Tiverton which he attended from 1905 to 1911, then went to Sidney Sussex College, Cambridge where he read Mathematics. Became a Lieutenant, Captain then Major in The Buffs (East Kent) Regiment and the Machine Gun Corps. Awarded the Military Cross. Later worked in Yokohama Japan as a Mercantile Assistant from the 1920s until the Second World War. Married in Seoul, Korea. Then moved to the USA. Died in the USA in 1965.

1902.5 – 1907.12 Philpot, Reginal Henry (1893-1968)

Reginald Philpot was born in Kingston in Surrey, the second son of Henry John Philpot, a member of the Stock Exchange who had himself been one of the Reverend Graham's early pupils at *Mount Lodge*. His parents lived in London. Spent 5½ years at *Dane Court* as a Boarder. His elder brother Godfrey Philpot was at *Dane Court* at the same time for three of those years. Attended Cheltenham College from 1908 to 1911, then the Royal Military College at Sandhurst. Commissioned in the 2nd Battalion of the Queen's Royal Regiment serving in South Africa and India. In the First World War he served in the 1st Battalion of the Queen's Royal Regiment in France, wounded on three occasions. Awarded the Military Cross. Mentioned in Despatches. Although retired, he re-joined his old regiment in its Depot during the Second World War. Known as Major R H Philpot. Died in Hampshire in 1968.

1902.5 – 1904.12 Scott, John Bodley (1890-1954)

John Scott was born in Christchurch, Hampshire, the son of Dr Thomas Bodley Scott, a General Practitioner and former Mayor of Bournemouth. His parents lived at *Aldington* in Poole Road, Bournemouth. Spent 2½ years at *Dane Court*, probably as a Day Boy. Died in Bournemouth in 1954.

1902.5 - 1903.3 Morley, Vivian Streatfield (1892-1945)

Vivian Morley was born in Warwick. His father's name and occupation are not known. His mother lived at *Simla* in Sea View Road when he came to the school. Only spent 10 months at *Dane Court* as a Day Boy. Later attended Dulwich College. In 1910 he entered the Royal Military College in Sandhurst and by 1911 was in the Royal Military Academy in Woolwich. He became a 2nd Lieutenant in the Dorset Regiment in 1912, a Lieutenant by 1914 and a Captain by 1917. He appears to have remained in the Army, by 1939 recorded as a retired Captain of the Dorset Regiment. Died in Surrey in 1945.

1902.6 – 1903.8 Dracopoli, John Chance (1890-1975)

John Dracopoli was born in Antibes in France, the son of an Italian father, Nicholas F Dracopoli, the Aide-de-Camp to the King of Montenegro. His English mother lived at *Holmwood* on Castle Hill in Parkstone while he was at *Dane Court*. He was 12 when he joined the school. Spent just over a year at *Dane Court* as a Day Boy before moving on to Malvern College from 1904 to 1906. Before the First World War he accompanied his brother Ignacio on hunting and exploring expeditions in Mexico and East Africa, then spent time in Paris and Antibes. Later enlisted in the Public Schools Battalion 1914, invalided 1915. He was an ambulance driver in the French Army from 1915 to 1918. Croix de Guerre. Later became a Sculptor and Painter of Synchromist paintings. Died in Suffolk in 1975.

1902.6 – 1908.7 Maxwell, Reginald (1894-1972)

Reginal Maxwell was born in Worthing in Sussex, the son of Lieutenant Colonel F D Maxwell, who had died by the time Reginald attended *Dane Court*. His mother lived at *Kimberley* in Balmoral Road, Parkstone. Spent just over 2 years at *Dane Court* as a Day Boy. Attended Repton School from 1908 to 1912. Became a Wireless Operator in the Merchant Service in 1914. Probationary Flight Sub-Lieutenant in the Royal Naval Air Service in 1916. In the Royal Naval Reserve in December 1916. On the H M Yacht *Iolaire* 1917/18. After the First World War he became a dental student at Guy's Hospital. Emigrated to Rhodesia as Dentist c1929. Had returned to UK by 1939. Died in Essex in 1972.

1902.6 – 1906.4 Davenport, John Forbes (1891-1959)

John Davenport was born in Eastbourne in Sussex, the son of Stewart Forbes Davenport who was of private means. He lived with his aunt, Miss Cecilia Davenport, at *Torvaine* in St Peter's Road, Parkstone. Spent nearly 4 years at *Dane Court* as a Day Boy. Had emigrated to Australia by 1925. Returned to Fordingbridge by 1939 living on his own means. Died in Bournemouth in 1959.

School year 1902-1903

1902.9 – 1908.7 Oakley, Philip John Bowen (1895-1963)

Philip Oakley was born in Parkstone, the son of Edward Benjamin Oakley, an Architect and Surveyor. His parents lived at *Dulverton* in Alton Road, Parkstone. Spent nearly 6 years at *Dane Court* as a Day Boy. Attended the Thames Nautical Training College on *HMS Worcester* at Greenhithe. Qualified as Second Mate of a Foreign-Going ship in the Merchant Service in 1914. Qualified as Master of a Foreign-Going Steamship in the Merchant Service in 1922. Died in Parkstone in 1963.

1902.9 – 1908.7 Batterham, Douglas John (1894-1968)

Douglas Batterham was born in St Leonards-on-Sea, the first son of Dr John William Batterham FRCS. His mother died in 1903 when he was 9 years of age while at *Dane Court*. Spent nearly 6 years at *Dane Court* as a Boarder. Attended Aldenham School from 1908 to 1912, then Caius College, Cambridge. Trained at St Bartholomew's Hospital. Served in France with the Friends' Ambulance in WW1 then as a Captain in the Royal Army Medical Corps in Mesopotamia and India. Became a Fellow of the Royal College of Surgeons in 1923. Surgical Specialist in the Rhine Army in 1924 and in Burma in 1927. Later practiced in Newton Abbott. In World War II he served with the rank of Major as a Surgical Specialist in France, Northern Ireland and West Africa. Died in Devon in 1968.

1902.9 – not known Moullin, Eric Balliol (1893-1963)

Eric Moullin was born in Parkstone, the son of Arthur Daniel Moullin, a Civil Engineer. His parents lived at *Fermain* on Constitutional Hill Road nearby. Came as a Day Boy. Date of leaving not known. According to his obituary he was educated at home for part of the time. The family had moved to Swanage by 1911. Later won a scholarship to Downing College, Cambridge and took First Class Honours in Mathematical Tripos, followed by the same in the Mechanical Sciences. Became a Lecturer in Engineering at Cambridge and Assistant Lecturer at King's College. Later became Professor of Electrical Engineering in Cambridge. Wrote books including *The Principles of Electromagnetism and Electromagnetic Principles of the Dynamo*. Several inventions including the Moullin valve voltmeter, perfected in the 1920s, which became a standard instrument for electrical laboratories. Also, an electrical torsiometer measuring the torsion of rotating shafts such as propellers. Further details on his life and work, plus photos, in *The Times* obituary of 20 September 1963. Died in Cambridge in 1963.

1902.9 – 1906.7 Drew, Vincent (1893-not known)

Vincent Drew was born in Wareham, Dorset, the second son of John Albert Drew, a Coal and Iron Merchant. His parents still lived in Wareham. Spent nearly 4 years at *Dane Court* probably as a Boarder. His elder brother, Albert John Kingman Drew overlapped with his time at the school. By 1911 he was a divinity student. He may have emigrated to Southern Rhodesia. No other details known.

1903.1 – 1904.4 Geidt, Frederick Bernard (1892-1955)

Frederick Geidt was born in Rangpur in India, the second son of Justice Bernard George Geidt, a High Court Judge in Calcutta. His mother died in 1894 when he was two. In 1901 he was living with his maternal grandmother at *Scotter* in Chine Crescent Road, Bournemouth. Spent one year and three months at *Dane Court* as a Boarder. His elder brother, Edward Wollaston Geidt, was already at the school when he joined. Attended Wellington College from 1907 to 1911, then Corpus Christi College, Oxford. Became 2nd Lieutenant rising to Major in the Royal Field Artillery Territorial Force Reserve from 1914 to 1917. Awarded the Military Cross. Mercantile Assistant with Bird & Co, Calcutta from 1920 to 1927. Later a statistician with the stockbrokers Morton Bros. in London. In the Royal Artillery from 1940 to 1943. Died in Hertfordshire in 1955.

1903.1 – 1904.4 Geidt, Charles Uppleby (1894-1918)

Charles Geidt was born in Darjeeling in India, the third son of Justice Bernard George Geidt, a High Court Judge in Calcutta. His mother died in 1894, the year of his birth. He joined the school with his brother Frederick Bernard Geidt and spent one year and three months at *Dane Court.* Attended Wellington College from 1908 to 1911. Then spent a few years fruit farming in British Columbia in Canada. Became a trooper with the 2nd Canadian Mounted Rifles from 1914 to 1915. From 1915 to 1918 he was a Lieutenant in the Queen's Own Cameron Highlanders. When asked to train as a Pilot, he asked to be trained in Egypt as he was born in India and was *'used to, and benefits by, a warm climate'*. The flying school used airfields near Alexandria at Aboukir and Heliopolis. Accidentally killed while flying with the squadron on 10 April 1918.

1903.1 – 1907.7 Stevens, Cecil James Duff (1893-1967)

Cecil Stevens was born in Aberdeen, the first son of Major Cecil Robert Stevens who worked for the Indian Medical Service in Bengal. His maternal grandmother in Auchterloss, Aberdeenshire was the contact when he was at the school. Spent 4½ years at *Dane Court* as a Boarder. Attended Charterhouse School from 1907 to 1911, then Trinity College, Cambridge. He was in the 7th Somerset Light Infantry during the First World War. Wounded. Emigrated to the USA in 1922. Later a Salesman with the Standard Oil Company in Chicago. Died in Australia in 1967.

1903.5 – 1903.7 Gregory, Christopher Clive Langton (1892-1964)

Christopher Gregory was born in Parkstone, the son of the Reverend J W Gregory who was Vicar of St Peter's Church for a time. His obituary noted that his education was much interrupted through illness. Went to Downing College, Cambridge. Served in France in the First World War. Became a Lecturer in Astronomy at University College, setting up the University of London Observatory at Mill Hill in 1929. Died in an accident in 1964.

1903.5 – not known Parish, Arthur Basil Okes (1891-1983)

Arthur Parish was born in Parkstone, the son of the Reverend William Samuel Okes Parish. The family lived at *Longfleet Vicarage* in Ringwood Road, Longfleet, Poole. Not known how long he attended *Dane Court.* He later became a Captain in the Lincolnshire Regiment. Died in Devon in 1983.

1903.6 – 1903.7 Rogerson, Sidney (1894-1968)

Sidney Rogerson was born in Winterborne Kingston in Dorset, the first son of the Reverend Sidney Rogerson. His parents had recently moved to Pateley Bridge in Yorkshire. Only at *Dane Court* for two months. He was then transferred to St. Cuthbert's College in Worksop. In the West Yorkshire Regiment from 1916 to 1919. Publicity Manager for the Federation of British Industry from 1923 to 1930. Worked for ICI from 1930 to 1952. Publicity and Public Relations Advisor to the Army Council, War Office from 1952 to 1954. Hon. Colonel 44th (Home Counties) Infantry Division Signals Regiment in 1955. Wrote several books, a number on war: *Twelve Days* (1933), *Last of the Ebb* (1937) and *Propaganda for the Next War* (1938). Died in Suffolk in 1968. Further details of his life and career are included in *The Times* obituary dated 28 November 1968.

School Year 1903-1904

1903.9 – not known Tayler, Noel (1894-not known)

Noel Tayler was born in Longfleet, Parkstone, the son of Richard Tom Tayler, a Bank Clerk. Not known how long he was at *Dane Court* as a Day Boy. He was a Science Student in Plymouth by 1911. May have emigrated to South Africa in the 1950s.

1904.1 – 1908.7 Gorst, Edmund Rann Kennedy (1895-1935)

Edmund Gorst was born in Fulham in London, the son of Harold Edward Gorst an Author and Journalist. His mother was Nina Cecilia Francesca Rose Kennedy, a Novelist and Dramatist. Spent 4½ years at *Dane Court* as a Boarder. Believed to have become a Diplomat. Died in 1935.

1904.1 – 1908.7 Phillips, Henry Walter (1894-1942)

Henry Phillips was born in Taunton, the son of Henry Walter Phillips, a Major in the Army Pay Department. His father had died in 1903, the year before he joined the school. His mother lived in Exeter. Attended *Dane Court* for 4½ years as a Boarder. Then attended Malvern College from 1908 to 1912. Became a Private in the London Regiment. Later a Bank Clerk in Drummonds Bank. Died in 1942.

1904.5 – 1910.9 Batterham, (Hugh) Willoughby (1896-1931)

Willoughby Batterham was born in St Leonards-on-Sea, the second son of Dr John William Batterham FRCS. His mother died in 1903, the year before he came to *Dane Court*. His brother Douglas John Batterham had started at the school in September 1902 and remained there until July 1908. Willoughby spent nearly 6 years at *Dane Court* as a Boarder. Attended Aldenham from 1910 to 1914, then the Royal Naval College in Dartmouth. Became a Lieutenant Commander in the Royal Navy until 1920. Died in Paddington in 1931. *Picture references: 41 and 59.*

1904.5 – 1907.12 Howes, Basil Edward (1894-not known)

Basil Howes was born in Fritton, Norfolk, the son of the Reverend Leonard P Howes. His parents lived in Long Stratton in Norfolk. Spent 3½ years at *Dane Court* as a Boarder. Attended St. Edwards School in Oxford after *Dane Court*, then Wadham College, Oxford. Became a Captain in the Royal Warwickshire Regiment. In 1939 he was a Planning Clerk for the Hoffman Ball Bearing Company.

1904.5 – 1907.7 Carpenter, John Philip Morton (1893-1916)

John Carpenter was born in Salisbury, the son of the Venerable Harry William Carpenter, Archdeacon of Sarum. His parents lived in Salisbury. Spent 2 years and 2 months at *Dane Court*. Attended Marlborough from 1907 to 1909, then Lancing College from 1910 to 1912. Became a 2nd Lieutenant in the 5th Battalion of the Wiltshire Regiment in 1914. In the Royal Field Artillery in 1915. Wounded at Sulva Bay in August 1915. Killed in action on the Somme 15 September 1916.

1904.5 – 1908.4 Wodehouse, Frederick Guy de Picquigny (1894-not known)

Frederick Wodehouse was born in Hertingfordbury in Hertfordshire, the sixth son of Charles Edward Wodehouse, a Justice of the Peace and Gentleman Farmer, to be taught by the Reverend Graham. His parents and grandfather lived at *Woolmer's Park* in Hertingfordbury. Spent 3 years at *Dane Court* as a Boarder. Attended Malvern College from 1908 to 1911. Enlisted in 1916 in the 4/R 9th F.A. Brigade in Queensland, Australia. Remained in Queensland as a factory worker.

1904.7 – 1907.7 Robinson, Frederick Roland Henry (1897-1944)

Frederick Robinson was born in Benhal in Buxar, India, the first son of Francis Richard William Robinson who worked for the Indian Civil Service. His parents lived in Rewah in India. Spent 3 years at *Dane Court* as a Boarder. Attended Abingdon School, then Bedford Grammar School. Married in Bombay in 1925. Manager in a motor manufacturer's depot by the 1920s and later a Director of Crescent Garages Limited. Died in Ealing in 1944.

1904.7 – 1907.7 Robinson, Louis Francis Woodward (1893-1917)

Louis Robinson was born in Benhal in Buxar, India, the second son of Francis Richard William Robinson who worked for the Indian Civil Service. Spent 3 years at *Dane Court* as a Boarder. Like his brother, he attended Abingdon School, then Bedford Grammar School. Obtained a commission in the Corps of Royal Engineers. In the British Expeditionary Force in August 1914, in Salonika from 1915 to 1916, then to France again in January 1917. Recommended for the Croix de Guerre. Missing believed killed in action 25 May 1917.

1904.7 – 1907.7 Robinson, Charles William Sydney (1895-1918)

Charles Robinson was born in Benhal in Buxar, India, the third son of Francis Richard William Robinson who worked for the Indian Civil Service. Spent 3 years at *Dane Court* as a Boarder. Like his brothers, he also attended Abingdon School, then Bedford Grammar School. Became an Air Mechanic with the Independent Air Force. Died on 8 August 1918 in hospital abroad following an accident in service.

School Year 1904-1905

1904.9 – 1909.4 MacGregor, Thomas Charles Stuart (1897-1917)

Thomas MacGregor was born in Lymington in Hampshire, his father was William Ord MacGregor who worked for the Indian Civil Service. Spent 4½ years at *Dane Court* as a Boarder. Attended Malvern College in 1910-1914. Commissioned November 1914 as a 2nd Lieutenant in the Highland Light Infantry. In France September 1915. In Ypres in winter 1915 and wounded on 10 May 1916. After three months leave, he joined the Royal Flying Corps. Killed in the air by a shell on 8 June 1917.

1904.9 – 1908.12 Sunderland, Harcourt Kingsley Pearce (1897-1926)

Harcourt Sunderland was born in British Columbia, Canada, the son of Captain Daniel Pearce Sunderland, a Captain in the 4th Hussars. His parents lived at *Beulah* in Ardmore Road. Spent 4 years and 4 months at *Dane Court* as a Day Boy. Returned to British Columbia later to be a Farmer and married there in 1922 although he died in Parkstone in 1926 where his parents continued to live.

1904.9 – 1906.7 Barker, Norman George (1894-1969)

Norman Barker was born in Christchurch, New Zealand, the son of Arthur Llewellyn Barker whose occupation is not known. His parents lived at *Heatherlands* in Parkstone for a short time. Spent nearly 2 years at *Dane Court* as a Day Boy. The family left for Wellington in New Zealand in 1906. Later became a sheep farmer. Died in New Zealand in 1969.

1904.9 – 1907.7 Rundle, (Cubitt) Noel (1893-1915)

Noel Rundle as born in Bengal in India, the second son of Colonel Cubitt Sindall Rundle who was a Surgeon in the Indian Medical Service. His elder brother was already at the school. Spent nearly 3 years at *Dane Court* as a Boarder. His parents retired to St Helier in Jersey and he then attended Victoria College in Jersey from 1907 to 1914. Enlisted in the South Wales Borderers but he was attached to the 5th Battalion of the Royal Scots. Killed in action at Gallipoli in the Dardanelles leading his platoon on 19 June 1915.

1905.5 – 1906.6 French, Arthur Cecil (1896-1974)

Cecil French was born in Little Blakenham in Suffolk, the son of the Reverend William Arthur French. His parents still lived there when he attended the school. Only spent just over a year at *Dane Court* as a Boarder. In 1915 became a 2nd Lieutenant in the Suffolk Regiment, later becoming a Lieutenant in the same regiment in 1922. Spent some time in India but by 1939 was a Secretary to the Territorial Army in Cambridge. Died in Cambridgeshire in 1974.

1905.5 – 1905.7 Helmore, Heathcote George (1894-1964)

Heathcote Helmore was born in Christchurch, New Zealand, the first son of George Henry Helmore, a Barrister and Solicitor. His parents still lived in Christchurch. Only spent the Summer Term of 1905 at *Dane Court* as a Boarder with his younger brother. Later attended Christ's College in Christchurch, New Zealand. Enlisted in the 1st Division of the New Zealand Army. Later became an Architect. Articled to Sir Edwyn Lutyens for two years. Became Senior Partner of Helmore and Cottrell, Architects. A thesis on this important architectural practice is available online. Died in New Zealand in 1964.

1905.5 – 1905.7 Helmore, Ernest Cresswell (1896-1917)

Ernest Helmore was born in Christchurch, New Zealand, the second son of George Henry Helmore, a Barrister and Solicitor. His parents still lived in Christchurch. Only spent the Summer Term of 1905 at *Dane Court* as a Boarder with his elder brother. Later attended Christ's College in Christchurch, New Zealand. Became a 2nd Lieutenant in the Notts and Derby (Sherwood Forresters) Regiment. He died of his war wounds on 1 January 1917 in Arras, France.

School Year 1905-1906

1905.9 – 1909.12 Belben, George Devereux (1897-1944)

George Belben was born in Poole, the first son of George Belben, a Miller with his own business. His parents lived at *Bark Hart* in Mount Pleasant Road, Poole, when he attended the school. His younger brother Thomas joined at the same time. Spent 4 years and 4 months at *Dane Court* as a Day Boy. Attended the Royal Naval College at Osborne House from 1909 to 1910. Later became Captain Belben. Awarded the DSO in 1918. DSC (posthumous), Albert Medal (posthumous), twice Mentioned in Despatches. Captain of armed merchant cruiser *HMS Canton* and light cruiser *HMS Penelope*. Drowned at sea in 1944. The citation when *HMS Penelope* was torpedoed and sunk off Naples on 18 February 1944 reads: *'Captain Belben lost his life from ultimate exhaustion as a result of his outstanding bravery and self-sacrifice in directing the rescue of survivors from the water'*. Sadly, all his medals and militaria were auctioned by Spink & Son in 2012.

1905.9 – 1910.4 Belben, Thomas Alan (1898-1936)

Thomas Belben was born in Poole, the second son of George Belben, a Miller with his own business. His parents at *Bark Hart* in Mount Pleasant Road, Poole when he attended the school. His elder brother George joined at the same time. Spent 4½ years at *Dane Court* as a Day Boy. Left for India in 1916. Became a 2nd Lieutenant in the Indian Army Reserve in 1917 and later a 2nd Lieutenant then Captain in the 4/6th Rifles, attached to the Remount Department. Married in Bengal 1930. Died in India in 1936.

1905.9 – 1907.7 Pillans, James Pritchard Scarth (1898-1953)

James Pillans was born in Chislehurst in Kent, the first son of Walter Scarth Pillans who lived on his own means. His parents lived at *Durrant House* in Durrant Road, Parkstone. Spent 2 years at *Dane Court* as a Day Boy. The family seems to have moved to Berkhampstead. Attended Berkhampstead Grammar School and the Faraday House Electrical Engineering College. Served in the Royal Engineers in the First World War. Received practical training at Plenty and Son in Newbury and C A Parsons and Co in Newcastle-upon-Tyne. He later worked for various electricity companies. In 1939 he was appointed as HM Electrical Inspector of Factories and then transferred to the Admiralty Electrical Engineering Department in Bath. Died in Middlesex in 1953.

1906.1 – 1912.4 Barton, John Mackintosh Tilney (1898-1977)

John Barton was born in Parkstone, the son of Tilney W Barton, a Church Missionary Society Missionary. Spent 6 years and 3 months at *Dane Court* as a Day Boy, although absent for nearly two years between 1908 to 1910 due to ill-health. Attended under the Reverend Graham and the Pooleys. Parents lived at *Crossways* in Wellington Road then 3 Belvedere Crescent, Parkstone.

Returned to the school in January 1910. Won an Open Historical Scholarship to Harrow School which he attended from 1912 to 1915, then went to Christ's College, Cambridge. Later a House Master of St Edmund's College in Ware. Ordained as a Priest in 1921. Wide-ranging career. Wrote a book called *Penance and Absolution*. Eventually became Canon of Westminster Cathedral from 1971. Known as the Right Reverend Monsignor Canon John Mackintosh Tilney Barton. Died in Berkshire in 1977. *Picture references: 58, 59, 75 and 162.*

1906.1 – 1913.7 O'Shea, Desmond Gerald George (1899-1966)

Desmond O'Shea was born in Plymouth, the son of the Reverend George James Jackson O'Shea who had the title The O'Shea of Kerry. His parents lived at *The Vicarage* in Canford Magna, near Wimborne. Spent 6½ years at *Dane Court* as a Boarder, although he left for two years from 1907 to 1909 as he could not come as a Boarder. Attended under the Reverend Graham and the Pooleys. Won a Foundation Scholarship to Marlborough which he attended from 1913 to 1917, then Exeter College, Oxford. Obtained a commission in the Royal Wiltshire Yeomanry in 1918. Became a Lieutenant in 1919. In the RAF by 1922. Succeeded to the title The O'Shea of Kerry in 1935. Education Officer in the RAF 1939. Promoted to Wing Commander in 1948. Died in Hampshire in 1966. *Picture references: 59, 60, 84, 85 and 86.*

1906.1 – 1911.4 Fawkes, Cecil Wentworth (1896-1981)

Cecil Fawkes was born in Alverstoke in Hampshire, the son of Lieutenant Colonel Montagu Fawkes of Queen Victoria's Royal Irish Fusiliers. His parents lived at *The White Lodge* in Sandringham Road, Parkstone. Spent 5¼ years at *Dane Court* as a Day Boy under the Reverend Graham. Became a 2nd Lieutenant in Queen Victoria's (Royal Irish Fusiliers) from 1914 to 1922. Had become an Assistant Master at Dorset House Preparatory School by 1939. Died in Kent in 1981. *Picture reference: 59 and 60.*

1906.5 – 1908.4 MacLeod, Hector John Roderick (1898-1925)

Hector MacLeod was born in Melbourne, Australia, the son of Roderick Maclean MacLeod. Parents lived at *Ulverstone* in North Road, Parkstone. Spent 2 years at *Dane Court* as a Day Boy. Attended Pelham House School in Folkstone from 1908 to 1911. Became a Lieutenant in the Cameron Highlanders. May also have served in India, where he married in 1921. He died in St Helier in Jersey in 1925 in a drowning accident.

1906.5 – 1907.7 Pillans, Albert Nelson (1899-1926)

Albert Pillans was born in Chislehurst in Kent, the second son of Walter Scarth Pillans who lived on his own means. His parents lived at *Durrant House* in Durrant Road, Parkstone. Spent just over a year at *Dane Court* as a Day Boy, at the same time as his elder brother. Then attended Berkhampstead Grammar School with his elder brother. In the Honourable Artillery Company in the First World War. Died in the USA in 1926.

1906.6 – 1908.12 Tennent, Hugh Patrick Lorraine (1899-1975)

Hugh Tennent was born in Rangitikei in New Zealand, the son of Patrick Hugh Lyon Tennent, a Retired Farmer. His parents lived at *Hazelmere* in Balmoral Road, Parkstone. Spent 2½ years at *Dane Court* as a Day Boy. Became a Lieutenant Commander in the Royal Navy.

School Year 1906-1907

1906.9 – 1907.7 Harington, Hubert Lionel (1892-1910)

Hubert Harington was born in Bishop's Waltham in Hampshire, the son of Colonel F W Harington. His parents lived in Bedfordshire. His guardian was a Miss Cox who lived at 36 Alexandra Road, Parkstone. Spent a year at *Dane Court* as a Day Boy, then attended Bedford Grammar School. Died aged 17.

1906.9 – 1910.4 Woodroofe, Thomas Borries Ralph (1899-1978)

Thomas Woodroofe was born in Adelaide in Eastern Cape, South Africa, the son of Dr George Borries Woodroofe, a Medical Practitioner. His mother lived at *Lisburn* in Sandecotes Road, Parkstone. Spent 4½ years at *Dane Court* as a Boarder. Attended St. Andrews College Grahamstown in South Africa from 1910 to 1916, then Clifton College from 1916 to 1917. Entered the Royal Navy 1917 rising to Lieutenant Commander by 1933. Commentator for the BBC from 1936 to 1939. Various positions in the Admiralty from 1939 to 1946. Wrote several naval stories including *Naval Odyssey, River of Golden Sand, Best Stories of the Navy* and several others. Died in Kensington in 1978. *Picture reference: 164.*

1907.1 – 1910.7 Mack, Joseph (1896-1916)

Joseph Mack was born in St. Kilda, Victoria in Australia, the first son of a Landowner and Farmer. His father was still in Australia while his mother brought Joseph and his younger brother Ian to Parkstone, living at *Airlie* in Kingsbridge Road then *Craddock* in Balmoral Road, Parkstone. Spent 3½ years at *Dane Court* as a Day Boy. Became a Sub-Lieutenant in the Royal Australian Navy. Killed on the Royal Navy ship *HMS Defence* at the Battle of Jutland.

1907.1 – 1907.7 Leonard, John Marius Ronald (1897-not known)

John Leonard was born in France. His father's name and occupation is not known. His mother lived at *The White Cottage* in Parkstone. He only attended *Dane Court* for six months as a Day Boy.

1907.5 – 1911.12 Hodgson-Stevens, Edmund James (1898-1977)

Edmund Hodgson-Stevens was born in Rio de Janeiro, Brazil, the son of George James Stevens, occupation not known. His parents were still in Brazil. The school's contact was his grandmother, Mrs Marguerite Hodgson-Stevens in Hampstead. Spent 4½ years at *Dane Court* as a Boarder, straddling the Graham and Pooley eras. Attended Brighton College from 1911 to 1915. Became a 2nd Lieutenant in the General List in 1917. Was then in the British Royal Air Force. Later a Clerk in Lloyds Bank. Died in London in 1977. *Picture references: 57, 58 and 70.*

1907.5 – 1912.7 Batterham, (Alexander) Gordon (1899-1931)

Gordon Batterham was born in St. Leonards-on-Sea, the third son of Dr John William Batterham FRCS. His mother had died in 1903 when he was 4 years of age. Spent over 5 years at *Dane Court* as a Boarder, overlapping with some of his brothers. He straddled the Graham and Pooley eras. Attended Aldenham School from 1912 to 1916. Became a Lieutenant in The Queen's Royal West Surrey Regiment. Later transferred to the RAF. Soon after the war he became ill and his health gradually deteriorated. He died in Newton Abbott in 1931. *Picture references: 41, 56, 60, 70 and 87.*

School year 1907-1908

1907.9 - 1908.12 Oakley, William Edward Bowen (1898-1960)

William Oakley was born in Parkstone, the second son of Edward Bowen Oakley, an Architect and Surveyor. His parents lived at *Dulverton* in Alton Road, Parkstone. His elder brother, Philip John Bowen Oakley, was still at the school when he joined. Spent one year and four months at *Dane Court* as Day Boy. Obtained his Royal Aero Club Aviators' Certificate in April 1917. Became a Flight Sub-Lieutenant in the Royal Naval Air Service. Died in Wiltshire in 1960.

1907.9 – 1908.4 Coleridge, Reginald Ernest (1898-1977)

Reginald Coleridge was born in Sumatra, the son of Henry Hill Coleridge, an Engineer. His mother lived in Bray near Maidenhead. Only spent 8 months at *Dane Court* as a Boarder. Attended Bradfield College from 1909 to 1912. Became a Lieutenant in the Royal West Kent Regiment in First World War. Attended Manchester University from 1919 to 1922. He is recorded as being a fitter of aeroplane cowls in 1939. Died in Cornwall in 1977.

1907.9 – not known Gwatkin, Norman Wilmhurst (1899-1971)

Norman Gwatkin was born in Dorchester, the son of Hugh Fortescue Wilmhurst Gwatkin, a Solicitor. Parents lived at *Fownhope* in North Road, Parkstone. Not known exactly how long he stayed at *Dane Court* as a Day Boy. Later attended a preparatory school in Westgate-on-Sea, then Clifton College from 1913 to 1916, followed by the Royal Military College at Sandhurst. Was in the Coldstream Guards in 1918. Subsequently joined the Royal Household. Assistant Comptroller of the Lord Chamberlain's Office. 5th Guards Armoured Brigade in Operation Overlord. DSO 1944. Extra Equerry to King George VI from 1950 to 1952 and same role in the household of Elizabeth II until his death in 1971. Knighted: known as Brigadier Sir Norman Wilmhurst Gwatkin. Died in Suffolk in 1971. *Picture reference: 159*

1908.1 – 1909.4 Tracy, Melvin Maxwell Carew (1901-not known)

Melvin Tracy was born in Graystones in County Wicklow, Ireland, the son of Major William Maxwell Tracy, a Major in the Indian Army, based in Cawnpore. Spent one year and three months at *Dane Court* as a Boarder. By 1911 his mother was living at *Carscadden* in St Clair Road, Canford Cliffs, Poole. In 1956 he was a Surveyor in Nairobi, Kenya.

1908.1 – 1908.7 Rogerson, George Carroll (1897-not known)

George Rogerston was born in Bingley, Yorkshire, the second son of the Reverend Sidney Rogerson. His parents lived in Yorkshire. Spent just six months at *Dane Court* as a Boarder with his elder brother Sidney. Attended St. Cuthbert's College in Worksop from later in 1908. Became a Lieutenant in the Royal Garrison Artillery from 1916 to 1923. Spent time in the Gold Coast as a Surveyor.

1908.1 – 1911.7 Burnier, Richard (1897-1918)

Richard Burnier was born in Willesden, Middlesex, the son of Carl Hugo Burnier a Dutch subject originally from Dusseldorf, a Teacher of Music. His mother, Adéle Burnier, was recorded in the 1911 Census as a *'Visiting School Mistress'* in Eastbourne. Spent 3½ years at *Dane Court* as a Boarder. Attended Bradfield College from 1911 to 1915. Went to the Royal Military College, Sandhurst. Became a 2nd Lieutenant, then Lieutenant in the 1st Battalion of the Royal Sussex Regiment from 1916 to 1918. Died in France of his wounds on 21 February 1918. *Picture references: 56, 57, 113.*

1908.9 – 1909.7 Heathcote, Geoffrey Arthur Unwin (1904-1977)

Geoffrey Heathcote was born in London, the second son of Major Arthur Unwin Heathcote. His parents lived in Maldon in Essex. Spent one year at *Dane Court* as a Boarder. Further education and career details not known. Died in Cambridgeshire in 1977. *Picture reference: 60.*

1908.5 – 1911.7 Heathcote, Michael Arthur Unwin (1902-1979)

Michael Heathcote was born in London, the first son of Major Arthur Unwin Heathcote. His parents lived in Maldon in Essex. Spent 3 years and 2 months at *Dane Court* as a Boarder. Became a Surveyor by 1929 and a Geographer by 1935. Died in Poole in 1979. *Picture reference: 56.*

1908.5 – 1909.12 Gorst, Harold John (1899-not known)

Harold Gorst was born in Battersea, the second son of Harold Edward Gorst, an Author and Journalist. His mother was Nina Cecilia Francesca Rose Kennedy, a Novelist and Dramatist. His parents continued to live in London. Spent 1½ years at *Dane Court* as a Boarder. His elder brother had previously attended the school. Attended Bradfield College from 1910 to 1912. Was later in the Royal Navy on *HMS Hibernia*. Became a Lieutenant Commander. Applied for US citizenship 1925.

School Year 1908-1909

1908.9 – 1913.12 Batterham, Arthur Graham (1900-1980)

Arthur Batterham in St Leonards-on-Sea, the fourth son of Dr John William Batterham FRCS. His mother had died in 1903. Spent 5 years and 4 months at *Dane Court* as a Boarder, overlapping with some of his elder brothers. Attended Aldenham School from 1914 to 1918 then Caius College, Cambridge. After service in the armed forces, he became an Assistant Master at

Dane Court Preparatory School in Pyrford between 1922 and 1930. Entered RADA in 1931 and toured in repertory for a time before returning to Dane Court Preparatory School around 1934 for many years. Known by Hugh Pooley as *'our beloved Batty'*. Several of his reminiscences are included in this book. *Picture references: 41, 70, 84, 85, 87, 107 and 165.*

1908.9 – 1914.4 Milner, Guy Sommerville (1901-1987)

Guy Milner was born in Parkstone, the son of Dr Vincent Milner, a Medical Practitioner. His parents lived at *Oak Lodge* in Bournemouth Road, Parkstone. Spent 5½ years at *Dane Court* as a Day Boy. Later attended Epsom College. In 1918 he was a Clerk with Wills Tobacco. By 1930 he was a Tobacco Merchant and in 1939 a Window Dressing Inspector. Died in Poole in 1987. *Picture reference: 78.*

1908.9 – 1909.7 Child, Claude Herbert (1900-not known)

Claude Child was born in Kennington in London, the son of Lieutenant Hubert Child of the Royal Navy. His parents lived at The *Brackens* on Bournemouth Road, Parkstone. Spent a year at *Dane Court* as a Day Boy. Later attended Clifton College from 1914 to 1917, then Wellington College in India from 1919 to 1920. In the Indian Army from 1920 to 1929, rising to the rank of Captain. Then he received two years of training with the Albion Motor Car Company in Glasgow from 1930 to 1932, towards qualifying as a Mechanical Engineer. Returned to India holding several posts in India and Ceylon. From 1946, he was Assistant Director of Mechanical Engineering for the British Commonwealth Occupation Forces in Japan.

1908.10 – 1910.7 Mack, Ian MacCallum (1900-1933)

Ian Mack was born in St Kilda, Victoria in Australia, the second son of a Landowner and Farmer. His father was still in Australia when he joined while his mother had brought his elder brother Joseph and him to Parkstone, living at *Airlie* in Kingsbridge Road then *Craddock* in Balmoral Road, Parkstone. Returned to Australia. Lived in Queensland. Worked as a District Patrol Officer. Speared by natives in Upper Rama, Papua New Guinea in 1933. His Patrol Reports were published in book form in 1994. The tragic events leading to his murder are described by Naomi McPherson in *Chapter 6: Wanted Young Man Must Like Adventure: Ian MacCallum Mack, Patrol Officer* in the collection edited by McPherson called *In Colonial New Guinea: Anthropological Perspectives*. *Picture references: 59.*

1909.6 – 1911.4 Belben, Stephen James (1902-1965)

Stephen Belben was born in Poole, the second son of George Belben, a Miller with his own business. His parents lived at *Bark Hart* in Mount Pleasant Road in Poole when he attended the school. His two elder brothers were still at the school when he joined. Spent just under 2 years at *Dane Court* as a Day Boy. Became Headmaster of Woodrough's Preparatory School in Moseley, Birmingham and then at Stanway Manor, Rushbury, Church Stretton. Died in Westminster in 1965. *Picture references: 59.*

School Year 1909-1910

1909.9 - 1912.7 Baker, Samuel (1893-not known)

Samuel Baker was born in Willesden, the son of a Retired Missionary, who was deceased by the time he came to *Dane Court*. His mother lived at *Rosalie* in Longfleet Road, Longfleet, Poole. Came to the school when he was 15. Spent 3 years at *Dane Court* as a Day Boy. Partially disabled and therefore behind with his studies. *Picture references: 70 and 87.*

1909.9 – 1912.7 Allen, Francis Lechampion (1902-1984)

Francis Allen was born in Bengal, India, the son of Edward Cuthbert Allen, occupation not known. His parents lived at *Sistina* in Ardmore Road, Parkstone. Spent 3 years at *Dane Court* as a Day Boy. Parents retired to Jersey. Married in New Zealand in 1927. Became a Priest. Died in Ashburton in New Zealand in 1984. *Picture references: 56 and 60.*

1910.2 – not known Hoey, Cedric Clinton (1899-1960)

Cedric Hoey was born in Solihull, the son of Denys Clinton Hoey, a Clerk in Holy Orders, by 1911 acting as the Diocesan Secretary of the Church of England Temperance Society. His parents lived in Hackney. His grandmother lived at *Montagu* in St Peter's Road, Parkstone, near the school. He was in the Royal Flying Corps from 1914 to 1922. Died in Kent in 1960. *Picture reference: 59.*

1910.5 – 1911.7 Erskine-Murray, James Alastair Frederick Campbell (1902-1973)

James Erskine-Murray was born in Edinburgh, the son of James Erskine-Murray, a Consulting Engineer. His parents moved to *The Oaks* in Church Road, Parkstone, opposite the school in Church Road. Spent one year and two months at *Dane Court* as a Day Boy. Attended Harrow from 1916 to 1920, then Glasgow University followed by the Royal Military College at Sandhurst. Became a Commander in 1922 in the Highland Light Infantry. Fought in World War II attaining the rank of Major. Later became a Fellow of the Society of Antiquaries in Scotland and a Fellow of the Zoological Society of Scotland. Succeeded to the title of the 13th Lord Elibank of Etrick Forest, Selkirk in 1962. Died in Scotland in 1973. *Picture reference: 60.*

1910.6 – 1911.3 Hobson, Frank Martin Carrington (1901-1969)

Frank Hobson was born in Trinidad and Tobago, the son of Leonard Manning Hobson, a Solicitor. He was a ward of a Miss Norris who lived at *The Moors* in Spur Hill Avenue, Parkstone, recorded in the 1911 Census as *'a guardian of children of friends abroad'*. Only spent 9 months at *Dane Court* probably as a Day Boy. He is believed to have spent some time farming in the 1920s, departing for Canada in 1929. By 1945 he was a 2nd Lieutenant in the Colonial Forces of the Caribbean Areas. He later became a Sugar Plantation Manager. In 1963 he was awarded the Colonial Police Medal for meritorious service as the Commandant of the St. Vincent Auxiliary Police Force. Died in St Vincent and the Grenadines in 1969. *Picture references: 56 and 60.*

1910.6 – 1912.7 Burn, Charles Scott (1896-1917)

Charles Burn was born in Kennoway in Fifeshire, the first son of George Frank Burn, a Civil Engineer and Managing Director of the Barbados Light Railway. His parents lived at *Pine Dene* in Mansfield Road, Parkstone. Entered the school aged 14. Spent 2 years at *Dane Court* as a Day Boy, then he was coached by a Mrs Higgins of Broadstone. Attended the Royal Military College, Sandhurst from January to July 1915. Became a 2nd Lieutenant in the Seaforth Highlanders in July 1915. Sailed for the Persian Gulf February in 1916. Invalided in India with cholera and dysentry in 1916. Became a Lieutenant in 1917. Killed in action in Mesopotamia on 3 November 1917. *Picture references: 70, 84, 85, 87 and 112.*

1910.6 – 1910.7 Politeyan, Cyril Dunhelm (1903-1985)

Cyril Politeyan was born in Durham, the son of the Reverend Jacob Politeyan. His parents lived in Didsbury when he joined the school. Only stayed a couple of months at *Dane Court* as a Boarder. Further schooling not known. Later went to Selwyn College, Cambridge. Became a Clinical Assistant in the Electro-Cardiographical Department and the Children's Department at St Thomas's Hospital. In the 1940s he was at the English Mission Hospital in Jerusalem. He returned to the UK in the 1950s. Died in Essex in 1985.

School Year 1910-1911

1910.9 – 1914.7 Chesshire, Robert Humphrey Hooper (1902-1999)

Robert Chesshire was born in Parkstone, the first son of Captain G H Chesshire of the Mercantile Marine Service. His parents lived at *Cotgrove* in Church Road East in Parkstone. Spent 4 years at *Dane Court* as a Day Boy. Attended Hurstpierpoint College from 1914 to 1917. Worked as a Clerk after college. Emigrated to Canada in 1924, marrying in Winnipeg, Manitoba in 1928. Held several positions in the Winnipeg Retail Store and the Fur Trade Department of the Hudson's Bay Company. General Manager of the Bay Stores in 1957. Died in Ontario, in 1999. *Picture reference: 60, 87 and 107.*

1910.9 – 1911.12 Luff, Cyril Edgar Evelyn (1902-1981)

Cyril Luff was born in Peasedown St. John in Somerset, the son of the Reverend Edgar Albert Luff. His parents lived in North Devon. Stayed with his aunt. Left when she moved as his father could not send him as a Boarder. Attended *Dane Court* as a Day Boy for one year and four months. Attended Exeter Cathedral Choir School in 1912. Employed at a motor works in Christchurch in 1920. By 1939 he was a Horticultural Nursery Propagator. Died in Gloucestershire in 1981.

1911.1 – 1912.7 Burn, George Frank (1897-not known)

George Burn was born in Kennoway in Fifeshire, the second son of G Frank Burn, a Civil Engineer and Managing Director of the Barbados Light Railway. His parents lived at *Pine Dene* in Mansfield Road, Parkstone. His elder brother was already at the school. Joined when he was 13. Stayed 18 months. Then coached by a Mrs Higgins of Broadstone from 1912 to 1913. Entered the offices of G D Belben in Poole in 1913. Worked at *Dane Court* helping with Preparation from Summer 1915 to Spring 1916, due to staff shortages. Attested under Lord Derby's Scheme in November 1915. Commissioned in 1916. Belgian Military Cross 1918. In the Army of the Rhine from 1918 to 1919. Trust Houses Limited 1920. *Picture references: 70, 84, 85 and 87.*

1911.1 – 1915.1 Norman, Hallion Addison (1901-1963)

Hallion Norman was born in Ditchingham, Norfolk, the son of Thomas Ostell Burton Norman, a Retired Indigo Planter in India. His parents lived at *Stretton Court* in Bournemouth Road, Parkstone. Spent 4 years at *Dane Court* as a Day Boy. Attended Marlborough College from 1915 to 1917. After Marlborough he entered a Munition Works in 1918. Worked at Poole Foundry in 1920, then BAT in South America from 1925. Died in Kent in 1963. *Picture references: 70, 87, 95 and 107.*

1911.3 – 1912.4 Gargery, Edwin John (1896-1983)

Edwin John was born in Dulwich, the son of Walter Thomas Gargery, an Estate Agent. His parents lived in Purley. Spent just over a year at *Dane Court* as a Boarder. Then received private tuition in Seaford. Attested 1917 at the 26th Training Reserve Battalion, then became a Private in the Army Ordnance Corps. Attended Keble College, Oxford in 1919. Ordained as a Priest and became a Curate in Cheam, Surrey. Died in Kent in 1983.

1911.5 – 1913.4 Scott, (John) Francis Robson (1902-1970)

Francis Scott was born in Tarrant Keynston in Dorset, the son of Major J S L Robson-Scott. His parents lived at *Thurnham* in North Road, Parkstone. Spent 3 years at *Dane Court* as a Day Boy. Left when his parents moved. Later won a Scholarship to Repton School which he attended from 1916 to 1920. Entered the Royal Military College Sandhurst in 1920 and then joined the Hussars. Died in Cumbria in 1970. *Picture references: 70, 74 and 87.*

1911.6 – 1913.7 Jones, Charles Allen Foulkes (1903-1944)

Not known where Charles Jones, the son of Allen Jones, whose occupation is not known. His mother lived at *Belparo* in Alexandra Road, Parkstone. Spent 2 years at *Dane Court* as a Day Boy. Left for *'special Swedish treatment and a governess'*. Later attended Hailey School in Bournemouth. Went to Canada with his mother in February 1915. By 1939 was running a guest house in Salisbury. Died in Wiltshire in 1944.

School Year 1911-1912

1911.9 – 1914.5 Ormerod, Edward Tyssen (1903-1942)

Edward Ormerod was born in Hove, the son of Dr Ernest William Ormerod, a Medical Practitioner. His parents lived in Wimborne. Spent just over 3½ years at *Dane Court* as a Boarder. *'Left to go to a larger school near Brighton with better air'*. Attended Wellington College from 1917 to 1921. Became a Tea Planter in Assam. He was later a 2nd Lieutenant attached to 2 Field Regiment of the Royal Indian Artillery. Died in 1942 in one of the campaigns. *Picture references: 87 and 88.*

1911.9 – 1915.9 Lassen, Eric (1903-1954)

Eric Lassen was born in Highgate in London, the son of Jens Jacob Lassen who was involved in engineering. Both his parents were born in Denmark. His parents lived in Hampstead when he was at the school. Spent 4 years at *Dane Court* as a Boarder. He was in Denmark on the outbreak of war and his family decided that he should stay there. Returned to England in 1918 to attend West Lavington Agricultural College. Attended University College School in 1919. At the Danish Agricultural College in 1920. Later became a Company Director. Died in London in 1954. *Picture references: 73, 87, 101 and 107.*

1911.9 – 1911.12 Fuller, Wilfred Robert (1896-not known)

Robert Fuller was born in San Francisco, the son of Wilfred Fuller, an Artist for a British newspaper there. His father died in 1911. His mother lived at *Nilgiri Lodge* in Alexandra Road, Parkstone. Wilfred was 15 when he joined so was over age for the school and only stayed one Term as a Day Boy. Then attended a Bournemouth secondary school. Obtained a commission in the Dorset Regiment in December 1914. Wounded in Flanders December 1915. Became a 2nd Lieutenant 1916 and a Lieutenant 1917. In the Gold Coast Regiment in West Africa in 1922. Later an Army Captain.

1911.9 – 1912.7 Greenlees, Campbell Glencairn Colville (1904-not known)

Campbell Greenlees was born in Edinburgh, the son of Daniel Colville Greenlees, a Retired Distiller. Parents lived at *Dunaverty* in Ardmore Road, Parkstone. Spent a year at *Dane Court* as a Day Boy. Withdrawn by his parents for a stammering cure and did not return. Later attended the Old Malt House Preparatory School in Langton Matravers in the Purbecks. Became an Assistant on a Rubber Estate in Penang in 1926. Was a Clerk in an Electricity Supply Company by 1939.

1912.1 – 1916.12 Ingram, David Caldicott (1903-1981)

David Ingram was born in Poole, the first son of Edgar Llewellyn Ingram, an Electricity Supply Engineer. His parents lived at *Caldicott* in Birchwood Road, Parkstone. Spent nearly 5 years at *Dane Court* as a Day Boy. Entered the Royal Naval College at Osborne House in December 1916. Later entered the submarine service. He was Lieutenant-Commander on *HMS Phoenix* from 1937 to 1940 based in Hong Kong then involved in patrols in the Yellow Sea and Kii-suido off Japan. He was then Lieutenant-Commander on *HMS Clyde* from 1940 to 1942 off Norway.

Acting Captain then Captain of *HMS Cyclops* from 1945 to 1946. DSC re attack on heavy enemy ship 1942. OBE in 1944 re midget submarine attack on the *Tirpitz*. CBE in 1945 for services in the Mediterranean. Chief of Intelligence Staff in the Middle East from 1948 to 1950. Deputy Director of Naval Intelligence from 1952 to 1953. Retired in 1955. Died in Surrey in 1981. *Picture references: 72, 86, 107, 111 and 115.*

1912.5 – 1913.4 Beal, Gilbert Roger Wallis (1902-1943)

Gilbert Beal was born in Upper Tooting, London, the son of Edward Beal, a Barrister. His parents lived at *Dophcot* in Highmoor Road, Parkstone. Spent a year at *Dane Court* as a Day Boy. Left to go as a Boarder away from Parkstone. Attended Winchester College from 1916 to 1921. Attached to the 1st Worcester Regiment 1923. With the 3/8th Punjab Regiment in the Indian Army from 1924 to 1938. Promoted to Captain in 1932. Retired in 1938. Died in Yorkshire in 1943.

School Year 1912-1913

1912.9 – 1914.7 Hagelstam, Tage (1900-not known)

Tage Hagelstam is believed to have been born in Denmark. His father's name and occupation are not known. His mother was living in Paris when he joined the school. Stayed at *Dane Court* for two years as a Boarder. Was to have stayed another year but his mother moved to Copenhagen and did not want to be parted from her son in time of war. Worked in business in Paris by 1920. *Sunrise* reported that some old boys visited him and his mother at his farm/vineyard in France in 1933. *Picture references: 87, 95, 99, 101 and 107.*

1912.10 – 1916.7 John, David Anthony Honore Nettleship (1902-1973)

David John was born in Liverpool, the first son of Augustus John, the painter, to attend the school. His mother died in 1907 before joining the school. His father and mistress lived at *Alderney Manor* on Ringwood Road when he attended the school. Spent 4 years at *Dane Court*, the first term as a Day Boy then as a Boarder. Later attended Westminster School. Attended the Architectural College in London. Later studied music and for a time was in the BBC Orchestra in Belfast. *Sunrise* reported that in 1961 he was working in the Head Office of the GPO. Died in London in 1973. *Picture references: 102, 107, 110, 111 and 116.*

1912.10 – 1916.7 John, Caspar (1903-1984)

Caspar John was born in Paddington, the second son of Augustus John to attend the school. His mother died in 1907 before he joined the school. As noted above, his father and mistress lived at *Alderney Manor* in Ringwood Road in Parkstone. Spent 4 years at *Dane Court*, the first term as a Day Boy, then as a Boarder. Attended the Royal Naval College at Osborne House from 1916 to 1917, then Dartmouth College from 1917 to 1920. Had a long and distinguished naval career, fully covered in the biography written by his daughter, Rebecca John. Knight Commander of the Order of the Bath in 1956. Admiral and Vice Chief of the Naval Staff in 1957. First Sea Lord and Chief of Naval Staff in 1960. Admiral of the Fleet in 1962. Knighted: Sir Caspar John. Died in Cornwall in 1984. Further details of his life and work are included in *The Times* obituary dated 13 July 1984. *Picture references: 95, 106, 107, 110, 111, 114, 116 and 156.*

1912.10 – 1918.7 John, Robin Thornton (1904-1986)

Robin John was born in Essex, the third son of Augustus John to attend the school. His mother died in 1907 before he joined the school. As noted above, his father and mistress lived at *Alderney Manor* in Ringwood Road in Parkstone. Spent 6 years at *Dane Court* mainly as a Boarder. Attended Malvern College from 1918 to 1919. Went to a school in Switzerland in 1920. At London University in 1925. According to *Sunrise* he was painting in Paris in 1934. By 1961 the magazine recorded that he was in the Bahamas teaching English. *Picture references: 93, 95, 107, 110, 111, 116, 119, 126, 128 and 137.*

1912.10 – 1919.7 John, Edwin (1905-1978)

Edwin John was born in Paris, the fourth son of Augustus John to attend the school. His mother died in 1907 before he joined the school. As noted above, his father and mistress lived at *Alderney Manor* in Ringwood Road in Parkstone. Spent nearly 7 years at *Dane Court* as a Boarder. Then attended the College de Normandie in France. Attended the Royal Academy Schools. Known as *'Teddy'*. Brief career as a Middleweight Boxer. *Sunrise* reported in 1931 that he was *'boxing in the ring with considerable success. A number of photographs of him have appeared in the daily press'*. In 1934, *Sunrise* reported that he *'is now painting in London and has just had a successful exhibition'*. Painted in Cornwall between 1946 and 1951.Then in 1961 *Sunrise* stated that he *'lives in Paris and paints pictures'*. According to his obituary, he inherited the estate of his aunt, the Painter Gwen John, and did much to restore her posthumous reputation. Further details of his life and work are included in *The Times* obituary dated 20 February 1978. Died in Shropshire in 1978. *Picture references: 107, 110, 111, 116, 117, 119, 122, 126 and 128.*

1912.10 – 1918.5 John, Romilly (1906-1986)

Romilly John was born in Normandy in France, the fifth son of Augustus John to attend the school. Spent 5½ years at *Dane Court* as a Boarder. His mother died in 1907 before he joined the school. As noted above, his father and mistress lived at *Alderney Manor* in Ringwood Road in Parkstone. Later attended school in France and Caius College, Cambridge. Served in the RAF. Briefly a Civil Servant. 1931 published a volume of poems. Wrote a crime novel with his wife, Katherine Tower, called *Death by Request*. In 1932 he published an autobiography called *The Seventh Child* with some recollections of *Dane Court*. Later served in the RAF and as a Civil Servant in the Ministry of Fuel and Power. His obituary described him as a Poet, Novelist and Eccentric. Further details of his life and work are included in obituaries in *The Times* dated 12 November 1986 and in *The Daily Telegraph* dated 13 November 1986. *Picture references: 95, 107, 116, 117, 126, 128 and 134.*

1913.1 – 1915.7 Everett, Henry (1903-1965)

Henry Everett was born at *The Manor House* in Wool near Wareham, the first son of the Marine Painter Herbert Barnard John Everett (known professionally as 'John Everett' from the time of his marriage in 1901). His parents lived at *Prospect* in Broadstone, also known as *Broadstone House.* His mother, Kathleen Olive Herbert (known as Katherine) was also a Painter. Spent 2½ years at *Dane Court* as a Boarder. Left to go Durlston Court School in Swanage, then St. Bees School. Later went to Cambridge. Became a Barrister. His mother Katherine Everett wrote interesting memoirs called *Bricks & Flowers* mentioning him. Died in Kent in 1965. *Picture references: 95, 107 and 111.*

1913.2 – 1917.7 Ingram, Bernard James (1905-1922)

Bernard Ingram was born in Poole, the second son of Edgar Llewellyn Ingram, an Electricity Supply Engineer. His parents lived at *Caldicott* in Birchwood Road, Parkstone. Spent 4½ years at *Dane Court* as a Day Boy. Attended St. John's School in Leatherhead from 1917 to 1922. Died of pneumonia at St John's School in Spring 1922. *Picture references: 107, 111 and 126.*

1913.5 – 1914.5 Wilson, Lyell Alexander Winder Otway (1904-not known)

Lyell Wilson was born in Western Australia, the son of Lyell Newton Wilson, a Metallurgist originally from New Zealand. His parents lived in Tarquah in South West Ghana. Spent one year at Dane Court as a Boarder. Left as *'Parkstone climate not suitable'* according to the School Register. Attended Blundell's School in Tiverton from 1917 in 1919. *Picture reference: 95.*

School Year 1913-1914

1913.9 – 1917.7 Brennand, Arthur Fynes (1904-1987)

Arthur Brennand was born in Blandford, the son of William Arthur Bedford Brennand, a Solicitor. His father had died in 1908. His mother, Ida Brennand, lived at *Firgrove* in Parkstone when he joined the school. She taught at *Dane Court* for a few years, having previously been the sole School Mistress at a small school in Blandford. Spent 4 years at *Dane Court* as a Day Boy. Attended the King's School in Canterbury from 1917 to 1923. Studied Mechanical Science at Cambridge. Became a Civil Engineer for the Caribbean Petroleum Company in Venezuela, part of Shell, from 1926 to 1929. In the Engineer's Department of London County Council from 1930 onwards. Died in Suffolk in 1987. *Picture references: 107, 111, 116 and 126.*

1913.9 – 1914.7 Watts, George Miles (1906-1939)

George Watts was born in Devonport, the son of George Watts, an Army Captain. His mother lived The Golf Club, Broadstone. Spent a year at *Dane Court* as a Boarder. Left in July 1914 as his parents were unable to keep him at the school owing to the war, while his grandfather was prepared to pay for him if he went to Newton College, which he then attended. Died in Oxfordshire in 1939.

1913.9 – 1919.7 Olivey, John Richard (1905-1968)

John Olivey was born in Poole, the son of Dr John Michael Abraham Olivey, a Medical Practitioner. His parents continued to live in Poole. Spent 6 years at *Dane Court* as a Day Boy. Later attended the King's School in Ely. Became a 2nd Lieutenant in the 1st Battalion of the Sherwood Foresters in Egypt and Libya. Lieutenant (Temporary Captain) Commanding Officer, C Company of the Rhodesian Volunteer Battalion. Awarded the Military Cross in 1942. He was a prisoner of war on Leros in November 1943 but managed to escape. Lieutenant in the Sherwood Foresters 1944. Awarded a Bar to his Military Cross. Wounded in the Middle East and then in Greece in 1945. Died in Zimbabwe in 1968. *Picture references: 106, 126, 128, 137 and 138.*

1913.9 – 1920.4 Taylor, Charles John (1906-1974)

Charles Taylor was born in Poole, the son of Alfred John Taylor, a Master Butcher and Farmer. His parents lived at *Denby Lodge* in Fernside Road, Poole. Spent 6½ years at Dane Court as a Day Boy. Attended Shaftesbury School from 1920 to 1922. Went into business in 1922. Later became a monk but was released from his vows. Became an Assistant Master at a school in Bedfordshire. In 1963, *Sunrise* reported: *'brought off his one man show of paintings at Letchworth'*. Died in Dorset in 1974. *Picture references: 107, 111, 116, 128, 137 and 138.*

1914.1 – 1916.7 Buller, Francis Warwick (1903-1967)

Francis Buller was born in Colchester, the son of Warwick Augustus Buller who was living on his own means. His parents lived at *Purbeck Lodge* in Parkstone. Spent 2½ years at *Dane Court* as a Boarder. Attended Malvern College from 1916 to 1919. Later became a Journalist in London. Died in Bournemouth in 1967. *Picture references: 107 and 111.*

1914.1 – 1916.3 Ellis, Godfrey Newell (1905-1941)

Godfrey Ellis was born in Mansfield in Nottinghamshire, the son of Newell William Ellis, a Bank Cashier. His parents lived at *Birklands* in Penn Hill Avenue, Parkstone. Spent just over 2 years at *Dane Court* as a Day Boy. His parents moved to Boscombe, and he then attended Gorse Cliff School there. Became a Serjeant in the Royal Artillery in WWII. Killed in 1941, details not known.

1914.1 – 1914.12 Everett, Anthony Blaze (1906-not known)

Anthony Everett (known as 'Tony Everett') was born in Swanage, the second son of the Marine Painter Herbert Barnard John Everett. His parents lived at *Prospect* in Broadstone, sometimes referred to as *Broadstone House*. His mother, Kathleen Olive Herbert (known as Katherine) was also a Painter. Spent 2½ years at *Dane Court* as a Boarder. His brother Henry was already at the school. His parents separated in September 1914. Pooley refused to take him later in 1914 as he was *'altogether subversive of discipline and fellowship among his mates'*. Attended Durlston Court School in Swanage instead. Enlisted for the Army in 1915 but was discharged in 1916 as unfit for duty having failed a test. Entered the Merchant Service. Later managed farms in Kenya. Mentioned in his mother's memoirs called *Bricks and Flowers*. *Picture references: 98 and 107.*

1914.5 – 1918.4 Fletcher, Thomas Simon (1904-1985)

Thomas Fletcher was born in New Sarum in Wiltshire, the first son of Wilfrid Fletcher, a Chartered Accountant with his own firm. His parents lived in Salisbury. Spent 4 years at *Dane Court* as a Boarder. Attended Rossall School in Fleetwood from 1918 to 1923, then Merton College, Oxford. Became a Chartered Accountant in his father's practice in Salisbury. Died in Salisbury in 1985. *Picture references: 111, 116, 126 and 130.*

School Year 1914-1915

1914.9 – 1916.3 Lloyd, Richard Eyre (1906-1991)

Richard Lloyd was born in India, the son of Lieutenant-Colonel William Edmund Eyre Lloyd of the 97th Deccan Infantry. His parents temporarily lived at *Vernon* in Sandecotes Road, Parkstone. Spent 18 months at *Dane Court* as a Day Boy. His parents then moved to Eastbourne in 1916 saying that the *'Parkstone climate was not good enough'*. Attended St. Cyprians, Eastbourne, Eton, the Royal Military Academy in Woolwich and Pembroke College, Cambridge. Joined the Bengal Sappers and Miners in 1930. Later commissioned in the Royal Engineers. Served in North-West Europe in the Second World War. Awarded the DSO. Assistant Chief of Staff for Intelligence in the British Army of the Rhine 1954. Chief of Staff for Middle East Land Forces in 1957. Director of Military Intelligence in 1959. Awarded a CBE in 1957. Companion of the Order of the Bath in 1959. Became Major-General Richard Eyre Lloyd. Further details of his life and career are included in *The Times* obituary dated 15 April 1991. *Picture references: 111 and 160.*

1914.10 – 1916.4 Freeman, John Horace Evans (1909-not known)

John Freeman was born in Natal in South Africa, the son of H B Freeman, occupation not known. Spent 18 months at *Dane Court* as a Day Boy. His mother lived temporarily at *Brinsworthy* in Danecourt Road, Parkstone. Left when his mother returned to South Africa.

1915.1 – 1920.3 Silley, Michael Leeson (1907-1972)

Michael Silley was born in Cuddington in Surrey, the son of Percival George Silley, an Architect. His parents lived in Ewell in Surrey. Spent just over 5 years at *Dane Court* as a Boarder. Left for an operation on his foot and did not return. Attended Gresham's School in Holt from 1921 and 1924. Went into business. In the Malay Police by 1929. Became a 2nd Lieutenant in the Royal Army Service Corps. Wounded and captured as prisoner of war in Thailand in 1942 and remained in prison until 1945. After the war became a Racing Correspondent. Died in Yorkshire in 1972. *Picture references: 111, 116, 119, 126 and 129.*

1915.1 – 1921.3 Margrie, Raymond John (1908-1921)

Raymond Margrie was born in Parkstone, the first son of a Bank Cashier. His parents lived at *Reca* in Glenair Avenue, Parkstone. Left in April 1915 after three months as his father transferred to Lloyds Bank in Burton-on-Trent. Returned with his brother in October 1919. Left March 1921. Died at home in the winter of 1921. *Picture reference: 139.*

1915.1 – 1917.4 Walford, John Neville (1902-1994)

John Walford was born in Newton Abbott, the first son of H N Walford, occupation not known. His parents lived in Milford in Surrey. Joined with his brother William Neville Walford. Spent 2 years 3 months at *Dane Court* as a Boarder. Fees paid at special rate by the Professional Classes War Relief Council. Later attended the Sloane School in Sloane Square, London. Became a Stock Jobber and Member of the London Stock Exchange. Emigrated to Canada. Died in Canada in 1994. *Picture references: 116 and 119.*

1915.1 – 1918.7 Walford, William Neville (1904-1983)

William Walford was born in the Isle of Wight, the second son of H N Walford, occupation not known. His parents lived in Milford in Surrey. Joined with his brother John Neville Walford. Spent 3½ years at *Dane Court* as a Boarder. Fees paid at special rate by the Professional Classes War Relief Council. Became a Stockbroker. Died in Somerset in 1983. *Picture references:111, 116, 126 and 137.*

1915.1 – 1916.4 Metophis, Georges (1906-not known)

Georges Metophis was born in Belgium, the son of Victor Metophis a Lieutenant in the Belgian Army. His father came to Poole Hospital in 1915 badly wounded. Georges entered the school free until September 1915, after which his father paid *'10 shillings a week for his keep'*. In 1916 his father was transferred to a post in France and his mother and son left for Le Havre. *Picture reference: 109*

1915.5 – 1916.7 Dixey, Maurice Boxwell Duncan (1903-1969)

Maurice Dixey was born in Quetta, the son of the Reverend Albert Duncan Dixey. His parents lived in Poole. Parents lived at *Ravenhurst* in Parkstone Road, Poole. Spent one year and two months at *Dane Court* as a Day Boy. Later attended Ely School. Became a Doctor. Worked in the Gold Coast from 1929 to 1931 where he wrote a report on Leprosy. *Sunrise* reported in 1936 that he was *'practicing as a doctor at Moreton Hampstead'*. Later practiced in Newton Abbott. Died in Cambridgeshire. *Picture references: 111.*

School Year 1915-1916

1915.9 – 1919.3 Fordham, (John) Hampden (1905-1967)

John Hampden Fordham (known as 'Bim') was born in Kennington, the son of Edward Wilfrid Fordham, a Barrister. His parents lived in Hampstead. Spent 3½ years at *Dane Court* as a Boarder. Later attended the Royal Naval College at Dartmouth, entering the Navy in 1920. Became a Commander in the Royal Navy. Appointed as a Principal Officer in the London Fire Brigade in 1933 and commanded the Southern Division of the brigade on the outbreak of war. Second in command of the London Fire Brigade during the Second World War. His obituary records that he *'had a great reputation as an energetic and fearless leader during the air raids in London'*. After the war he became Chief Fire Officer of Kent. Awarded the CBE. Several of his reminiscences of *Dane Court* are included in this book. Died in Hertfordshire in 1967. Further details of his life and career are included in *The Times* obituary dated 3 October 1967. *Picture references: 116, 117, 126, 133, 137 and 166.*

1915.9 – 1915.12 Logan, Reginald Francis Arthur (1906-1928)

Reginald Logan was born in Woolwich, the son of Lieutenant Colonel Francis Douglas Logan CB CMG DSO. His parents temporarily lived at *Springfield* on Castle Hill in Parkstone. Only stayed 3 months at *Dane Court* as a Day Boy. Was to have stayed two Terms but left after one Term on Doctor's orders owing to chest trouble which developed during the Christmas holidays. Believed to have served in the army in Bengal, India where he died in 1928.

1915.9 – 1922.7 Yeatman, Graham Neville (1908-1992)

Graham Yeatman was born in Poole, the first son of Neville George Yeatman, a Flour Miller with his own business. His parents lived at *Temple Lodge* in Longfleet Road, Longfleet, Poole. Spent 4½ years at *Dane Court* as Day Boy then transferred to Pyrford where he stayed for a further year and three months. Later attended Blundell's School in Tiverton from 1922 to 1926. Became involved in his father's flour milling business from Summer 1926. *Sunrise* reported that in 1930 he was a 2nd Lieutenant in the Dorset Heavy Brigade RA. Promoted to Lieutenant. Later promoted to Major. Appointed as High Sheriff of Dorset in 1978. Died in Wimborne in 1992. *Picture references: 116, 124, 126, 128, 131, 137, 138 and 139.*

1915.9 – 1916.4 Harper, Austin Byers (1908-1992)

Austin Harper was born in King's Norton in Warwickshire, the son of George Byers Harper who was of private means. His parents lived at *The Driffold* in King's Avenue, Parkstone. Only spent 7 months at *Dane Court* as a Day Boy. Left due to his parents leaving Parkstone. Became a Government Official in Jamaica. Police Officer in 1945. Died in Somerset in 1992.

1915.11 – 1923.4 Van Namen, Maxwell Newton (1909-1975)

Maxwell Van Namen was born in Parkstone, the son of Richard Dudgeon Van Namen, a Diamond Merchant. Spent 5½ years at *Dane Court* as a Day Boy and then transferred with the school to Pyrford in April 1921 where he stayed for a further 2 years. His father, who was born in New York in the USA, was killed on 16 January 1919 in France. His mother lived at *Harbour View* in Parkstone Road, Poole. Attended Cranleigh School from 1923 to 1926. By 1926 he was involved in a wood business in Bradford, then at Ogden's in 1927. In 1933 *Sunrise* reported that he was a Lieutenant in the South Staffordshire Regiment. Marine Sales Manager at a Boat Building business in Cowes after the war. *Picture references: 116, 126, 137, 138 and 139.*

1915.11 – 1919.7 Crockett, John Oliver (1905-1924)

John Crockett was born in Croydon, the son of the Reverend Oliver Goodman Crockett. His parents lived at *St Paul's Vicarage* in Poole. Spent nearly 4 years at *Dane Court* as a Day Boy. Attended Monkton Combe School in Bath from 1919 to 1921. Killed in a motorcycle accident near Poole in 1924. *Picture references: 116, 119, 126 and 137.*

1916.1 – 1917.12 Routledge, Bryan Howard (1903-1955)

Bryan Routledge was born in Paddington, the son of Ernest Bird Routledge, a Stockbroker's Clerk. His parents lived in Hampstead. Spent nearly 2 years at *Dane Court* as a Day Boy. Attended the King's School, Canterbury, from 1918 to 1921. Worked for the Indian police from 1922. Later he was the Superintendent of Police in Lakhimpur, Assam. Subsequently, he returned to the UK and took up Market Gardening near Swindon. Died in Newton Abbott in 1955. *Picture references: 116, 119 and 126.*

1916.1 – 1918.3 Douglas, Kenneth Christie (1906-not known)

Kenneth Douglas was born in Scotland, the son of James Douglas, occupation not known. His father had died in 1911. His mother lived in Farnham in Surrey. His fees were paid at a special rate by the Professional Classes War Relief Council. Spent just over 2 years at *Dane Court* as a Boarder. Later he attended Clark's College, Eastbourne, then a veterinary college. Married in Honolulu in 1925. No other career details. Died in Hawaii, year not known. *Picture references: 116, 119 and 126.*

1916.1 – 1921.7 Cope, (Alfred Arthur) David (1908-1976)

David Cope was born in Cheam in Surrey, the son of Alfred John Cope, a Chartered Accountant with his own firm. His parents lived in Ewell, Surrey. Spent 5¼ years at *Dane Court* as a Boarder and transferred to Pyrford for his final Term. Attended Repton School from 1921 to 1926. Became a Paymaster Sub-Lieutenant in the Royal Navy Volunteer Reserve. Later became a Chartered Accountant in his father's business. Died in Kent in 1976. *Picture references: 116, 126, 132, 137, 138 and 139.*

1916.1 – 1918.7 Dawson, Reginald Arthur (1908-1988)

Reginald Dawson was born in Southsea, the son of Commander A M Dawson, a Royal Navy Commander. His parents lived at *Moyola* in Penn Hill Avenue, Parkstone. Spent 2½ years at *Dane Court* as a Day Boy, then attended a school near Hindhead. Further education not known. Became Sales Manager for Hoover. Died in Lincolnshire in 1988. *Picture references: 124, 126 and 127.*

1916.5 – 1921.7 Braithwaite, (Francis) Joseph St. George (1907-1956)

Joseph Braithwaite was born in Clacton-on-Sea, the first son of Francis Joseph Braithwaite, an Army Major. His mother lived at *Newton Lodge* in Newton Crescent, Parkstone. Spent just over 5 years at *Dane Court* as a Day Boy and transferred to Pyrford for his final Term. Attended Bradfield College from 1923 to 1926 and then studied Mechanical Sciences at Cambridge. Joined the RAF in 1929. In 1930 *Sunrise* reported that he had been posted to No 13 Squadron, Netheravon. He was a torpedo specialist for much of his career. Awarded the CBE in 1946. Air Vice-Marshal in 1954. Commander in charge in Singapore. Killed in a solo air accident on the Indonesian island of Palau Batam in 1956. *Picture references: 116, 126, 131, 138, 139 and 158.*

1916.5 – 1921.4 Scutt, (John) Melville (1907-1995)

Melville Scutt was born in Poole, the son of Homer Scutt, a Corn and Seed Merchant. His parents lived at *Seldown Towers*, Seldown Road, Longfleet, Poole. Spent 5 years at *Dane Court* as a Day Boy. Then attended Monkton Combe School in Bath and St. Edmund's Hall, Oxford from 1926 to 1929 followed by Wycliff Hall. Ordained as a Priest in 1931. Rector of Worthing from 1936 to 1938. During World War II he was an RAF Chaplain in North Africa, Italy and France. Mentioned in Despatches. Vicar of Christ Church Worthing from 1945 to 1949. Rector of Edgware from 1949 to 1960. Vicar of Woodford Wells in Woodford Green, Essex from 1960. Wrote a book called *Melville's Memoirs - I Saw, I Conquered* which includes reminiscences of *Dane Court*. Died in Biggleswade in 1995. *Picture references: 116, 119, 126, 128, 138 and 139.*

1916.5 – 1923.7 Selous, Edric Medley (1909-1945)

Edric Selous was born in New Milton, the son of Dr Cuthbert Fennesey Selous, a Retired Physician and Surgeon. His parents lived at *Munster Lodge* in Munster Road, Parkstone. Spent just over 5 years at *Dane Court* as a Day Boy and transferred to Pyrford for a further 2 years. Then attended Pembridge Hall School. Later he worked in Sarawak as Secretary for Chinese Affairs in the Sarawak Civil Service. In 1945 he died while interned by the Japanese in Sarawak. *Picture references: 116, 118, 131, 137, 138 and 139.*

1916.5 – 1920.4 Fletcher, Richard (1906-not known)

Richard Fletcher was born in New Sarum in Wiltshire, the second son of Wilfrid Fletcher, a Chartered Accountant with his own firm. His parents lived in Salisbury. Spent 4 years at *Dane Court* as a Boarder. Later attended the Rossall School in Fleetwood from 1920 to 1924, then Pembroke College, Oxford from 1925 to 1929. Became a Coffee Planter in Kenya, according to *Sunrise* in 1947. Then joined the civil service. *Picture references: 116, 119, 122, 126, 128, 130, 137 and 138.*

1916.6 – 1921.4 Hearder, Robin Dixon (1909-not known)

Robin Hearder was born in Australia, the son of Captain Dixon Hearder of the Australian Imperial Force, later Major Hearder. His parents lived in London. Spent around 5 years at *Dane Court* as a Boarder. Attended King's School Canterbury in 1923-1927. Returned to Australia in 1927 attending the Royal Military College in Dentroon. Entered the Army. In 1932 returned to England and joined the Tank Corps at Wool. In 1934 transferred to India. By 1949 he had taken up an Army appointment in Singapore, having been made Lieutenant Colonel in 1944. *Picture references: 116, 121, 122, 124, 126, 138 and 139.*

School Year 1916-1917

1916.9 – 1918.4 Sitwell, Isla William Hurt (1909-1975)

Isla Sitwell was born in Bengal, the son of Sidney Ashley Hurt Sitwell who worked for the Bank of Bengal in Rangoon. His parents still lived in Rangoon. He lived with a relative in Parkstone. Spent just over 18 months at *Dane Court* as Day Boy. Later attended Seaford School. Became a Merchant in India and then in Japan. Died in Dorset in 1975.

1916.9 – 1919.12 Phillips, John Henry Lawrence (1910-1985)

John Phillips was born in Plumstead in Kent, the son of the Reverend Henry Lawrence Phillips. His parents lived at a rectory in Poole. Spent 3¼ years at *Dane Court* as a Day Boy. Later attended Weymouth College, then Trinity Hall, Cambridge. He was at Ridley Hall Theological College from 1932 to 1934. Ordained as a Priest in 1934, becoming a curate in Yorkshire. He joined the Royal Naval Volunteer Reserve as Chaplain during World War II later becoming Director of Service Ordination Candidates. Archdeacon of Nottingham from 1949 to 1960. Bishop of Portsmouth from 1960 to 1975. Member of the House of Lords from 1967. Died in Ipswich in 1985. Further details of his life and career are included in *The Times* obituary dated 16 November 1985. *Picture references: 126, 137, 138 and 163.*

1916.9 – 1917.7 Mairis, Henry Shuckburgh (1910-1993)

Henry Mairis was born in Gormeldon in Wiltshire, the son of Edward Shuckburgh Mairis a Major in the Royal Marines. His mother lived in London. Spent a year at *Dane Court* as a Boarder. Left to go his brother's school in Ramsgate. In the Cheshire Regiment in World War II. Died in Middlesex in 1993. *Picture reference: 126.*

1916.9 – 1916.12 Kite, Charles Macadam Bagehot (1908-1989)

Charles Kite was born in Taunton, the first son of Edward Bagehot Kite, a Solicitor. His mother lived at *Wayside* in Churchfield Road, Parkstone. His younger brother joined a month later. Only spent a term at *Dane Court* as a Day Boy. Left the school when his mother moved from Parkstone. His mother died in 1917. Became a Solicitor in his father's practice in Taunton. Died in Taunton in 1989.

1916.9 – 1919.4 Browne-Poole, Edward Gerald (1906-not known)

Edward Browne-Poole was born in Southsea. His father's name and occupation are not known. His mother lived in Blackheath. Spent 2½ years at *Dane Court* as a Boarder. Later attended a college in Reading. In December 1936, *Sunrise* gave his address as Surrey Car Sales, High Road, Byfleet, Surrey. By 1950, *Sunrise* reported that he was living in Constantia, South Africa and by 1954 he was a Farmer in South Africa. *Picture references: 126, 131 and 137.*

1916.9 – 1922.4 Christie, Donald Drayton (1908-2001)

Donald Christie was born in London, the son of Harold Christie, a Civil Engineer. His parents lived in Epsom in Surrey. Spent 4½ years at *Dane Court* and a year in Pyrford. Attended St. Paul's School and Rendcomb College. Became an Assistant Master at Hailey School, Bournemouth. By 1929 he had become a Monk, known as Benedict Christie at Farnborough Monastery, but was later released from his vows. In December 1932, *Sunrise* reported that he was a *'Schoolmaster in Hove and is about to publish his first book While the World Revolves'*. In April 1933, *Sunrise* reported that he had *'taken up residence at old Dane Court, Parkstone as a Modern Languages Master'*. By November 1934, he was at The Old Ride School in Branksome Park. He wrote a couple of books on French usage and practice and one or two travel books. Also, a children's book based on episodes at *Dane Court* called *Andy Was Eight*. Died in Poole in 2001. *Picture references: 124, 132, 137, 138 and 139.*

1916.9 – 1918.7 Dry, Edward Nelson (1906-1985)

Edward Dry was born in Parkstone, the son of (Ernest Frederick) Kenneth Dry who was of private means. His parents lived at *Coolhurst* on Sandbanks Road in Lilliput, Parkstone, then *Rosemont* in Fernside Road, Parkstone. Spent 2 years at *Dane Court* as a Boarder. Attended Wimborne Grammar School. By 1939 he is recorded as being an Engineer's Bench Hand. Died in Bodmin in Cornwall in 1985. *Picture references: 126 and 137.*

1916.9 – 1924.4 Field-Richards, Peter John (1910-1994)

Peter Field-Richards was born in Highcliffe in Hampshire. His father's name and occupation are not known. His mother lived at *The Five Ways* in Parkstone. Left after three months in December 1916 and re-entered in May 1919 and stayed until April 1924. Spent 2 years and 2 months in total at *Dane Court* and a further 3 years at Pyrford. Attended Sherborne School from 1924 to 1929, then the Royal Military College at Sandhurst in 1930. Became a member of the Royal Aero Club in 1930. In the South Staffordshire Regiment until 1933. An RAF Squadron-Leader in the Second World War. After the war he was Chief Test Pilot at A V Roe & Co. Repair Organisation. *Picture references: 138 and 139.*

1916.10 – 1916.12 Kite, Edward de Cheveley (1910-1997)

Edward Kite was born in Taunton, the second son of Edward Bagehot Kite, a Solicitor. His mother lived at *Wayside* in Churchfield Road, Parkstone. His elder brother had joined a month earlier. Only spent part of a term at *Dane Court* as a Day Boy. Left the school when his mother moved from Parkstone. His mother died in 1917. Became a Lieutenant in the Royal Army Medical Corps in 1940. Died in Eastbourne in 1997.

1917.1 – 1919.7 Salmon, Geoffrey Fitzjohn (1905-1962)

Geoffrey Salmon was born in Hampstead, the first son of Henry Thomas Salmon, a Chartered Accountant. His parents lived in Cricklewood. Spent 2½ years at *Dane Court* as a Boarder. Later attended St. Paul's School. Articled to his father's firm of Chartered Accountants. Qualified as a Chartered Accountant in 1930. *Sunrise* reported in May 1930 that he had been admitted as Partner in the firm of Messrs Salmon, & Barnaschoné, Chartered Accountants. Became Accountant and Auditor for Dane Court Preparatory School in Pyrford. Died in Rickmansworth in 1962. *Picture references: 119, 122 and 137.*

1917.1 – 1917.7 Wills, Phillip Francis James (1905-1990)

Phillip Wills' place of birth and his father's name and occupation are not known. His mother lived at *Hessle* in Bournemouth Road, Parkstone. He joined the school when he was nearly 12. Only spent 6 months at *Dane Court* as a Day Boy. Attended a Bournemouth Secondary School as a Boarder. Had become a Nursery Foreman in Alton in 1939. Died in Hampshire in 1990. *Picture reference: 126.*

1917.1 – 1918.4 Linklater, Robert Hugh (1909-not known)

Robert Linklater was born in Witchampton in Dorset, the son of Hugh Linklater, a Farmer, who was originally from Lerwick in the Shetland Islands. His parents lived at *The Maples* in Broadstone. Spent one year and three months at *Dane Court* as a Day Boy. Later attended Hubbington House School in Fareham, then Fettes College in Edinburgh. In the Dorset Regiment by 1929. In 1933 he was an Army Officer living in India and got married there a year later. Became a Lieutenant-Colonel. *Picture references: 126 and 128.*

1917.1 – 1918.9 Chronander, Carl Robert (1910-2002)

Carl Chronander was born in Westminster, the son of Gunnar Chronander, Director of the Swedish Manual Treatment. He was from Sweden. His mother lived at *Wilmer Nook* in Spencer Road, Parkstone. Spent 18 months at *Dane Court* as a Day Boy. He is believed to have gone to Cambridge University later. Became a member of the Royal Aero Club in 1931. In July 1936, *Sunrise* reported that he was *'working on stresses and strains with Fairey Aviation'*. In December 1936, *Sunrise* further reported that he *'has designed and built with two other people an all-metal low-wing monoplane called the CWA Cygnet'*. In July 1938, *Sunrise* indicated that he *'is now working for General Aircraft Ltd who have taken over the manufacturing rights of his CW Cygnet monoplane'*. Died in Slough in 2002. *Picture references: 126 and 137.*

1917.5 – 1917.11 Lobley, John Oliver Hargreaves (1909-2000)

John Lobley was born in Holford in Somerset, the son of (John) Hodgson Lobley, a Painter best known for his work as an Official War Artist for the Royal Army Medical Corps during the First World War, painting 120 pictures. The family lived at *Westland House* in Poole but also had a London address. Only spent 6 months at *Dane Court* as a Boarder as he had to leave owing to a recurrent medical condition. By 1939 he was acting as a Flying Instructor and is believed to have had a career in Civil Aviation. Died in Poole in 2000. *Picture references: 124 and 126.*

1917.5 – 1919.5 Byers, Jack (1904-not known)

Jack Byers' place of birth is not known. He was the son of Norman R Byers whose occupation is also not known. Removed after five days on doctor's orders to have a few months rest, later returned. Spent a little less than 2 years at *Dane Court* in total, as a Boarder. *Picture reference: 119.*

1917.5 – 1922.7 Saben, Derek Russell (1908-1993)

Derek Saben was born in Accrington in Lancashire, the son of the Reverend Percival Saben. Spent 4 years at *Dane Court* as a Boarder, then transferred to Pyrford for a further year and three months. Later attended St. Edmund's School in Canterbury, then London University. By 1939 he had become an Electrical Engineer involved in radio and television development in Coventry. Later in 1939 he was a 2nd Lieutenant Royal Corps of Signals. Wrote two books: *The Saben, Saban, Saborne Family of Herts and Essex* (1969) and *The Saben family of Staffordshire* (1971). Died in Coventry in 1993.

School Year 1917-1918

1917.9 – 1920.12 Burbury, Thomas Evelyn Thornley (1907-1973)

Thomas Burbury was born in Wakefield, the son of Henry Herbert Thornley Burbury, a Linen Manufacturer. His parents continued to live in Wakefield. Spent 3¼ years at *Dane Court* as a Boarder. Later attended Oundle School in Northamptonshire. Entered his father's textile manufacturing business. Between 1929 and at least 1945 he was mainly in Canada and appears to have been a Farmer in Lunenberg, Nova Scotia, where his father-in-law lived. Around 1958-9 he was ordained as a Priest. Died in Yorkshire in 1973. *Picture references: 137 and 138.*

1917.9 – 1925.7 Pooley, (Henry) Peter Krohn (1912-1996)

Peter Pooley was born at *Dane Court*, the son of Hugh Francis Pooley, the Headmaster. Lived at *Dane Court* for 9 years, attending the school for 3½ years before continuing at Pyrford for a further 4¼ years. Attended Gresham's School in Holt then University College, Oxford as a Graves Scholar (Cecil Graves was Head of the BBC Empire Service and later a joint Director-General of the BBC). Worked for the BBC between 1939 and 1947, being the Founder and first Editor of the BBC's Radio Newsreel. He was also an Empire Announcer. Associate Producer with the Crown Film Unit 1947 to 1951. Joined NATO's London office in 1951, moving to Paris in 1951. Assistant Director of the NATO Information Service until 1967 in Paris, then in Brussels. Awarded an OBE 1977. Retired in 1977 to Fontainebleau south-east of Paris. Further details of his life and career are included in obituaries in *The Times* dated 5 March 1996, *The Independent* dated 8 February 1996 and *The Daily Telegraph* dated 20 February 1996. *Picture references: 86, 95, 107, 111, 116, 126, 137, 138 and 139.*

1917.9 – 1922.7 Pritchard, Charles Arthur (1908-not known)

Charles Pritchard was born in Manildra in New South Wales, Australia, the son of Hope Pritchard, whose occupation is not known. His parents had addresses in Australia and in London. Spent 3½ years at *Dane Court* as a Boarder and then transferred to Pyrford where he spent a further year and three months. Went into business in 1925. Left for Australia in 1928. Then returned to the UK. Became a member of the Royal Aero Club obtaining his licence in 1935. In the 600 Squadron Auxiliary Air Force 1936 and called to full-time service in 1939. As Acting Flight Lieutenant, he was involved in several bombing missions during 1940 and 1941. Shot down in his Blenheim on 10 May 1940 during an attack on a Rotterdam airfield. He managed to evade capture and returned to England. Awarded the DFC in June 1941. Wing Commander at Cranfield September 1941. Released from RAF 1945 as Wing Commander. In the 1950/51 edition of *Sunrise* he was reported as *'now living in Southern Rhodesia'*. By 1959 he was resident in South Africa and recorded as a Director of the Banking Co of Sydney. Believed to have remained in South Africa. *Picture references: 121,122, 128, 132, 137, 138 and 139.*

1917.9 – 1919.12 Strange, John Clement (1911-1989)

John Strange was born in Christchurch, the son of the Reverend C A Strange. His parents lived at 96 Alexandra Road in Upper Parkstone when he joined. Left in April 1918 as his parents were leaving Parkstone. Re-entered for one term in Sept 1919, so in total spent about a year at *Dane Court* as a Day Boy. Became a Tea Planter in India from age 18 in 1929 until at least 1953. Died in Sussex in 1989.

1917.11 – 1919.12 Lawton, Patrick Herbert (1911-2000)

Patrick Lawton was born in Delhi. His father's name and occupation are not known. His mother lived at *Fairoaks* in Parkstone. Spent 2 years at *Dane Court* as a Day Boy. By 1939 he was working in the telephone industry. Died in Worthing in 2000.

1917.11 – 1922.7 Wiggins, Henry Desmond (1908-1988)

Henry Wiggins was born in Mansfield in Nottinghamshire, the son of Robert Henry Wiggins, a Solicitor. His parents lived at *Inglenook*, 7 Chester Road, Branksome Park as well as an address in Mansfield. Spent 3½ years at *Dane Court* as a Day Boy and a further a year at Pyrford. Later attended Bembridge School on the Isle of Wight. By 1939 he was working as an Automobile Engineer. Died in Essex in 1988. *Picture references: 137 and 139.*

1918.1 – 1924.7 Braithwaite, Michael Robert (1910-1974)

Michael Braithwaite was born in Grimsargh in Lancashire, the second son of Francis Joseph Braithwaite, an Army Major. His parents lived in Parkstone. His elder brother had started at the school two years before. Spent 2½ years at *Dane Court* initially as a Day Boy. He left in April 1918 and returned in September 1918 as a Boarder. He transferred to Pyrford in April 1921 where he spent a further 3¼ years. Attended Bradfield College from 1924 to 1928. By 1931 he was in the Norfolk Regiment (9th Foot). He was a prisoner of war in Malaya from 1942 to 1945 when a Major. Mentioned in Despatches. Became Lieutenant-Colonel in 1953. Died in Norfolk in 1974. *Picture references: 138 and 139.*

1918.1 – 1920.7 Philps, (Alan) Seymour (1906-1956)

Seymour Philps was born in Potters Bar, the son of Francis John Philps, the Editor of the *Financial Times*. His fees were paid by the Professional Classes War Relief Council. His parents lived in Radlett. Spent 2½ years at *Dane Court* as a Boarder. Attended Aldenham from 1920 to 1922. Received his medical training at St. Bartholomew's Hospital. Became a FRCS 1931. He was an Ophthalmic Surgeon at Victoria Hospital for Children, Chelsea and the Miller General Hospital, Greenwich in 1932. Then Chief Assistant in the eye department of St. Bartholomew's in 1934. He was Assistant Surgeon at Moorfields in 1938 and a Full Surgeon in 1940. In the Royal Army Medical Corps during World War II, he was involved in the invasion of Normandy in 1944. Assistant Ophthalmic Surgeon then Full Surgeon in 1948 at St Bartholomew's Hospital as well as acting as Consulting Surgeon at Mid-Herts Hospital Group. Wrote a book called *Ophthalmic Operations* illustrated with his own drawings and photographs. Died in Hampstead in 1956. Further details of his life and work are included in *The Times* obituary dated 30 April 1956. *Picture references: 128, 129, 137, 138 and 139.*

1918.1 – 1920.7 Levey, Sydney Henry Wilfred (1907-1986)

Sydney Levey was born in London, the first son of Joseph Henry Levey, a Lieutenant-Colonel in the Army. His parents continued to live in London. Spent 2½ years at *Dane Court* as a Boarder. Later attended Westminster School. Taught in a preparatory school as an Assistant Master in 1926. Went to Canada aged 21 in 1928 with the intention of going into farming. He had become an Insurance Underwriter in Canada by 1931. By 1934 he had returned to England and settled in Oakleigh Park near Barnet. Later moved to Port Elizabeth in South Africa where he was to remain as an Insurance Underwriter. He also became a cricket commentator and pundit often heard on the South African Broadcasting Corporation. Wrote two books: *The Fires Are Burning Low* (unpublished) with reminiscences of *Dane Court* and a history of the cricket club in Port Elizabeth. Several of his reminiscences are included in this book. Died in South Africa in 1986. *Picture references: 137, 138, 139, 140, 167 and 170.*

1918.1 – 1923.12 Levey, Maurice Emmanuel (1910-1979)

Maurice Levey was born in London, the son of Joseph Henry Levey, a Lieutenant-Colonel in the Army. His parents continued to live in London. Spent 3¼ years at *Dane Court,* then transferred to Pyford where he stayed for a further 3 years and 8 months. Later attended Westminster School. Died in London in 1979. *Picture references: 132, 138 and 139.*

1918.1 – 1920.7 Chesshire, George Pountney Peregrine (1910-1980)

George Chesshire was born in Parkstone, the second son of Captain G H Chesshire of the Mercantile Marine Service. His parents lived at *Cotgrove* in Church Road East in Parkstone. Spent 2½ years at *Dane Court* as a Day Boy. His elder brother had attended the school some years earlier. His parents left Parkstone. Later attended Gorse Cliff School in Boscombe. Attested for the Royal Artillery in 1938. After the war became a Solicitor in Southampton. Died in Southampton in 1980. *Picture references: 137, 138 and 139.*

1918.1 – 1919.12 Chesshire, John Barnabas (1911-1993)

John Chesshire was born in Parkstone, the third son of Captain G H Chesshire of the Mercantile Marine Service. His parents lived at *Cotgrove* in Church Road East in Parkstone. Spent 2 years at *Dane Court* as a Day Boy. Died in Bournemouth in 1993. *Picture reference: 138.*

1918.5 – 1925.12 Van Namen, Claude Dudgeon (1912-1991)

Claude Van Namen was born in Parkstone, the second son of Richard Dudgeon Van Namen, a Diamond Merchant. Spent 3 years at *Dane Court* as a Day Boy, then transferred with the school to Pyrford where he spent a further 4 years and 8 months. His father, who was born in New York, was killed on 16 January 1919 in France. His mother lived at *Harbour View* in Parkstone Road, Poole. Attended Harrow from 1926 to 1931. The December 1932 edition of *Sunrise* reported that he had *'joined his father's firm of diamond merchants in St James's'*. Then the November 1934 issue stated that he was *'working at the Ford factory at Dagenham'*. He was in the Royal Artillery in Second World War as a Lieutenant, Captain then Major. Wounded and captured in Greece. Later worked for Huntley & Palmer as an Export Manager. Awarded the OBE. Died in Berkshire in 1991. *Picture references: 139.*

1918.5 – 1925.4 Yeatman, Maurice (1911-1986)

Maurice Yeatman was born in Poole, the second son of Neville George Yeatman, a Flour Miller with his own business. His parents lived at *Temple Lodge* in Longfleet Road, Longfleet, Poole. Spent 3 years at *Dane Court* as Day Boy then transferred to Pyrford where he stayed for a further 4 years. Attended Blundell's School in Tiverton from 1925 to 1929. The July 1936 edition of Sunrise reported that he was *'practicing as a Solicitor in Poole'*. Died in Parkstone in 1986. *Picture references: 137, 138 and 139.*

1918.5 – 1926.4 Philby, Frank Montague (1912-1964)

Frank Philby was born in Bombay, the son of Ralph Montague Philby, a Lieutenant-Commander in the Royal Navy. His parents lived at *Cullissa* in Parkstone. Spent 3 years at *Dane Court* as a Day Boy, then a further 5 years at Pyrford. Went to Pangbourne Nautical College in 1926. Joined the Royal Navy 1930. The September 1931 edition of *Sunrise* stated that he had been *'promoted to Midshipman in the Royal Navy'*. The July 1936 edition stated that he had *'assisted in conveying the Emperor of Abyssinia from his country'*. Later became a Lieutenant-Commander and was awarded the DSC. Died in Hampshire in 1964. *Picture references: 137, 138 and 139.*

1918.5 – 1921.7 Jones, (John) Russell (1910-1987)

Russell Jones was born in Bournemouth, the son John Henry Jones, a Building Contractor with his own business. His parents lived at *Hadleigh* in Alumhurst Road in Bournemouth. Spent 3 years at *Dane Court* as a Day Boy. Later attended Gorse Hill School in Boscombe. Died in Sussex in 1987. *Picture references: 137 and 138.*

1918.5 – 1921.4 West, John Andrews Stallon (1911-1996)

John West was born in Poole, the son of Percy West, a Draper's Manager. His parents lived at 59/61 High Street, Poole. Spent 3 years at *Dane Court* as a Day Boy. Left when the school moved to Pyrford. By 1939 he was a Bank Clerk in Southampton. Died in Poole in 1996. *Picture references 137, 138 and 139.*

1918.5 – 1919.7 Gerfalk, Ole Bernth (1906-not known)

Ole Gerfalk was born in Denmark, the son of Axel Gerfalk, a London Editor for Scandinavian newspapers. His parents lived in London when he was at the school. Spent 14 months at *Dane Court* as a Boarder. Left when his parents returned to Denmark. Later attended the Metropolitan Skollen in Copenhagen. *Picture references: 137.*

1918.5 – 1919.4 Deekers, Jacques (1907-not known)

Jacques Deekers was born in Belgium, the first son of Emile Deekers, occupation unknown. His parents lived at *Easterton* in Sandringham Road, Parkstone. Spent a year at *Dane Court* as a Day Boy. Left when his parents returned to Belgium. *Picture reference: 137.*

1918.5 – 1919.4 Deekers, Christian (1907-not known)

Christian Deekers was born in Belgium, the second son of Emile Deekers, occupation unknown. His parents lived at *Easterton* in Sandringham Road, Parkstone. Spent a year at *Dane Court* as a Day Boy. Left when his parents returned to Belgium. *Picture reference: 137.*

1918.5 – 1919.7 Carter, (William Henry Charles) Philip (1910-1986)

Philip Carter was born in Hendon, the first son of Charles Cyril Carter, an Encaustic Tile Manufacturer. His parents lived *Belle Vue* in Poole. Spent 14 months at *Dane Court* as a Day Boy. Left when his parents were unable to find a home in Parkstone. Later became a Schoolmaster. Died in Hereford & Worcester in 1986. *Picture references: 137 and 138.*

1918.5 – 1919.7 Carter, (John) David Armishall (1913-2004)

David Carter was born in Hendon, the second son of Charles Cyril Carter, an Encaustic Tile Manufacturer. His parents lived at *Belle Vue* in Poole. Spent 14 months at *Dane Court* as a Day Boy. Left when his parents were unable to find a home in Parkstone. Died in Wiltshire in 2004. *Picture references: 137 and 138.*

1918.5 – 1919.4 Braithwaite, John Duncan (1910-1981)

John Braithwaite was born in Hampstead, the son of William John Braithwaite, a Civil Servant with the Inland Revenue. Spent a year at *Dane Court* as a Day Boy. Left when his parents left Parkstone. Later attended a preparatory school in Shropshire. By 1939 he had become a Forest Officer. Died in Gloucestershire in 1981. *Picture reference: 137.*

1918.5 – 1918.12 Penrose, Derek John Wetherston (1910-1983)

Derek Penrose was born in Calcutta, the son of John Ernest Penrose, a Merchant. His parents lived at *The Nook* in Penn Hill Avenue, Parkstone. Only spent seven months at *Dane Court* as a Day Boy. Died in Surrey in 1983. *Picture reference: 137.*

School Year 1918-1919

1918.9 – 1920.4 Clark, Roger Land (1907-1969)

Roger Clark was born in Bournemouth, the son of Hugh Richard Clark, a Commercial Traveller in the gloves trade. Parents lived at *Inglenook* in Parkstone. Spent just over 18 months at *Dane Court* as a Day Boy. Then attended the Bournemouth Collegiate School. By 1939 he was a Retail Confectioner. Died in Suffolk in 1969. *Picture references: 138.*

1918.9 – 1922.7 Salmon, Richard Henry (1908-1982)

Richard Salmon was born in Willesden, the second son of Henry Thomas Salmon, a Chartered Accountant. His parents lived in Great Missenden in Buckinghamshire. Spent 2½ years at *Dane Court* as a Boarder and then transferred to Pyrford for a further 15 months. Later attended St.

Paul's School. Became a Chartered Accountant and later a partner in Truman & Knightley. Died in London in 1982. *Picture reference: 139.*

1918.9 – 1921.4 Lewis, Norman Kingsbury (1910-1982)

Norman Lewis was born in Poole, the son of Harry Lewis, a chemist. His parents continued to live in Poole at 209 High Street. Spent 2½ years at Dane Court as a Day Boy. Left when the school moved to Pyrford. Attended Weymouth College. Attested for the Royal Artillery in 1938. Later ran a chemist's shop in Poole. Died in Bournemouth in 1982. *Picture reference 138.*

1918.9 – 1918.12 Dobson, Kenneth Blair Austin (1907-1981)

Kenneth Dobson was born in Shanghai, the son of the Reverend George Francis Clement Dobson. His parents lived at *Tranent* in Spencer Road, Parkstone. Spent only three months at *Dane Court* as a Day Boy. Left when his parents decided to move back to St Leonards. Later attended Clifton College in Bristol and Oriel College, Oxford. Worked for the Colonial Service in Tanganyika from 1930 to 1957. His daughter, Julia Tugendhat, wrote a book *My Colonial Childhood in Tanganyika* describing her father's work. Died in Kent in 1981.

1918.9 – 1923.4 Le Good, Dennis Ivan (1911-not known)

Dennis Le Good was born in Bristol, the son of William Dennis Le Good, an Insurance Manager. His parents lived at *Flaxholme* in Glenair Avenue, Parkstone. Spent 2½ years at *Dane Court* as a Day Boy and then a further 2 years at Pyrford. By 1939 he was a Clerk in a Public Works Contractor in Enfield. *Picture references: 138 and 139.*

1918.9 – 1921.4 Evans, John Edward (1910-not known)

John Evans's place of birth and father's name and occupation are not known. His parents lived at *Fairhaven* in Clifton Road, Parkstone. Spent 2½ years at Dane Court. Left the school when it moved to Pyrford. *Picture reference: 138.*

1918.9 – 1921.4 Bell, Francis Graham (details not known)

Francis Bell's place of birth is not known. He was the son of Graham Bell, a Mining Engineer. Parents lived at *Newton Lodge*, Newton Road in Parkstone. Spent 2½ years at *Dane Court* as a Day Boy. Left the school when it moved to Pyrford. *Picture reference: 138.*

1918.9 – 1918.12 Dupret, George Henri (1909-not known)

George Dupret was born in Belgium, the first son of M Dupret, occupation not known. He just stayed one term at *Dane Court* as a Day Boy. His parents returned to Brussels in January 1919 at the end of the war.

1918.9 – 1918.12 Dupret, Robert (1910-not known)

Robert Duprest was born in Belgium, the second son of M Dupret, occupation not known.

He just stayed one term at *Dane Court* as a Day Boy. His parents returned to Brussels in January 1919 at the end of the war.

1918.9 – 1918.12 Dupret, Jean (1911-not known)

Jean Dupret was born in Belgium, the third son of M Dupret, occupation not known. He just stayed one term at *Dane Court* as a Day Boy. His parents returned to Brussels in January 1919 at the end of the war.

1919.1 – 1920.12 Egremont, (Alan) Godfrey (1906-1971)

Godfrey Egremont was born in Fordingbridge, first the son of J Godfrey Egremont, a Farmer. Spent nearly 2 years at *Dane Court* as a Day Boy. Later attended Shaftesbury School. Worked on his father's farm by 1939. Died Hampshire in 1971. *Picture reference 138 and 139.*

1919.1 – 1919.7 Crokaert, Pierre Jacques Leopold (1907-2008)

Pierre Crokaert was born in Belgium, the son of M Crokaert, a Diamond Cutting Merchant. He only spent six months at *Dane Court* as a Boarder. He left the school when his parents returned to Belgium. Involved in the diamond industry all his working life, starting out in the family cutting business in Antwerp and subsequently working in London and Africa. A Director of De Beers for many years. Died in South Africa in 2008. *Picture reference: 138.*

1919.1 – not known Pope, Norman William (1911-1997)

Norman Pope's place of birth and name and occupation of father are not known. His mother lived at *Logan* in Hermitage Road, Parkstone. It is not known how long he was at *Dane Court* nor his further education. By 1939, he was a General Motor Mechanic in Dover. Died in Kent in 1997. *Picture reference: 138.*

1919.1 – 1919.7 Tarver, Charles Herbert (1908-1982)

Charles Tarver's place of birth not known. He was the son of Colonel Tarver of the Indian Army. His parents continued to live in India. Spent six months at *Dane Court* as a Boarder. He had become an Officer in the Indian Army by 1938 where he remained until at least 1953. Reached the rank of Brigadier in the Indian Army. Later became Major-General Charles Herbert Tarver CB CBE DSO. Died in Buckinghamshire in 1982. *Picture reference: 138 and 161.*

1919.3 – 1920.4 Hawkins, Raymond Summerfield (1910-1986)

Raymond Hawkins was born in Berkeley in Gloucestershire, the son of Colonel Hawkins who was from Australia. His parents lived at *Blakedene* in Parkstone. Spent a year at *Dane Court* as a Day Boy. Later attended Weymouth College. By 1930 he was in the Royal Engineers. Died in Sussex in 1986. *Picture reference: 138.*

1919.5 – 1920.4 **Flemmich, Peter Max Davy (1911-1973)**

Peter Flemmich was born in Curry Rivel in Somerset, the son of Max Flemmich of private means. Spent a year at *Dane Court* as a Boarder. By 1930 he was trading as a Builder. Died in Bolton in 1973. *Picture reference: 138.*

1919.5 – 1920.12 **Crockett, Hugh (1913-not known)**

Hugh Crockett's place of birth is not known. He was the second son of the Reverend Oliver Goodman Crockett. His parents lived at *St. Paul's Vicarage* in Poole. Spent just over 18 months at *Dane Court.* Emigrated to Canada in 1930 to become a farmer. By 1939 he was an Inspector of Shells in Shrewsbury. *Picture reference: 138.*

1919.5 – 1923.7 **Fletcher, David (1909-1990)**

David Fletcher was born in New Sarum in Wiltshire, the first son of Wilfrid Fletcher, a Chartered Accountant with his own firm. His parents lived in Salisbury. Spent 2 years at *Dane Court* as a Boarder and a further 2 years and 2 months at Pyrford. Attended the Bedales School in Petersfield, the Merton College, Oxford. Attended the Bristol School of Architecture part-time from 1931 to 1935. In 1937 he became an Associate of the Royal Institution of British Architects. He was in the Royal Signals in the Middle East and Italy from 1941 to 1945. Worked as an Architect in London after World War II. Died in Salisbury in 1990. *Picture references: 138.*

1919.5 – 1923.7 **Ship, Dudley Stuart (1910-1974)**

Dudley Ship was born in Weymouth, the son of Charles Henry Ship, a Hotel Proprietor. His parents lived in Bournemouth. Spent 2 years at Dane Court as a Boarder and a further 3 years and 2 months at Pyrford. Later attended Wrekin College. In April 1933, *Sunrise* reported that he was a 2nd Lieutenant in the RASC. *Picture references: 138 and 139.*

1919.6 – 1921.7 **Tolson, Richard Frederick Herman Shlesinger (1909-1992)**

Richard Tolson's place of birth is not known. He was the son of F Tolson, occupation not known. Spent 2 years at *Dane Court* as a Day Boy. Later attended King's School, Taunton. Died in Leicestershire in 1992. *Picture references: 138 and 139.*

School Year 1919-1920

1919.9 – 1920.12 **Thomas, Lewis George Alfred (1907-1987)**

Lewis Thomas was born in Bath. His father's name and occupation not known. Living on own means by 1939. Died in London in 1987. *Picture reference: 139.*

1919.9 – 1920.7 **Hamilton, Benjamin Charles (1910-not known)**

Benjamin Hamilton was born in Sussex, the first son of Commander Claude Hamilton. His father was at the Russell Cotes Nautical School in Parkstone. Spent a year at *Dane Court* as a

Day Boy. Later attended the King's School in Canterbury from 1924 to 1926, then the Nautical College in Pangbourne. Went into the Merchant Navy on the Union Castle Line. *Picture reference: 139.*

1919.9 – 1927.7 Hamilton, Anthony Norris (1913-1991)

Anthony Hamilton was born in South Stoneham in Hampshire, the second son of Commander Claud Hamilton. Spent 18 months at *Dane Court* as a Day Boy, then re-joined the school at Pyrford in September 1924 where he spent a further three years. Attended Kelly College in Tavistock. In July 1936, *Sunrise* reported that he was a Master at Clifton College. By 1939 he was a House Tutor at Clifton College. Became Headmaster of Dorchester Grammar School. Died in Cumbria in 1991. P*icture reference:139.*

1919.9 – 1921.4 Margrie, James David (1910-1967)

James Margrie was born in Parkstone, the son of Thomas William Margrie, a Bank Cashier. His parents lived Burford in Oxfordshire. Spent just over 18 months at *Dane Court* as a Boarder. Left the school when it moved to Pyrford. Became a Bank Official. Obtained a Royal Aero Club Aviator's Certificate in 1939. He was in the Royal Airforce Volunteer Reserve in 1941. Worked as a Hotel Manager in South Africa after the war. In July 1949, *Sunrise* reported that he was *'Manager of the Carlton Hotel in Grahamstown in the Union of South Africa'*. Died in Kent in 1967. *Picture reference: 139.*

1920.1 – 1921.4 May, Peter (dates not known)

Peter May's place of birth and his father's name and occupation are not known. Spent 15 months at *Dane Court* as Day Boy. Later attended Bedford School and London University. Joined the RAF. In October 1931 *Sunrise* reported that he was a Pilot Officer. *Sunrise* later stated that he had gone to the Flying Training School at Digby. Killed in World War II. *Picture reference: 139.*

1920.1 – 1921.2 Swatman, Philip Stenning (1910-2002)

Philip Swatman was born in Bournemouth, the first son of Harry Raigersfeld Swatman, a Bank Manager. Spent 15 months at *Dane Court* as a Day Boy. Later attended Salisbury Choir School. Further education not known. Had become a Solicitor by 1939. *Picture reference: 139.*

1920.1 – 1921.4 Swatman, Michael Raigersfeld (1911-1996)

Michael Swatman was born in Christchurch, the second son of Harry Raigersfeld Swatman, a Bank Manager. Spent 15 months at *Dane Court.* By 1939 he was working as a Bank Clerk. Died in Poole in 1996. *Picture reference: 139.*

1920.1- 1921.4 Swatman Peter Phillimore (1913-1993)

Peter Swatman was born in Christchurch, the third son of Harry Raigersfeld Swatman, a Bank Manager. Spent 15 months at *Dane Court.* Joined Morris Motors Limited as an apprentice in 1932 and then moved to SU Carburettor Co. as a Technical Assistant in 1935. Appointed

Joint Works Manager in 1945 and Works Manager in 1952. Later appointed as a Director of SU Carburettor Co. Died in Gwynedd in 1993. *Picture reference: 139.*

1920.1 – 1921.12 Smith, William Josef Maurice (1908-not known)

William Smith was born in Radlett. His father's name and occupation not known. Spent 15 months at *Dane Court* as a Boarder and a further 9 months at Pyrford. Attended Aldenham in 1922. Emigrated to South Africa in 1925. *Picture reference: 139.*

1920.1 – 1921.4 Bell, Neil Graham (1913-not known)

Neil Bell's place of birth not known. His father was Graham Bell, a Mining Engineer. Spent 15 months at *Dane Court* as a Day Boy. He was however absent for the summer term of 1920. Left the school when it moved to Pyrford. Emigrated to South Africa with his family.

1920.5 – 1924.12 Budge, Vincent Alexander Prideaux (1913-1981)

Vincent Budge was born in Plymouth, the son of Hubert Lionel Budge. His father had been killed at the Somme in July 1916. Spent a year at *Dane Court* as a Day Boy and then 3 years and 8 months at Pyrford. His mother lived at *Bay View* in Mount Road, Parkstone. Later attended a school in Brighton. Became a Royal Aero Club Member in 1934. Later he was a Brigadier in the Grenadier Guards. Awarded the CBE and MVO. Died in London in 1981.

1920.5 – 1920.12 Barton, Guy Trayton (1908-1977)

Guy Barton was born in Ningpo in China, the son of the Reverend H Barton. His parents lived in Parkstone. Spent 7 months at *Dane Court* as a Day Boy. Later attended Weymouth College. Matriculated at Selwyn College, Cambridge in 1927. Became a Civil Servant in Nigeria during the 1930s. In the 1950s he was Assistant Colonial Secretary in Barbados and Chief Colonial Secretary from 1958 to 1961. Awarded CMG and OBE. Wrote a book *The Prehistory of Barbados* in 1953. Died in Essex in 1977. *Picture reference: 139.*

1920.5 – 1922.7 Gervis, Geoffrey Rawlinson (1907-1969)

Geoffrey Gervis was born in Hampstead, the son of Dr Arthur Gervis, a Surgeon and Physician. His parents lived in Hampstead. Spent a year at *Dane Court* as a Boarder, then a further 15 months at Pyrford. Worked for Express Dairy in 1925. Area Manager in 1939 living in Enfield. Died in Petersfield in 1969. *Picture reference: 139.*

1920.5 – 1920.12 Egremont, Humphrey (1909-1971)

Humphrey Egremont was born in Rockbourne in Hampshire, the second son of J Godfrey Egremont, a Farmer. His parents lived at Braemore in Hampshire. Spent 7 months at *Dane Court* as a Boarder. Later attended Sherborne School. By 1939 he was a Bank Clerk in Andover. Died in Andover in 1971. *Picture reference: 139.*

1920.5 – 1927.12 Pooley, Ole Krohn (1914-2015)

Ole Pooley was born at *Dane Court*, the son of Hugh Francis Pooley, the Headmaster. Lived at *Dane Court* for 7 years, the last year as a pupil. Attended the school at Pyrford for a further 6 years and 8 months. Later attended Gresham's School from 1928 to 1931. Known as 'Olaf' quite early on. He was at the Architectural Association in 1931. Studied painting at the Chelsea School of Art and the Academie Colarossi in Paris in 1934. In December 1936, *Sunrise* reported that he was *'working in the Art Department of Herbert Wilcox Films at Pine Wood Studios, Iver'*. After the Second World War he had a wide-ranging career as an Actor on the stage, on TV and in films in numerous supporting roles. Also, a Script Writer. He returned to painting in later life. Emigrated to Santa Monica in California in 1986, where he remained. *Picture references: 107, 111, 116, 126, 138 and 139.*

1920.5 – 1924.7 Field-Richards, Michael Jackson (1912-1990)

Michael Field-Richards was born in Southbourne. His father's name and occupation are not known. His elder brother Peter had started at the school a few years earlier. Spent a year at *Dane Court* as a Boarder, then transferred to Pyrford where he stayed a further 3¼ years. Later attended Sherborne School from 1926 to 1929. Received his technical training as a Mechanical Engineer with J I Thorneycroft Co. Ltd in Basingstoke starting in 1929. Later became a Lieutenant in the Royal Army Ordnance Corps in Cyrenaica then he was a Lieutenant in the Royal Electrical and Mechanical Engineers. Later promoted to Major. Died in Sussex in 1990. *Picture references: 139.*

1920.5 – 1921.4 Evans, David (dates not known)

David Evans' place of birth and his father's name and occupation are not known. His mother lived at *Tranmere* in Birchwood Road, Parkstone. Spent a year at *Dane Court* as a Day Boy. *Picture reference: 139.*

School Year 1920-1921

1920.9 – 1921.4 Lawton, Graeme Monk (1913-1955)

Graeme Lawton was born in Longfleet, Poole, the son of Harold Lawton, a Civil Engineer on the Indian railways. His parents had a house in Parkstone. Spent 7 months at *Dane Court* at a Day Boy. Become a Solicitor in the Local Government Service by 1939. He was a 2nd Lieutenant in the Royal Regiment Artillery of the Indian Army in 1942. Mentioned in Dispatches in 1946 while serving in Burma. He then worked for the Colonial Legal Service as the Registrar of the High Court in Northern Rhodesia. In 1952, he became Registrar of the High Court in Kenya. Died in Parkstone in 1955.

1920.9 – 1925.7 Rosenberg, David John (1911-1993)

David Rosenberg was born in London, the son of August Rosenberg, occupation not known. His parents continued to live in London. Spent 7 months at *Dane Court* as a Boarder, then transferred to Pyrford where he stayed a further 4 years and 3 months. Later attended Oundle

School in Northamptonshire. Became an Accountant. Emigrated to Trinidad in 1946. Died in London in 1993.

1920.9 – 1920.11 De Woolfson, Robert St. John Green (1907-1976)

Robert De Woolfson was born in Eton, the son of Dr Green de Woolfson. His parents lived at *Clovelly* in Parkstone Road in Poole. Only spent a couple of months at *Dane Court* as a Day Boy.

1920.9 – 1921.4 Cowie, (Kenneth) David (1908-1975)

David Cowie was born in Warwick, the first son of Kenneth Vere Cowie, a Bank Clerk. Spent 7 months at *Dane Court* as a Day Boy. Parents lived at *Milton Lodge* in Parkstone. Later went to Wadham College, Oxford. Worked in Rangoon, Burma as a Conservator of Forests from 1930 to 1935. Died in Bishop Stortford in 1975.

1920.9 – 1921.4 Cowie, Samuel Richard (1912-1979)

Samuel Cowie's place of birth is not known. The second son of Kenneth Vere Cowie, a Bank Clerk. Spent 7 months at *Dane Court* as a Day Boy. Died in Kent in 1979.

1920.9 – 1921.4 Pooley, Richard Warner (1912-2003)

Richard Pooley was born in Ecclesall Bierlow in Yorkshire, the first son of Dr G H Pooley, a Surgeon. His parents lived in Sheffield. Spent 7 months at *Dane Court* as a Boarder. Left the school when it moved to Pyrford. Later attended Charterhouse School, then Pembroke College, Cambridge. Became a Micro-Paleontologist with Royal Dutch Shell Group between 1934 and 1959 working in Sarawak, Dutch New Guinea, Cairo, Maracaibo and Caracas in Venezuela. Died in Oxfordshire in 2003.

1920.9 – 1921.4 Pooley, Thomas Brooke (1914-1974)

Thomas Pooley was born in Ecclesall Bierlow in Yorkshire, the second son of Dr G H Pooley, a Surgeon. His parents lived in Sheffield. His younger brother joined at the same time. Spent 7 months at *Dane Court* as a Boarder. Later attended Charterhouse School, then Pembroke College Oxford. Had become a Bank Clerk with Barclays in London by 1939. He was a Corporal in the Royal Army Ordnance Corps in 1941, later promoted to the ranks of Major. After the war he worked for Barclays Bank in Tanzania in 1947, Mauritius in 1951, Tanganyika in 1956-63 and Dar-es-Salaam in 1964. Died in Spain in 1974.

1920.11 – 1927.7 MacLaurin, Robert Hall (1913-not known)

Robert MacLaurin's place of birth and father's name and occupation are not known. His mother lived at *Boxmoor* on Longfleet Road, Poole. Spent 6 months at *Dane Court* as a Day Boy, then returned to the school as a Boarder in Pyrford in May 1925, staying for a further 2¼ years. Later attended St Edwards School in Oxford. Emigrated to Kenya working as a Civil Engineer in the 1950s, later in South Africa. The 1952/53 edition of *Sunrise* reported that he was a *'Civil Engineer, Nairobi, Kenya'*.

1920.11 – 1928.7 MacLaurin, Stuart Glare (1915-1979)

Stuart MacLaurin's place of birth and father's name and occupation are not known. His mother lived at *Boxmoor* on Longfleet Road, Poole. His elder brother joined at the same time. Spent 6 months at *Dane Court* as a Day Boy, then returned to the school as a Boarder in Pyrford in May 1925, staying for a further 3 years and 3 months. Had become a Farmer in Rhodesia by 1935. He was in the Somerset Light Infantry in 1940. The 1952/53 edition of *Sunrise* reported that he was farming in Karoi, Southern Rhodesia. Died in 1979.

1921.1 – 1921.4 Oakley, Edwin Herbert (1915-not known)

Edwin Oakley was born in Veracruz in Mexico, the son of E T Oakley, a Merchant. Only spent 3 months at *Dane Court* as a Boarder. Went back to Veracruz in Mexico with his parents in 1921. Travelled to the UK in 1935 when working in insurance. By 1939 he was a working as Coal Lorry Driver in Brentford.

1921.1 – 1921.4 Evans, Frederick (1911-not known)

Frederick Evans's place of birth and his father's name and occupation are not known. His parents lived at *Pirbright* in North Road, Parkstone. Only attended *Dane Court* as a Day Boy for 3 months. Left the school when it moved to Pyrford.

BIBLIOGRAPHY

Main sources

The main sources include the following in the possession of the Pooley family:

- School Registers maintained by the Reverend Graham from 1867 to 1911;
- School Registers maintained by Hugh Francis Pooley from 1911 to 1921;
- photograph albums relating to Dane Court Preparatory School relating to 1909 to 1920;
- Annual Reports relating to the Dane Court Preparatory School from 1911 to 1915;
- copies of the school magazine *Sunrise* from 1930 to 1981 where available.

Other key sources are drawings, photographs and other information in the possession of the Phipps family.

In addition to the above, other original sources are referred to in the notes to each chapter. The Author has used information from national and local newspapers and certain details from some of the books listed below, as referred to in the notes to each chapter, as well as genealogical information as required.

The information in the Supplement is drawn from the Dane Court Preparatory School Registers; updates on old boys in the school magazine, *Sunrise*; relevant public school registers, where published; books written by or about the boys; obituaries in national or local newspapers; censuses and other genealogical records; military and naval websites and other relevant information online.

Book referred to and of general interest:

Agnew's. *Turner Watercolours: A Loan Exhibition to mark the occasion of Evelyn Joll's retirement from Agnew's* at Easter 1994. London, 1994. Agnew's.

Ball Clay Heritage Society. *The Ball Clays of Devon and Dorset.* Newton Abbott, 2003. Cornish Hillside Publications.

Brannon, Philip. *Illustrated Historical & Picturesque Guide to the Town & Harbour of Poole* by Philip Brannon. 1855, Bournemouth. R Sydenham

Brown, Kenneth D. *The Trade Union Tariff Reform Association 1904-1913*, published in *The Journal of British Studies Volume IX Number 1.* 1969, Hartford. Trinity College, Hartford, Connectiicut

Carter, Herbert S. *I Call to Mind. Poole,* 1949. J. Looker Ltd.

Cannon, Richard. *Historical Record of The Sixty-Seventh or The South Hampshire Regiment.* Parker, Furnivall & Parker, London. 1849

Cathery, Frank. *Parkstone Illustrated with Historical Sketch by W K Gill, Esq.* Fred Cathery, Parkstone. c1910

Corbett, Charles – *A History of My Family*. Privately published. Includes information on John Dracapoli

Davies, W.J.K. *Pike Bros. Fayle & Co. Ltd Furzebrook.* 1957, Narrow-Gauge Railway Society

Densham, W and Ogle, J. *The Story of the Congregational Churches of Dorset.* 1899, Bournemouth. W. Mate & Sons Limited

Edgington, M.A. *Bournemouth and the First World War: The Evergreen Valley 1914-1919.* 1985, Bournemouth. Bournemouth Local Studies Publications

Everett, Katherine. *Bricks and Flowers: An Anglo-Irish Memoir.* First published in 1949. Reissued 2018, Cork. Somerville Press

Graham, Mary. *The Royal National Hospital: The Story of Bournemouth's Sanatorium.* Bournemouth, 1992. Bournemouth Local Studies' Publications.

Falls, Cyril. *The Life of a Regiment Volume IV: The Gordon Highlanders in the First World War 1914-1919.* 1958, Aberdeen. Aberdeen University Press

Foot, Samantha. *The Alexandra Hospital for Children with Hip Disease.* London, 2011. Institute of Historical Research, University of London. Online only.

Haggard, H. Rider. *On Going Back* published in Volume LXI in the November 1887 issue of *Longman's Magazine.* 1887, London. Longmans, Green & Co.

Haggard, Lilias Rider. *The Cloak That I Left: A Biography of the Author Henry Rider Haggard K.B.E.* 1951, London. Hodder and Stoughton

Higgins, D.S. *Rider Haggard: The Great Storyteller.* 1981, London. Cassell

Holroyd, Michael. *Augustus John A Biography.* 1974, London. Heinemann Ltd.

John, Rebecca. *Caspar John.* 1987, London. Collins

John, Romilly. *The Seventh Child.* London, 1932. Heinemann

Kidner, R.W. *The Railways of Purbeck (Third Edition).* Usk in Mon, 2000. Oakwood Press

Legg, Chris. *The Furzebrook Railway of Pike Brothers' Dorset Clay Works.* 2016, Truro. Twelveheads Press.

Legg, Rodney. *Dorset in the First World War.* 2012, Somerset. Dorset Books

Mitchell, Sally. *Dinah Mulock Craik.* 1983, Boston. Twayne Publishers.

McPherson, Naomi. *Chapter 6: Wanted: Young Man Must Like Adventure – Ian MacCallum Mack, Patrol Officer in In Colonial New Guinea: Anthropological Perspectives.* 2001, Pittsburgh. University of Pittsburgh Press

Moffat, Ian C.D. *The Allied Intervention in Russia, 1918-1920: The Diplomacy of Chaos.* 2015, Basingstoke. Palgrave Macmillan

Morris, Iris. *Looking Back: A Social History of the Village of Ashley Cross in Parkstone, Poole, Dorsetshire from 1833 to the Present Day.* 1996, Poole. Old Thyme Publishing

Mumm, Susan. *Stolen Daughters, Virgin Mothers: Anglican Sisterhoods in Victorian Britain*. 1999, London. Leicester University Press

Murray, Peter. *Home from the Hill: Three Gentlemen Adventurers*. 1994, Victoria, Canada. Horsdal & Schubart. Part of the book is about Warburton Pike, the explorer

O' Sullivan, Norah. *The Clay Boats and Clay Trade*. 1987, Poole. Poole Maritime Trust.

Parish, William Okes. *Records of the Church of Saint Peter, Parkstone*. 1926, Parkstone. Ralph & Brown

Pike Bros Fayle & Co. Ltd. *The Clay Mines of Dorset Worked by Pike Bros. Fayle & Co. Ltd of Wareham 1760-1960*. 1960, Wareham. Harley Publishing Company

Prochaska, Frank. *Philanthropy and the Hospitals of London: The King's Fund, 1897-1900*. 1992, Oxford. Oxford University Press.

Scott, John Melville. *Melville's Memoirs: I saw, I conquered.* Privately published c1986

St. Barnabas Hospital. *St. Barnabas Hospital: A Short History*. Mid-1980s, Saltash. St. Barnabas Hospital

Sturdy, Giles. *A Biography of Major Ambrose Edward Sturdy M.B.E.* 2016, Wareham. Privately published.

Tugendhat, Julia. *My Colonial Childhood in Tanganyika*. 2011. Private published.

Ward, Ted. *Augustus John: Artist & Bohemian – Alderney Manor Poole 1911-1927*. Undated, Poole. Chatsworth Publications. Copy available in Dorset History Centre, Dorchester.

Waters, Jeremy. *Parkstone-on-Sea: Salterns, Sandbanks & Seaplanes.* 2014, Poole. Poole Historical Trust.

Wheway, Edna. *Edna's Story – memories of life in a Children's Home and in Service in Dorset and London*. 1984, Dorset. Word and Action (Dorset) Ltd

NOTES

Prologue

1. Brick field – marked on the 1844 Tythe Map
2. Poole, Dorset with Corfe Castle in the Distance by J M W Turner, watercolour heightened with touches of bodycolour. Private Collection. According to the catalogue for an exhibition by Agnew's on 26 February – 25 March 1994 called *Turner Watercolours: A Loan Exhibition to mark the occasion of Evelyn Joll's retirement from Agnew's at Easter 1994*, the view is taken from Canford Heath, above Fleets Corner, looking towards Poole with Brownsea Island just visible on the extreme left. Turner based the watercolour on a pencil sketch on p14 of the 1811 *Devonshire Coast No.1 Sketchbook* now in the Turner Bequest in the Clore Gallery.
3. Early 19th century Canford Manor Estate Map – Dorset History Centre reference D-WIM/JO827
4. Buckland Chapel – according to *The Story of the Congregational Churches of Dorset from Their Foundation to the Present Time* by W Densham and J Ogle, 1899, the chapel was financed by *'a wealthy lady residing in Poole, Mrs Bunn, the aunt of the late Mrs Martin Kemp-Welsh'*. Mrs Bunn's maiden name was Buckland. *'The late Mr George Gollop was architect and builder; under him Mr David Tuck took the contract for the masonry'*. Further historical details on the chapel are included in the book.
5. *Heathfield* – the date is c1840 according to *An Inventory of Historical Monuments in the County of Dorset Volume Two South-East Part 2*, published by the Royal Commission on Historical Monuments (England), 1952, p239 (under the entry relating to 'Danecourt Rooms').
6. Reverend Walter Gill – the advert read as follows:

   'PARKSTONE, NEAR POOLE, DORSETSHIRE.

   The Rev. Walter Gill, having (by medical suggestion), relinquished for a season, the stated duties of the ministry, intends devoting himself to the work of Tuition.

   Extensive and most healthily situated premises have been secured at the above-mentioned pleasant village, the salubrity of which is universally acknowledged. The spot selected has the highest medical sanction attached to it as eminently favourable, especially for young persons of delicate constitution.

   The course of instruction is intended to be such as will meet the growing requirements of the age. Pupils confided to the care of Mr Gill (who has had many years' experience in education) will be diligently prepared for a college course, or for commercial or professional life.

   Prospectus and terms (including a list of references of the highest respectability) may be had on application.

   Duties will commence on February 1 and allowance will be made for the shortness of the quarter'.

Chapter 1

7. Learned papers – according to *Plarr's Lives of the Fellows Online* his papers included *Observations on Diseases of Infants 1840, Treatise on the Conformation of the Brain in Infancy 1840, Advice to Opium Eaters, showing its Injurious Effects on the System* 1841 and papers on diphtheria in *The Lancet* in 1859.

8. Many public appointments – *Plarr's Lives of the Fellows Online* states that at the time of his death he was Admiralty Medical Officer to the Coastguard and Naval Reserve, Physician to the Town and County Gaol; Medical Officer of Health, Rural District Great Canford and Kinson; Surgeon to the Great Canford Dispensary, the Police, the South-Western Railway Company, and the Dorset County Reformatory; Medical Inspector (Marine Department), Board of Trade; Medical Examiner, Government Insurance; and Medical Referee to numerous Assurance Societies.
9. *Brontë House* description – taken from an advert for the property in the 4 August 1864 issue of the *Dorset County Chronicle* when it was included in an auction to be held on 15 August 1864 at the London Hotel in Poole.
10. Area north of Ashley Cross largely undeveloped – as evidenced by the 1851 and 1861 Census and Kelly's 1849 *Directory for Dorsetshire*. There were some cottages and smaller properties but the larger Victorian villas in the vicinity were mainly built in the 1880s and 1890s.
11. London Court of Bankruptcy – as described in *The Leisure Hour* in 1858, quoted on the victorianlondon.org website.
12. Frank Cathery – *Parkstone Illustrated with Historical Sketch by W K Gill, Esq*. Published & illustrated by Fred Cathery.

Chapter 2

13. Costume of the 67th Foot – plate facing page 1 of a *Historical Record of The Sixty-Seventh or The South Hampshire Regiment* compiled by Richard Cannon. Parker, Furnivall & Parker, London. 1849
14. Since 1864 – Richard Morgan Humfrey is referred to in the bankruptcy proceedings as the tenant of *Brontë House* and he is also mentioned in the advert for the auction of the property in August 1864. He is then listed in the Register of Electors in 1865 and 1866 and continues to be shown as the contact for viewings of the property when advertised in 1866 and 1868.
15. Arrived in Parkstone c1851 – *Hunt & Co. Directory of Dorsetshire 1851* in the Dorset History Centre.
16. *Beulah Villa* – he is shown at this address in the 1861 Census with his wife and niece Lucy Robinson Humfrey.
17. Lucy Robinson Humfrey – she is mentioned in Richard Morgan Humfrey's will.
18. Joseph Allen – details per the 1871 Census.
19. George Rennison – details per *The Post Office Directory of Hampshire including The Isle of Wight, Wiltshire & Dorsetshire*. London. 1875, Kelly & Co.
20. Coroner's Inquest – the details of the inquest are based on an article entitled *Lamentable Suicide of R M Humfrey Esq*., in *The Poole & South Western Herald* on 12 January 1871.
21. George Braxton Aldridge – details per *The Post Office Directory* referred to above.
22. John Sidney Hudson – details per *The Post Office Directory* referred to above.
23. *Holly Lodge* - the property still exists situated on the south side of Commercial Road 100 yards after Chapel Road when travelling west.

24. Niece joined her in January - *The Bournemouth Visitors' Directory & Poole & Christchurch Saturday Advertiser* included a list of residents' names and addresses each week for Bournemouth and Parkstone, space permitting. The 21 January 1871 issue records Mrs R M Humfrey and Miss Humfrey residing at the property.
25. Mr & Mrs Harvey and family – Mrs R M Humfrey and Miss L R Humfrey are last recorded at the property in the 28 October 1871 edition of *The Bournemouth Visitors' Directory* referred to above. The 4 November 1871 issue records Mr & Mrs Harvey and family residing there. They had vacated the property by the time of the 6 July 1872 issue.

Chapter 3

26. Augustin Ley – he married (Sarah) Lucy Du Buisson, the youngest daughter of Richard Ley's sister, Charlotte Anne Dunning Du Buisson (née Ley) and Caroline's elder brother Reverend Edmund Du Buisson
27. Pronounced 'Lee' – according to a descendant of Richard Ley's younger brother, Ernest James Ley who emigrated to Australia in 1845.
28. Thomas Hunt Ley – there are some amusing anecdotes about him in the document *Incumbents and Patrons of Maker and Rame* on the Rame History Group website based on people who knew him.
29. Running a small preparatory school – page 248 of *Mercer's Directory of Buckinghamshire 1853* (available on disc) indicates that *'the living is a perpetual curacy, held in connection with Brill; the Reverend Richard Ley is the officiating minister'*. Under 'Trades' of Brill, there is a listing for *'Ley, Rev Richard, preparatory school'*.
30. Priest at Cumnor – *Crawford's Clerical Dictionary 1858*
31. Du Buisson pronunciation – according the great grand daugher of her sister Charlotte.
32. Glynhir Estate – by arrangement with his elder brother Thomas Du Buisson (1778-1843), William Du Buisson (Caroline Ley's father) inherited the *Glynhir* estate in 1812 instead on the death of their father. Her uncle Thomas Du Buisson (1778-1843) was heavily involved in the family firm later known as Henckell, Du Buisson & Co. based in London, and subsequently Thomas's son James Du Buisson (1812-1879), grandson Thomas Du Buisson (1848-1933) and great grandson James Melmoth Du Buisson (1889-1976) were also. The firm traded in sugar, hemp, hides and skins. William Du Buissson became Deputy Lieutenant of Carmarthenshire in 1815 and High Sheriff in 1826.
33. Caroline Du Buisson, the mother of Caroline Ley – information regarding her setting up of a school is based on a family history document held at the *Glynhir Mansion*.
34. Living in Gloucestershire – a summary prepared by Hereford Record Office of the diary of Richard Ley's niece, Edith Caroline Du Buisson (daughter of Richard Ley's sister Charlotte) states that in August 1865 Edith went to see *'Aunty Carry and Uncle Dick in Gloucestershire where she was taken to see many churches'*. The original diary was later removed by the family.
35. *Stewarton Lodge* – the house was later called *Burford Glen* and the site is now occupied by an annex to the Town Hall, on the right when travelling west just after the bridge over Braidley Road (which had not been constructed at the time of the 1874 map).

36. Book on the National Hospital – *The Royal National Hospital: The Story of Bournemouth's Sanatorium* by Mary Graham. Bournemouth, 1992. Bournemouth Local Studies' Publications.
37. Conveyance dated 6 June 1873 – held at Dorset History Centre under reference D-1229 – Collyer Bristow, Solicitors.
38. *Stewarton Lodge* particulars – the house was put up for auction on 16 October 1872 and the advert in the *Bournemouth Visitors' Directory* indicated that it was *'a substantially-erected residence of pleasing elevation, containing Entrance Hall, Drawing Room with bay window, handsome and spacious Dining-Room, Breakfast Room, Library, ten bed and dressing rooms', etc. It has a conservatory, lawn, pleasure grounds and shrubberies and a plot of pasture or garden land, the whole comprising just over an acre'.*
39. House auction – held on 8/9 December 1874 at *Brontë House*.
40. *The Alexandra Hospital for Children with Hip Disease* by Samantha Foot. London, 2011. Institute of Historical Research, University of London
41. *Philanthropy and the Hospitals of London: The King's Fund, 1897-1900* by Frank Prochaska. Oxford, 1992.
42. The Lease of *Brontë Cottage* dated 22 April 1874 is in the Bart's Archives in London.
43. Treatment of hip disease – pages 34 and 35 of Samantha Foot's study referred to above.

Chapter 4

44. 16 North Street in Wareham – the house still exists.
45. Craik's diaries – relevant extracts of these were kindly provided to the author by Janice Taylor and Karen Bourrier of the University of Calgary. They were in the process of digitising over 1,000 of Craik's letters in 2016.
46. Pike's obituary – it first appeared in the *Wareham Advertiser* and was reprinted in the *Poole & Dorset Herald* early in September 1884.
47. Paul Brannon's print – it appeared in his book *Illustrated Historical & Picturesque Guide to the Town & Harbour of Poole* by Philip Brannon. c1855, Bournemouth. R Sydenham.
48. Sloop Hill – on Parkstone Road now part of Commercial Road.

Chapter 5

49. Sir Barry Jackson – a fascinating book that covers his early years and career is *The Birmingham Repertory Theatre* by T C Kemp. 1943, Birmingham. Cornish Brothers Limited
50. *Pen-Craigh* – this red-brick Victorian villa was situated on the corner of The Avenue and Lindsay Road. It was demolished when the large roundabout was constructed near County Gates in the late 1960s.
51. Civil Engineer – on James Jackson's marriage certificate 7 September 1878.
52. Family moved around a lot – based on the birth certificates of his children and the 1851 Census: Sarah born in Hammersmith in 1835; Mary Ann 1838 and George 1840 in Deptford; James Frederick in Hurstpierpoint 1842; Emma in Worcester 1844, Ellen in 1846 and Catherine Susannah in 1848 both in Cambridge.
53. At the *Plough Tavern* for a couple of years – according to the London Post Office directories in

the Guildhall Library in London.

54. Branksome Conservative Club – according to his obituary in the 7 September 1906 edition of the *Western Gazette.*

55. James Jackson may have sent his three sons to Heathfield School. It is not possible to prove this as the school records have not survived and James Jackson and his family arrived just after the 1891 Census and left before the 1901 Census.

Chapter 6

56. Tour of the house – included in the Centenary Edition of the school magazine, *Sunrise*, in 1967.

57. Arthur Graham Batterham – reminiscences also included in the Centenary Edition of *Sunrise* in 1967.

58. Herbert Carter – page 7 of his book *I Call to Mind* published in 1949.

59. After some illness – according to *The Cloak That I Left: A Biography of the Author Henry Rider Haggard K.B.E* by his daughter, Lilias Rider Haggard. 1951, London. Hodder and Stoughton

60. Biographer D S Higgins – *Rider Haggard: The Great Storyteller* by D S Higgins. 1981, London. Cassell.

61. Susan Mumm's study of the Anglican Sisterhoods – *Stolen Daughters, Virgin Mothers: Anglican Sisterhoods in Victorian Britain* by Susan Mumm. 1999, London. Leicester University Press.

62. *Paton's List of Schools and Tutors* – not listed in 1904 and 1907 editions, for example.

63. *The Trade Union Tariff Reform Association 1904-1913* – the history of this organisation is set out in a paper with that title by Kenneth D Brown in *The Journal of British Studies Volume IX Number 1* dated November 1969.

64. Postcard dated 19 July 1907 – the sort of item that comes up on a well-known online auction website.

Chapter 7

65. The Boy's Room pictures – the small pictures around the walls depict various school plays in which the boys had performed over the years.

66. The Schoolroom – the boys appear to be working on a General Knowledge quiz on the blackboard.

67. The Dane Court Scout Troop – none of the *Dane Court* boys were involved in the famous camp held on Brownsea Island.

68. Edna Wheway's fascinating memoirs – *Edna's Story – Memories of Life in a Children's Home and in Service in Dorset and London* by Edna Wheway. 1984, Dorset. Word and Action (Dorset) Ltd.

69. Alderney Manor – as described in *Augustus John: Artist & Bohemian – Alderney Manor Poole 1911-1927* by Ted Ward. Undated, Poole. Chatsworth Publications. Copy in the Dorset History Centre.

70. Biography of Augustus John – page 22 of *Augustus John A Biography* by Michael Holroyd. 1974, London. Heinemann Ltd.

71. Hugh Pooley later remembered – *A Short History of the School 1867-1967* by Hugh Pooley printed in the Centenary Edition of the school magazine, *Sunrise*, in 1967.
72. Romilly John later commented – on page 62 of *The Seventh Child* by Romilly John. London, 1932. Heinemann.
73. Biography of Caspar John – page 35-6 of *Caspar John* by Rebecca John. 1987, London. Collins.
74. *Prospect* – there is a photograph of the house in Katherine Everett's memoirs called *Bricks and Flowers: An Anglo-Irish Memoir* by Katherine Everett. First published in 1949. Reissued 2018, Cork. Somerville Press.
75. Iris Morris's book on Ashley Cross – *Looking Back: A Social History of the village of Ashley Cross in Parkstone Poole Dorsetshire from 1833 to the Present Day*. 1996, Poole. Old Thyme Publishing.
76. *Bournemouth and the First World War: The Evergreen Valley 1914-1919* by M A Edgington. 1985, Bournemouth. Bournemouth Local Studies Publications.
77. *Dorset in the First World War* by Rodney Legg. 2012, Somerset. Dorset Books.
78. Mrs Everett's memoirs – *Bricks and Flowers* as noted above.
79. Melville Scutt's memoirs – *Melville's Memoirs: I saw, I conquered* by J Melville Scutt, privately published c1986.

Chapter 8

80. Ambrose Edward Sturdy – one of his descendants, Giles Sturdy, wrote *A Biography of Major Ambrose Edward Sturdy MBE* based around Ambrose Edward Sturdy's numerous letters and documents and those of other family members. 2016, Wareham. Privately published.
81. History of the Gordon Highlanders – *The Life of a Regiment Volume IV: The Gordon Highlanders in the First World War 1914-1919* by Cyril Falls. 1958, Aberdeen. Aberdeen University Press.
82. Battle of Ancre – described by Cyril Falls on pages 108 to 113 of the above-mentioned book.
83. 18 or 19 November 1916 – the records are inconsistent. The Gordon Highlanders Museum has indicated that *'the war diary indicates no contact with the enemy on the day of his wounding'. However, Cyril Falls states that 'the battle was continued until November 19th'.* His Casualty Form indicates the date of the casualty as '19.11.16' whereas the hospital admission record states the *'onset'* of the condition was '18.11.16'.
84. Allied Intervention in Russia – the complex background and history of this intervention has been covered by Ian C D Moffat in his book *The Allied Intervention in Russia, 1918-1920: The Diplomacy of Chaos*. 2015, Basingstoke. Palgrave Macmillan
85. Cecil William Ayerst continued the school for a couple of years – he is recorded as the Headmaster of *Dane Court Preparatory School* in the 1934 and 1935 editions of Kelly's Directory.

Chapter 9

86. *Glenquaich* - her youngest daughters continued to live at the house until the mid-1930s.
87. Diaries of Lucy de Buisson – in Hereford Record Office.
88. *St. Barnabas Hospital and Convalescent Home* – information recorded in *St. Barnabas Hospital: A Short History* published by the hospital in the 1980s. There was also an article entitled *Spotlight on St.Barnabas Hospital* in the *Saltash Journal* in March 1966.
89. Rose Ellen Gemmer – she was the daughter of Frederick Gemmer, an actor. The precise circumstances in which she ended up in the All Hallows Orphanage are not clear.
90. *East Down House* – per the 1911 Kelly's Directory for Dorsetshire.
91. Laurence Warburton Pike - Laurence's wife Eleanor continued to live at *Furzebrook* House for a further eleven years. She then moved to a house called *Holmhurst* in Highcliffe where she remained until her death in 1933. There was a sale of the house contents in 1934 at *Holmhurst.* The site is now a housing estate.
92. Arnold Pike – when Eleanor Pike moved to *Holmhurst* in 1911, Arnold Pike, his wife Bertha Louisa and their daughter Phyllis Penelope Pike moved into *Furzebrook House* where they remained until Arnold and Bertha died in 1930. According to the 1911 Census, Arnold Pike previously lived at *Netton Lodge,* Durlston Road in Swanage.
93. Chris Legg – *The Furzebrook Railway of Pike Brothers' Railway of Pike Brothers' Dorset Clay Works* by Chris Legg. 2016, Truro. Twelveheads Press.
94. William Lewison Pike's obituary – in the 2 January 1902 edition of the *Exeter and Plymouth Gazette.* The obituary further states that he had a keen interest in the salmon fishing industry at Appledore. As well as his charitable activities, he was involved in the Bideford Horse Show, the Bideford Chrysanthemum Society and the Instow and Appledore Regatta.
95. High profile divorce case – press reports may be found on www.britishnewspaperarchive.co.uk
96. James Frederick Jackson – Director of a Provision Merchant, according to the 1911 Census.
97. The Saben family – *The Saben, Seban, Saborne Family of Herts and Essex* (1969) and *The Saben Family of Staffordshire* (1971).
98. *While the World Revolves* published by Burns Oates & Washbourne in 1932.
99. Cecil William Ayerst – biographical information based on *Crockford's Clerical Dictionary 1949-50.*

INDEX

All references are to page numbers. References highlighted in bold relate to the pages where relevant illustrations appear. Names of people who lived or spent significant time at *Dane Court*, or the cottage and lodge in the grounds, are highlighted in bold, indicating their status and the dates they were there.